Women at the Edge
of Discovery

Women at the Edge of Discovery

40 True Science Adventures

KENDALL HAVEN

LIBRARIES
UNLIMITED
A Member of the Greenwood Publishing Group
Westport, Connecticut • London

10/2 2/2005

Library of Congress Cataloging-in-Publication Data

Haven, Kendall F.
  Women at the edge of discovery : 40 true science adventures / Kendall Haven.
    p. cm.
  Includes index.
  ISBN 1–59158–015–3 (alk. paper)
  1. Women scientists—Biography. 2. Science—History—20th century. I. Title.
Q141.H368   2003
509.2'2—dc21   2003054570

British Library Cataloguing in Publication Data is available.

Library of Congress Catalog Card Number: 2003054570
ISBN: 1–59158–015–3

First published in 2003

Libraries Unlimited, 88 Post Road West, Westport, CT 06881
A Member of the Greenwood Publishing Group, Inc.
www.lu.com

Printed in the United States of America

The paper used in this book complies with the
Permanent Paper Standard issued by the National
Information Standards Organization (Z39.48–1984).

10   9   8   7   6   5   4   3   2   1

This book is dedicated to the thousands of women who loved the sciences so much they forced their way into science schools, science jobs, and science careers, opening the doors of science to all women who followed. Women pioneers of science undertook the greatest adventure of all.

Contents

Foreword

As someone who has made the recognition and celebration of women's historic accomplishments the focus of my work and life, I was eager to read *Women at the Edge of Discovery*. My information about twentieth-century women scientists was limited, but I had no idea how limited or how much my knowledge base would be expanded by the stories I read. Women were and are the pioneers in so many scientific fields, and yet most of these women had escaped my discovery.

Through Kendall Haven's writing, I experienced the freezing Arctic wind; the oozing toxic air and caustic cave mud; the hot, wet, sticky rain forest, each bringing life-threatening danger to the scientist. Amazing courage and daring emerged as almost universal qualities of these women, along with a willingness to try, try, and try again. Reading about one remarkable woman after another, I was astonished at the many female stereotypes exploded by the actions of these scientists. Without exception each of these women demonstrated a fearless drive for knowledge and discovery. Each had a determined eagerness to pave new paths and do what had never been done before.

These stories encouraged my own sense of wonder and appreciation for the skills related to scientific observation. I wondered how men and women might solve problems differently; and I considered the impact of having the female and male experience represented in developing scientific theories and methods of experimentation. Since women's experience in biological field studies rewrote the manual for success, does that mean that women relate to animals differently than men relate to animals?

This wonderful collection presents an extraordinary array of scientific topics to explore and many thought-provoking questions for research and discussion. In addition, it provides an index for year, name, and field of discovery and an expansive bibliography for each story. Having said this, my hope is that this engaging resource will not be used exclusively in science classes. Instead, it should be required pleasure reading for those who daily make assumptions about who women are and what they have achieved.

The telling of the accomplishments of women of the late twentieth century is long overdue. Because these stories are about women in science, this resource is all the more valuable. Each story is different from the next. Yet, together these stories help create a vivid mosaic of women scientists of the twentieth century, and present women as problem solvers and essential contributors to the quality of life for the twenty-first century.

I thank Kendall Haven for using his tremendous talent as a scholar and writer to tell the stories of these women and their discoveries.

Molly Murphy MacGregor
President and Cofounder
National Women's History Project
www.nwhp.org

Introduction

Each time I ask students what makes a story fun to read, one of the first replies they offer is "adventure!" Thrilling stories of adventure makes reading, itself, an exciting adventure.

But what is adventure? Dictionaries describe adventure as an unusual event or events that create excitement and danger. Facing a charging rhino in the wild is an adventure. Swinging by a vine across a river of molten lava is an adventure. Hacking your way across an uncharted jungle island is an adventure.

But can ordinary science work be a thrilling adventure? Certainly, science involves lots of careful, hard work and study. Certainly reputable scientists try to take only carefully calculated risks and proceed to face dangerous moments only after as much study and preparation as possible. Many famous and productive scientists never face what we would call "adventures."

But many do. The process of doing many types of science work inherently involves more risk and danger than most types of careers.

Any leap into the unknown for the sake of discovery can become an adventure. Science exploration and moments of discovery are always exciting, always unusual. Always the very real possibility exists that something unforeseen will happen and turn the moment into a dangerous disaster.

Kids typically think of science as boring, as endless tables, lists, theorems, and formulas to memorize and regurgitate. True, that is part of *learning* about science. But the process of *doing* science can be very different. It is creative, imaginative, inventive, and—yes—adventurous.

The *doing* of science is all about observing, about guessing, about venturing beyond the bounds of existing knowledge. Scientists often act like crime detectives, piecing together scant clues, trying to reconstruct an accurate picture of what *really* happened (or is going to happen), playing hunches as they leap from one shred of evidence to the next in that attempt. Often, years of careful work lead a scientist to one experiment, to one moment, when their efforts and ideas will either produce discovery and fame or failure. Such moments are always exciting adventures for the scientists involved.

This book contains stories of forty women who have faced considerable adventure and, in doing so, have advanced our science knowledge. Many think of men as the ones to face danger and adventure. At least in the world of science this is not necessarily true. Women scientists can and do claim equal share in the dangers and adventures of science. The forty women presented here are far from the only forty to do so. These stories describe only one of the many adventures each of these women has had.

I wrote these stories and this book with the following five goals in mind:

- To demonstrate the thrilling adventure to be found in the world of science.
- To inspire girls (and women) to pursue science careers.
- To help readers appreciate the contributions of women to science.
- To help readers appreciate the great effort required for each advance in our science knowledge.
- To help readers appreciate the immense struggle it has taken for women to gain their rightful place as prominent members of the science community. Women have gained general acceptance in most fields of science over the past fifty years and now comprise an equal share of each year's graduating class of science majors. The percentage of working women scientists is steadily growing. But the struggle for real equality is far from over. As of the year 2000, only 5 percent of the members of the National Academy of Sciences were women. Only 12 percent of university science department chairs were women.

How were these particular forty women and adventures selected for inclusion in this book? After initial research, we compiled over 300 possible stories that could be used. Whittling that number down to forty involved many difficult choices. For every story that is in the book, there are several others I would have liked to include.

Because they will have more relevance to today's young readers, I decided to emphasize recent science events and so only allowed three stories to stray back toward the beginning of the twentieth century, while fifteen occurred within the past ten years. Many of the stories have happened within the past few years. I hope that that gives readers a better image of what it looks like to do science work today.

I also wanted to maintain a balance between the three general branches of science—physical, life, and earth sciences. Certainly, several stories blur the boundary between two of these areas. Still, I felt it was important to provide a glimpse into the workings of each of these major areas of science. The same was true for balancing the stories between field and laboratory work.

Furthermore, I wanted to present as full a range as possible of the kinds of adventures women scientists can experience during a science career. Some happen in the lab, some in the field. Some happen while conducting experiments, some while gathering data and making observations.

Lastly, I wanted to balance between famous scientists and ones who have done (or are doing) important work but who are not well known outside of their own field of specialty. Some of these women's names will be familiar to young readers. Many will not. These forty stories are the result of that process of compromise and balance.

Each of these stories focuses on the *process* of doing science. What does it look like and feel like to do it? What are the methods and procedures used in the doing of science research? What are the concerns and struggles of scientists engaged in original research? How do they go about doing what they have to do?

Students can use this book and these stories as a reference work, as a research tool for learning about either individual scientists or about the different fields and specialties of science. But don't forget to view these stories as fun stories you can read for pleasure. Teachers can use these stories as springboards to launch science units or to augment and expand an existing unit.

Look at this book as a fun and exciting walk on the adventurous side of the world of science. Use these stories as starting points for research into specific fields of science or into these specific scientists. Use them as inspiration for your own career in science, or as studies in the process of doing science. Use them as part of your education about the sciences.

I owe thanks to many who helped in locating the research, sources, and information I needed to complete these stories. In particular, I offer my deepest thanks to the following women. Barbara Ittner shaped and focused this book and inspired me to write it. Her insights and editorial crafting shine on every page. Roni Berg, the love of my life, reviewed and critiqued several drafts of each story, vastly improving them in the process. She also deserves credit for creating my story titles. The librarians at the National Women's History Project were, as always, invaluable as sources of reliable, in-depth information. Finally, I want to thank my six teacher-reviewers and their classes who read and critiqued these stories: Nancy Ferris, Linda Young, Gretchen Krieg, Melissa Taylor, Judy Leffert, and Dianne Yoesting. Each story is much improved because of the contributions of each of these women and by their students.

Finally, my thanks to you, the reader. Enjoy these stories and the struggle and adventure they represent. Observe through them the process and activity of science. Then search for your own science adventure stories to share. Thousands exist. These are only forty.

Stories by Year of Occurrence

Year	Name	Field
1902	Marie Curie	Physics
1910	Alice Hamilton	Industrial Medicine
1918	Florence Sabin	Histology
1924	Margaret Mead	Anthropology
1932	Lise Meitner	Physics
1942	Dorothy Hodgkin	X-Ray Crystallography
1944	Grace Hopper	Mathematics
1948	Rachel Fuller Brown	Biochemistry
1949	Eugenie Clark	Marine Biology
1950	Ruth Patrick	Limnology
1950	Barbara McClintock	Genetics
1951	Annie Wauneka	Community Health
1952	Rosalind Franklin	X-Ray Crystallography
1956	Chien-Shiung Wu	Physics
1961	Jane Goodall	Biology
1965	Jocelyn Bell Burnell	Astronomy
1967	Dian Fossey	Primatology
1967	Cynthia Moss	Biology
1970	Vera Cooper Rubin	Astronomy
1972	Candace Pert	Brian Chemistry
1975	Mary Leakey	Archeology
1978	Rose Kellman	Biology
1979	Sylvia Earle	Marine Biology
1985	Jane Kirkwalter	Physics

1988	Helen Thayer	Climatology
1990	Holly Lisanby	Neurological Research
1994	Christina Allen	Ecology
1995	Ann Bowles	Bioacoustics
1996	Shannon Lucid	Chemistry
1997	Karen Tejunga	Biology
1999	Marta Aznar	Volcanology
1999	Darlene Ketten	Marine Biology
1999	Anna Roosevelt	Archeology
2000	Judith Bernard	Marine Biology
2000	Barbara Bond	Plant Biology
2000	Louise Hose	Speleology
2000	Teri Roth	Biology
2001	Janet Harrington	Insect Biology
2001	Karen McComb	Biology
2001	Cindy Lee Van Dover	Marine Ecology

Women Scientists by Field

Name	Field
Physical Sciences	
Jocelyn Bell-Burnell	Astronomy
Rachel Fuller Brown	Biochemistry
Marie Curie	Physics
Rosalind Franklin	X-Ray Crystallography
Dorothy Hodgkin	X-Ray Crystallography
Grace Hopper	Computer Languages
Jane Kirkwalter	Physics
Shannon Lucid	Chemistry
Lise Meitner	Physics
Vera Cooper Rubin	Astronomy
Chien-Shiung Wu	Physics
Life Sciences	
Christina Allen	Ecology
Judith Bernard	Marine Biology
Barbara Bond	Plant Biology
Ann Bowles	Bioacoustics
Eugenie Clark	Marine Biology
Sylvia Earle	Marine Biology
Dian Fossey	Biology
Jane Goodall	Biology
Alice Hamilton	Industrial Medicine

Janet Harrington	Insect Biology
Rose Kellman	Biology
Darlene Ketten	Marine Biology
Holly Lisanby	Neurological Research
Barbara McClintock	Genetics
Karen McComb	Biology
Cynthia Moss	Biology
Candace Pert	Brain Chemistry
Teri Roth	Endangered Species Breeding
Florence Sabin	Histology
Karen Tejunga	Biology
Annie Wauneka	Community Health

Earth Sciences

Marta Aznar	Volcanology
Lousie Hose	Speleologist
Mary Leakey	Anthropology
Margaret Mead	Anthropology
Ruth Patrick	Limnology
Anna Roosevelt	Archeology
Helen Thayer	Climatology
Cindy Lee Van Dover	Oceanography

Christina Allen

Hide and Seek:
A Science Adventure

Rain Forest
Ecologist

A remote rain forest ecosystem edges toward collapse as local villagers destroy native fruit palms. Christina Allen, a lone graduate student, works in the middle of the Peruvian rain forest, amid panthers, pit vipers, spiders, and slugs—in the pitch-black night. She has only one month to prove the importance of the fruit palms in order to save both them and the local ecology.

A Science Adventure in the South American Rain Forest

In May 1994 the Peruvian rain forest was hot . . . and wet . . . and sticky. But then, the rain forest always felt hot, wet, and sticky—even in the darkest hours of night.

Twenty-four-year-old ecologist Christina Allen hunched through the pitch-black night on a rickety, seven-foot-high observation platform she had fashioned that afternoon. She had piled a canteen, compass, and site survey map at her side. A flashlight swung from her belt. So did a machete if she needed it—which she rarely did. The floor of the rain forest—dimly lit even during the day because of the thick layers of trees stretching several hundred feet overhead—stayed relatively open of entangling undergrowth.

Holding her breath so as not to make a sound, refusing to move and make the flimsy platform creak, Christina tried to peer through the impenetrable dark toward a palm fruit cache she had piled on the forest floor just at dusk. Did she hear breathing? Movement? Was something down there sniffing? Nibbling? If she clicked on her flashlight to see, she might scare away countless other creatures of the night. If she didn't, she might miss identifying what was gobbling her fruit.

This was the sixth onsite day of Christina's study. As part of her Master's degree program, the young scientist hoped to document the effects to the local ecosystem as humans systematically chopped down fruit palm trees in the area.

Palm tree fruit was a main food source for many rain forest animals. But which animals? How much palm fruit did each animal eat? How important was that one food source? What would happen if that one food source were severely reduced or removed? No one in the government or in either of the nearby villages seemed to know. And yet the trees were already being cut.

Christina had set up this palm fruit cache to see which animals would visit it at night. As she perched through the night, the impenetrable dark magnified the sounds of the forest.

In turn, each sound magnified her imagination. Christina could almost *feel* bloodsucking leeches drop from the trees to suck her dry (as she had heard they would in Malaysian rain forests). She felt a rising fear of unseen animals circling closer—spiders, slugs, snakes, panthers. Each sound became a threatening monster. Howls, screeches, soft hisses drifted through the muggy night air. Some were far off, some so close they seemed right on top of her. She felt a need to constantly glance over her shoulder.

It felt creepy and scary!—mostly because she couldn't tell if something was there. She felt defenseless, and very visible to the night forest that she could not see.

Christina longed to click on her flashlight. But she knew her light would scare away the very animals she hoped to observe and ruin any value of her survey. The point was to find out what naturally ate palm fruit at night. But she wasn't learning anything in the dark.

She sighed and clicked on the powerful beam. Light stabbed through the dark and caught several rabbits and five smaller rodents— each scurried away into the cover of darkness. She also spotted three slugs, each bigger than her hand, slithering across her fruit.

Instantly, Christina felt safer. Still, a grueling knot churned in her stomach. Her survey wasn't working.

At first light Christina dropped from the platform to study the ground for tracks and to study the half-eaten fruit. But the tracks were impossible to read in the dust and leaf mold. Bite marks alone couldn't be tracked back to a specific animal.

She needed a new plan. But, because there was no established methodology for conducting this type of survey and study, she'd have to invent one on her own. How could she tell for sure what role palm fruit played in the local ecosystem?

Six days ago, Christina had begun her work by laying out study area boundary markers and then a survey grid with markers on trees. She carefully hiked the entire site over the course of two days, marking food sources, and searching for evidence of which animals ate various food sources. As she could, she counted the species and populations present in the area, but she knew that most of them were far better at hiding than she was at finding.

A part of Christina had become comfortable traipsing through the thick rain forest with its sounds and patterns. Another part of her cringed with each step, waiting for something creepy and unseen to plop onto her shoulder or lock onto her ankle.

Christina had interviewed local villagers about their hunting practices, changes in game they had noticed, what species they saw, or didn't see; met, or didn't meet; found, or didn't find. Mostly the villagers shrugged, unable to provide any specific information.

Now she had tried direct observation at a food cache, and she *still* didn't know who ate palm fruit and who didn't.

Then it hit her. What she needed was to see clear footprints of each animal that approached a fruit tree. Clear footprints were only made in mud.

Christina knew she needed help if she was going to ring each of the dozens of fruit palm tree with mud each day.

In the nearest village she organized a bucket brigade to haul water from a nearby stream. Hand-carrying sloshing buckets of water over rough forest trails was slow, backbreaking work. Her team members were soon drenched in sweat. By late afternoon they had hauled only enough water to turn the ground surrounding each fruit palm tree in a one-acre plot into a moat of mud. One acre was a small sample area, but it would have to do.

Christina carefully cleared away leaves and raked the souplike mud smooth. Now every footprint through the night would be recorded for her to study in the morning.

The next morning, eight clear sets of prints were frozen in the hardened mud around the first tree she checked. She could identify approximate size and age as well as species for each. Her mud circle invention worked!

But that was only one night, and only in one acre. As a scientist, Christina knew she would need to collect data over as many nights and over as wide an area as possible if her findings were to have merit. Then she realized that she was only counting fruit eaters that walked on the ground.

As the afternoon light began to wane, she shinnied up trees to string bat nets across the open space between trees and find out how many fruit-eating bat species lived in the area. Climbing one tree she felt a quick prick on her shoulder. She shifted her weight and turned to look. Nothing. She even shone her hardhat headlamp through the growing gloom. Nothing.

Thirty minutes later, hiking back to camp, Christina's arm began to drag. Waves of dizziness and nausea swept over her. That night in the small camp she shared with the four local workers she had hired to assist her study, Christina couldn't concentrate enough to write in her daily study logbook. She lay panting and sweating through the night.

Next morning a local snake expert examined her shoulder and identified the markings of a pit viper bite, a highly poisonous forest predator. For some unknown reason, the snake had injected only a tiny drop of poison into Christina. A normal dose would have killed her.

Late that afternoon, and still feeling weak from the effects of the venom, Christina and several local tribesmen climbed that same tree. They found a five-foot viper wrapped around a branch, its tongue flicking the air as its cold black eyes glared at them. Before they could capture this killer, it slithered high up the trunk and disappeared into thick foliage above.

Christina began to climb trees more warily, stomping, calling, shaking branches ahead of her to give snakes ample chance to slither away. While checking her last bat net of the afternoon three days later, she rattled a nest as well as a branch. A dozen wasps roared into the open. Three dove for Christina. One stung her hand as she wildly flailed at the attackers. One struck next to her eye. The eye swelled shut in five minutes. Her whole head throbbed for hours.

Despite the dangers, Christina established a daily study pattern. Early in the morning she climbed trees to inventory the previous night's bat catch. Next she recorded each set of prints left in the hardening mud at each tree. In the afternoon she and her local "bucket brigade" rewatered the mud and raked it smooth. Then she reset her nets between trees before retiring to camp to enter the days findings in her study logs under a flickering gas lantern.

After Words

Within three weeks Christina had completed her groundbreaking survey of forest activity and population. She had created a new technique for forest ecological study. Additionally, she had compiled detailed and valuable information on forest ecology and the role of fruit palms for the Peruvian government and for other researchers. Science is rarely about the big, glamorous discoveries. Science progresses because of small advances made through individual studies in specific areas, advances that later combine to into general leaps forward in our understanding. Most scientists work on such small specific projects as Christina's that contribute small, but important, pieces to our general knowledge.

* * *

Suggested Topics to Explore

This story deals with tropical rain forests and forest ecology. Here are starting questions that will help you discuss and research both.

1. If you had to study a forest (or desert, or prairie) ecosystem, how would you find out what lived there? How do modern ecologists survey a site? What do they look for?

2. What are the major elements in a food web? How could you build a picture of a local food web? How could you find out what each animal in the ecosystem eats? Because most animals eat more than one thing, how could you decide how important a single type of plant is to the local ecosystem?

3. Research the concept of ecosystem diversity. What does this term mean? How important is it to ecosystem stability?

For Further Reading About This Story

Baker, Lucy. *Life in the Rain Forest.* New York: Franklin Watts, 1992.

Banks, Martin. *Conserving Rain Forests.* New York: Steck-Vaughn Library, 1990.

Forsyth, Adrian. *Portraits of the Rain Forest.* New York: Scholastic, 1992.

George, Jean. *One Day in the Tropical Rain Forest.* New York: Crowell Books, 1993.

Green, Jen. *Rain Forest.* New York: Garth Stevens, 1999.

Greenwood, Elenor. *Rain Forest.* Chicago: D K Publications, 2001.

Kovacs, Deborah. *Noise in the Night: The Habits of Tropical Bats.* Washington, DC: Smithsonian Institution, 2001.

O'Mara, Anna. *Rain Forest.* Boston: Bridgestone Books, 1996.

Senior, Kathryn. *Rain Forests.* New York: Franklin Watts, 1999.

Stille, Darlene. *Tropical Rain Forests.* Danbury, CT: Children's Press, 1999.

Marta Aznar

Fire and Ice: Volcanologist
A Science Adventure

Imagine hiking down sheer cliff walls into a seething volcano crater filled with hissing sulfur fumes and boiling plumes of rising gas and smoke in order to collect needed scientific data. Marta Aznar made such a trip less than two weeks after a small explosion of gas and car-sized rocks signaled that the volcano was nearing another major eruption.

A Science Adventure in a Volcano

A helicopter neared the ragged rim of the Central Mexico volcano at an altitude of 18,500 feet on a September morning in 1999. One moment the air was dazzling clear and a deep, ethereal blue that made Marta Aznar know she was halfway up to space. The next second, loose snow boiled into a near whiteout and built quickly on the helicopter windows as the pilot jockeyed to keep the frail craft even in the buffeting gusts of wind and to settle onto the narrow crater rim.

"Heavy turbulence," the pilot yelled. Marta clutched her safety straps and assumed that meant the landing would be scrubbed. But the pilot continued to hover as the motor whined, the chopper rocked like a cradle in gusts that roared off the crater wall, and the snow howled like a frozen hurricane at the windows. Then—plop—the helicopter lightly touched down on the snow-packed rim of this giant volcano.

"Everybody out!" yelled the pilot. Thirty-three-year-old University of Mexico volcanologist Marta Aznar along with her team of three other scientists tumbled out lugging backpacks and hard-shell cases jammed with high-tech equipment. Each team member wore a hardhat and crampons (spikes attached to the bottom of boots) for walking across ice fields at the top of the world.

Instantly the motor roared. The chopper sprang back into the air and shot down the long, glacier-covered slope of Popocatepetl volcano toward the central Mexican plain, 15,000 feet below.

Marta shielded her face from the blast kicked up by the helicopter. The snow settled and the jagged rim of Popocatepetl emerged as if from a retreating fog. The helicopter's "landing pad" had been less than six feet wide. One of the chopper's landing skids had settled on the glacial ice of the volcano's steep outer slope. The other had rested on the inside of the lip that rolled quickly into a near-vertical inner wall that encircled the seething cauldron and steaming crater lake of Popo's innards. They stood on the knife's edge of the crater's jagged, circular rim that stabbed into the sky like a broken bottle.

The first thing that hit Marta was the silence—as if the air were too thin to carry even the moan of the ever-present wind. Her second observation was that it was impossible to breathe at over 18,000 feet. She gasped for air, sucking huge lungfuls that seemed devoid of life-giving oxygen. She felt dizzy, nauseous. Even standing seemed too great an effort. One of the other team members lurched and staggered, trying to arrange their packs of equipment.

Hugo Granados, fifty-year-old senior volcanologist, smiled—seemingly unaware of, and unaffected by—the thin air at this altitude.

"Don't move or you'll pass out. Ten minutes ago you were three miles lower. Bend over and get your head down by your knees."

One of the other assistants, Lorenzo Ortiz, collapsed to the snow and gasped, "If we can't breathe, what can we hope to get done up here?"

Still bent over and panting, Marta answered, "Satellite images show that the ice fields up here are melting. The mountain is heating up. We need to collect samples and set up a monitoring station to provide more accurate data than satellite or long-range sensors can provide."

Oritz pointed down into the steaming crater. "Is it dangerous being up here? I've never been up on a cone volcano before."

Hugo shrugged. "Sure. It's an active volcano that shows signs of building toward a major explosive eruption. But if we're going to get the data, *someone* has to come up here."

"But it's safe now. Right? When was the last explosion?"

"Two weeks ago. Nothing catastrophic, but plenty to kill us all if we had been here."

Popocatepetl is one of the three giant, cone-shaped volcanoes that dot the mid-Mexican plain. Two (Popo and Pico de Orizaba) remain very active. Popo had erupted in December 1994, and had periodically spewed towering plumes of ash and gas ever since. Without more sensitive and precise monitoring data, the scientists feared that they would not be able to accurately warn of the next major eruption.

Marta motioned for her team to gather. "I asked Hugo to lead this expedition since he has more experience than anyone on high-altitude volcanoes. We've got a lot of work to do and can only stay up here a couple of hours—three at the most."

A team member asked, "Why? What will happen?"

Hugo counted off the dangers as casually as if he were reading the ingredients in a breakfast cereal. "Sulfur inhalation is toxic. Fluid can build up in your lungs or brain—both deadly—from the low pressure and low O_2 levels, plus the usual migraines, nausea, and blurred vision. Then, of course, storms do come up—deadly whiteout storms that can rise in a couple of minutes."

Marta passed out their assignments. Lorenzo Ortiz would record a series of ground temperatures using a two-foot-long probe. He would also dig holes and erect two bright yellow poles. Being visible from a distant base camp station, the poles could be used to detect movement or swelling (bulging) of the volcanoes magma chamber.

Hugo would set up a differential GPS (Ground Positioning Satellite) station and a laser receiver and transmitter aimed at other laser bases over twenty miles away. These would provide a better "fix" on the mountain and allow researchers back in the city to monitor even slight movements of the mountain as well as changes in the ice fields and pattern of tremors.

Marta and Hugo's assistant, Juan Venegas, would descend into the crater to collect gas and water samples.

Marta roped herself to Juan—a safety precaution for their trek down ice-covered steep rocks in gusting winds and past unknown and unseen crevasses (cracks or splits in the ice—many only three or four feet deep, but some over eighty).

Hugo cautioned, "Remember. Popo is an angry volcano. Don't hesitate to run if you feel or sense anything."

Marta smiled, "*Run?* In this thin air? I'll be lucky to walk."

Hugo unpacked the three hard cases and spread out the steel-cased modules, small antenna dish, and connectors of the differential GPS station. He drilled anchor bolts for the station's antenna through snow and into the rocky mountaintop.

Meanwhile, Lorenzo Ortiz cautiously edged his way down both exterior and interior slopes jamming his crampon spikes deep into the ice on every step and periodically wedging his slim temperature probe several feet into the earth. "Wow!" He hollered toward Hugo. "A foot under the ice, it's ninety-four degrees!"

Cupping his ears in the growing wind, Hugo cried, "How hot?"

"Ninety-four degrees Fahrenheit. Much hotter than you measured a year ago!"

Marta led Juan down the steep interior slope. Steam and sulfurous gasses hissed from a dozen fumarols (small holes). It was difficult to see through the fumes and smoke. Marta had to jam her pick deep into the ice before she took each step to be sure she wasn't about to walk into a deadly crevasse thinly covered by ice.

Halfway down, the ground shook and then groaned. Billows of smoke and steam belched from a thin fissure fifty feet to the volcanologists' right. Sounding like thunder, several great boulders broke free and tumbled down the sheer cliff wall on the far side of the cauldera. Each time they struck the cliff wall, a roaring explosion of rocks rumbled across the crater.

Marta ducked low and hugged a convenient rock to keep from being knocked off her feet. She huddled there a full minute after quiet returned before daring to stand and continue.

The crater reeked of rotten eggs, a sure sign of the dense sulfur gasses being emitted from the volcano. Nearing the bottom and the steaming crater lake, Marta felt another tremor beneath her feet. More rocks crashed off the rim wall and exploded in gas and steam when they hit bottom. Marta was surrounded by sauna-hot smoke, hissing steam, yellow sulfur fumes, and ice. It felt like the ultimate moment of doom when the Earth would be consumed by fire.

The two scientists threaded their way around yellow pools of bubbling mud surrounded by walls of smoothed ice. Sulfur fumaroles hissed gas like steam kettles, staining the ice and rock nearby a deep yellow. Never could a place look and feel more like inferno. Marta thought that this hellhole couldn't possibly be part of the same Earth that sprouted trees, grass, and flowers.

In the crater's lake, deep, aquamarine water bubbled. Marta's thermometer measured 166 degrees Fahrenheit. Steam swirled from the scalding surface. "Careful," she reminded herself. Touch the water and she'd be burned. Fall in and she'd be cooked. As Marta crouched on an oven-hot rock to scoop her water samples from the lake, giant bubbles wobbled their way upward only to belch sour-smelling gasses when they broke the surface.

Finally, Marta and Juan had filled their glass sample containers and wedged them into padded backpacks for the return trip.

"It's good there's so much off-gassing," Marta said.

Juan tapped his chest and replied, "The sulfur burns my lungs."

"Better that than to die in an eruption. Eruptions and explosions happen when the gas can't escape and builds up pressure inside the mountain."

The two scientists followed their footsteps in reverse up the slope to the rim. They stopped every four steps to pant during this steep uphill climb. Marta poked the ice ahead of her before taking each step.

Halfway up the treacherous climb, her pick broke through a crust of ice that shattered into the narrow crevasse it hid, chiming like broken glass as it fell. Marta lost her balance and tumbled forward. Juan dug his heels into the snow and yanked back on their connecting rope. The jerk pulled Marta aside, so that she fell into the snow next to the hidden crevasse instead of head first into it to her death.

As Juan crawled up to peer over the edge, steam and fumes gushed from the chasm, driving him back. "This is the same way we descended. How did we miss this on the way down?"

Marta sat up rubbing her sore elbow. "Steam vents shift. Ice cracks along new fissures. . . . It's never safe inside an active volcano."

As the two trudged back toward the top, boiling storm clouds materialized over the western rim and swirled into the crater. Snow began to fall. Some flakes hissed as they hit super heated spots of rock and dirt. Within moments Marta and Juan walked in a blinding fog, barely able to see the ground in front of them. Snow and wind obscured their trail. Marta had to bend low to make sure she followed the trail back to Hugo and Lorenzo. To get lost in the cauldera was also deadly.

When they finally crawled onto the rim where the wind howled and snow swirled horizontally, they were just fifteen minutes late, but it felt like days had passed. Hugo trudged out of the white, materializing like a smiling ghost.

"Popo's got everything, eh? Fire, ice, smoke, boiling water, and snow—all at once!"

Hugo had to shout to be heard. "We're finished here. We'll tie onto you two and begin our descent."

Lorenzo asked, "Isn't the helicopter going to pick us up?"

Hugo gestured at the slashing storm. "Not now and we can't afford to wait. A thousand feet down the mountain it might be clear and warm. Safer to hike down 'til we're well below the clouds."

Fifty minutes later the team had snaked their way down to the 15,000-foot level and had found a landing space well below the storm clouds swirling 2,000 feet above. Marta called for the helicopter over her handset radio. Their work this day on Popo was over.

After Words

Dr. Aznar's team had spent less than two-and-a-half hours on the mountain. It felt like days. Still the data they collected, and the stations they created to provide long-term monitoring data, have proved invaluable to scientists assigned to both understand and monitor Mexico's dangerous volcanoes. Data have faithfully flowed from Hugo's GPS and laser stations, allowing vastly improved monitoring of the volcano's progress toward a major eruption. With a volcano, nothing is certain except that someday it will violently explode. The more scientists are willing to risk the mountain's dangers, the better able others will be to protect the people below.

* * *

Suggested Topics to Explore

This story deals with volcanology. Here are starting questions that will help you discuss and research that topic.

1. Where are there active volcanoes? Mark their location on a world map. List recent eruptions for each. Did you find any undersea volcanoes? Are there any volcanoes that rise from the bottom of the ocean? Make a list of famous eruptions over the past 2,000 years.

2. What are the physical signs of an impending eruption? Research the techniques vulcanologists use to monitor volcanoes and to predict eruptions.

3. Where do the heat, gas, and magma of volcanoes come from? Why do some volcanoes explode while others simple spew out streams of lava? What are the different types of volcanoes?

For Further Reading About This Story

Asimov, Isaac. *How Did We Find Out About Volcanoes?* New York: Walker & Company, 1988.

Clarkson, Peter. *Volcanoes.* Stillwater, MN: Voyager Press, 2000.

Decker, Robert. *Volcanoes.* New York: W H Freeman, 1988.

Fisher, Richard. *Out of the Crater.* Princeton, NJ: Princeton University Press, 1999.

Green, Jen. *Volcanoes.* Brookfield, CT: Copper Beach Books, 2000.

Harrison, David. *Volcanoes: Natures Incredible Fireworks.* Honesdale, PA: Boyd's Mill Press, 2002.

Llewellyn, Claire. *Volcanoes.* Portsmouth, NH: Heinemann Library, 2000.

Meister, Cari. *Volcanoes.* New York: Abdo Books, 1999.

Thompson, Dick. *Volcano Cowboys: The Rocky Evolution of a Dangerous Science.* New York: St. Martin's Press, 2000.

Van Rose, Suzanne. *Volcanoes.* New York: Altea, 1993.

Judith Bernard

Shark Bait: Marine Biologist
A Science Adventure

Judith Bernard does her work in choppy ocean waters infested with great white sharks. Her job? To lure the sharks closer. How would you feel if you were trying to study a twenty-five-foot-long monster shark as it circled closer and closer—studying you for its next meal?

A Science Adventure with Great White Sharks

The summer fog bank had receded a mile or more offshore when thirty-eight-year-old University of California biologist Judith Bernard's sixty-foot work boat, the *Jenny Mae,* muscled through the chop outside San Francisco's Golden Gate Bridge and veered north along the coast. Judith's shoulder-length amber hair was tied back in a ponytail and jammed under a Stanford baseball cap.

"Not heading for the Farallons today?" asked Walter Jennings, Judith's sixty-two-year-old pilot. Weathered by years at sea, with a crew cut and a "Popeye" pipe clamped between his teeth, Jennings had piloted this boat for the Stanford Marine program for a decade.

The Farallon Islands—scarcely more than chunks of rock thrust above the water ten miles outside San Francisco Bay—is one of the three best places on Earth to find great white sharks. (The other two are Dangerous Reef in Australia and Dyer Island off South Africa.)

Judith answered, "Bodega Bay Marine Lab reported an unusually large seal population near Tomales Bay. We'll hunt up there today." She scanned the sky on this August afternoon in the year 2000. "Besides it's a great day to sail up the coast."

"No sails on board the *Jenny Mae*," Jennings grumbled. "It's 2,500 horses of diesel all the way."

Two undergraduate summer interns had volunteered to assist with this expedition. One of them, twenty-year-old Josh Landers, a marine economics major, asked, "Why not just kill the great whites? It'd be a lot safer for humans and for marine mammals. It would make ocean recreation safer and more popular"

Judith answered, "No data *at all* has been collected on *c. carcharias* (great whites) over ninety-five percent of their natural range. Their population is plummeting worldwide. This creature has survived for over six hundred million years. It is the undisputed king of the ocean. One great white could turn an adult blue whale into bite-sized scraps."

"All the more reason to eradicate them," Josh smiled impertinently.

Judith snapped, "If we're not careful, humans will wipe out great whites inside fifty years. We know *nothing* about their population dynamics or reproductive behavior. These creatures are the most efficient, high-tech hunters on Earth."

"High-tech?" interrupted Carol Martinez, a nineteen-year-old sophomore who had just decided to apply for a fisheries major. "I thought fish were pretty dumb."

"*We* should be learning from *them*. They are swimming computers that can sense light, sound, electrical fields, magnetic fields, and vibrations. They sense every creature within a half mile. Great whites have no fat, are almost totally disease-free, and are one of only eight shark species that are warm-blooded—and we don't how they do it. We'd freeze. Besides they're highly intelligent. What better creature could there be to study?"

Josh folded his arms and shrugged, "One that doesn't want to eat me."

Carol fidgeted with the notebook she carried. "I've only studied small, freshwater fish. What will we do if we find a shark?"

"Oh, we'll find plenty of great whites," Jennings called over his shoulder as he steered from the pilothouse.

Judith said, "I want to tag as many as possible. I want to inventory age, size, and sex of all we see. I want to observe their behavior and social interactions and organization. I want to collect live tissue and blood samples."

Josh Landers interrupted, "Collect *live* tissue? Doesn't that mean you'll have to get *real close* to the shark?"

Jennings throttled back when they reached a depth of 120 feet near the entrance of Tomales Bay. Gentle swells rolled out of the west-north-west on a light breeze.

Carol and one of the deck hands spent the last hour of their northward cruise mixing a smelly brew of tuna blood, fish guts, and crushed sardines. Josh had begged off, saying that the smell made him sick. Now the deckhand ladled the sludge into the water off the stern diving platform, creating a tantalizing trail that led to the *Jenny Mae*.

Under Dr. Bernard's supervision, Carol prepared a box of barbed, oval marking tags. With luck, they would be hooked into the dorsal fins of three or four sharks before the *Jenny Mae* headed home.

Dr. Bernard ordered Josh to rig the back half of a tuna onto a floating bait line and buoy. Judith filled out a data sheet with the day's environmental parameters: air and water temperature, wind speed, water visibility, current, and seal activity she could detect through powerful field binoculars.

Tense and silent minutes followed while the boat inched forward on idle—Judith waited eagerly, straining to see a dorsal fin cut through the rolling ocean swells. Both interns half-hoped the man-eating monsters would never come near.

Carol cried, "Look! A fin!"

"Aye. She's a great white," Jennings confirmed.

Judith ordered, "Launch the floater. Toss out the rubber duck [a bright yellow float with attached wooden flippers painted to look like a duck]."

Josh asked, "What's the duck for?"

"Great whites explore the world with their mouth. It's called test biting—sort of like picking up an unknown object with your hands to study it more closely. We don't know enough about this behavior."

"What's to know besides don't-let-it-happen-to-you?" Josh grinned.

Judith answered, "Great whites smell far better than humans. They can sense minute changes in electrical and magnetic fields through the water—even those caused by a human heartbeat. Their hearing is phenomenal. And yet for some reason they have to mouth things in order to understand them. And we don't know why. Watch."

The dorsal fin disappeared. The boat gently rocked with the steady swells.

"It's gone," Carol sighed, trying to build her enthusiasm for a close encounter with a deadly shark.

"No. It's circling—studying us from below, spiraling in closer and closer."

Almost as if bored, the shark's snout eased out of the water. Even from twenty feet, the sight of this great predator was chilling. The tuna float was pulled into its gaping mouth. The shark held for a second and let go. Again it seized the float, shook lightly, and again let go, sinking out of sight into the blue. It hadn't eaten the tuna but left great rips where its serrated teeth sawed through the meat.

"See?" said Judith. "It was only testing the float."

Josh stammered, "But that could have been my leg!"

Judith nodded. "Yes. That's what happens to most humans who are attacked. Great whites test bite and let go. If a great white was really after you, you'd never live to tell the tale." She called to a deckhand, "Drag the duck to the stern. We'll try to get the shark to come close."

Judith climbed onto the diving platform, a wooden ledge behind the stern railing. The platform ran the width of the boat, was three feet wide, and rested six inches above the waterline.

"You want the shark *closer?*" gasped Josh.

Judith chuckled and shook her head, "Interns . . . "

The shark cruised past the stern of the *Jenny Mae.*

"A five-meter female," Judith announced, squinting down at the dark silhouette now drifting a few feet under the surface in a counterclockwise circle around the boat. It looked like the shadow of a passing cloud. Judith tossed a hunk of tuna into its path, hoping to lure the shark to the surface. It looped past, ignoring the bait.

"Look it's been tagged!" She pointed to Josh. "Get the tag number." She turned to Carol. "Take notes."

The shark rose to nudge the tuna with its snout. Kneeling less than four feet away on the platform, Judith called out scars, markings, approximate age.

And then the tuna was gone, almost like a magician's trick. In the blink of an eye, the shark sucked it under and down its gullet.

Suddenly, the *Jenny Mae* began to feel overly small and fragile to the two interns. In their eyes, the shark had grown to a whale-size monster with a craving for human flesh.

Judith splashed her hand in the water.

"What are you doing?" cried Carol. "The shark's still down there!"

Judith explained, "I have to draw it closer if I'm to study how a great white explores its world."

"Yeah. Like how it eats," added Josh, standing well back from the rail.

Again Judith splashed—lightly, almost as if strumming her fingers on the surface. Both interns stood wide-eyed, frozen in fear.

"It knows my hand is here. No human can touch the ocean without some shark sensing it."

Judith stared past the sunlight dancing off the surface into the deep, dark waters below. "Come on, girl," she murmured, rhythmically splashing her fingers again. A deep, expectant quiet settled over the *Jenny Mae,* broken only by the soft lapping of the swells against the hull.

The water under her hand seemed to bulge slightly. Reflexively, Judith jerked her hand up just as the snout and gaping mouth of this sixteen-foot, three-ton predator broke vertically through the surface of the ocean, like a slow-motion submarine-launched missile, and hung there for a moment as if wondering where Judith's hand had gone.

Water streamed off its snout and gurgled from its mouth as it rose higher. The snout was deeply scarred—perhaps from test-biting one too many shark cages and boat motor mounts. The mouth was still bloody from its last feast. The finger-long serrated teeth almost glowed, pearl white against pink gums.

Judith reached out and held its snout, now even with her shoulders. With a quick jerk of its head, the shark tried to flip her hand into its waiting mouth. Judith gripped the rough skin of the snout and held on. She thrilled at the raw power of this mighty creature—not evil—just determined and purposeful. She let go, and it sank back underwater with a final, more violent thrash.

Smiling, Judith turned to her interns, who stood frozen in disbelief at the rail. "Great whites are really very curious and playful."

"*Playful?!*" Carol blurted. "She tried to eat you! Trout fingerlings never did that."

Judith asked, "Did you get the tag number?"

Josh stammered, "No, ma'am. I . . . I forgot to look."

"Don't forget this time!" Judith instructed, "Hand me the tissue pole [an eight-foot metal pole with an "O"-shaped surgical blade on the end to punch out a small core sample of tissue and blood]."

Judith knelt on the dive platform holding the tissue pole like a harpoon. The shark seemed to wander away, then wheeled on its right pectoral fin and glided back toward Judith. It paused and rose out of the water, treading water with its tail while one black eye stared at the boat. Then it flopped forward as if to say, "Put your hand back in my ocean. I'm ready to play again."

"Did you *see* that?" Carol exclaimed. "That was . . . weird."

Judith answered, "It's called spyhopping. Quite normal for great whites. They do it mostly to search for seals." Again she focused on the shark. "Come on back, girl. . . . A little closer . . . "

The dark shadow of the shark knifed toward Judith and the diving platform. In a lightning quick strike, Judith jabbed her pole forward. Before the shark could react, the pole was back out of the water and Judith was transferring the tissue sample into a glass test tube for shipment to the lab.

"I think the tag said D9865," whispered Josh.

"D?" Judith questioned. "That's not one of ours. We'll look it up on the registry when we get back."

Judith called to Jennings. "Bring out the shark cage. We're going in."

She pointed at Carol. "You want to get into fisheries. Get in a wet suit. This is your chance to see one of the world's greatest fishes up close."

"You won't make me leave the cage, will you?" she asked.

"Not today."

Josh asked, "Isn't this a little dangerous?"

Judith answered, "We can't observe social—group—interactions from up here."

"You mean sharks act like a . . . a family?" Carol asked. "Don't you mean a *school?*"

Judith said, "Sharks are smart. They may show some pack identity and loyalty. But we don't know. They may hunt in coordination like lionesses do and that's why they tend to gather in small, specific areas. We don't know if there they have a social hierarchy, how different generations interact, if they are gregarious . . . nothing. That's why we have to watch them in their natural environment—underwater."

Judith Bernard and Carol Martinez carefully checked each other's equipment. Judith said, "Watch carefully down there."

"You mean so we don't get eaten?"

Judith smiled. "I mean watch the way individuals and the group behave and interact. Watch what they do and how they do it. Watch and help humanity learn." She turned to the other interns. "Stay alert and watch for opportunities to tag."

Walter Jennings lowered the steel-barred cage with a power winch. Two wet suited divers rolled off the dive platform and down through the open top of the cage. Their bubbles rose to the surface. Five great whites lazily circled below and beside them, curious, playful, planning. It was just another day of shark research.

After Words

Only a dozen researchers scattered across the world are studying great white sharks. At that rate, it will take decades to amass the necessary data to be able to understand and protect the king of the ocean from its one natural predator—humans. The research continues—as does the steep decline in great white populations.

* * *

Suggested Topics to Explore

This story deals with marine biology and sharks. Here are starting questions that will help you discuss and research both.

1. Should we work to save great white sharks or let them become extinct? Search for arguments on both sides of this question.

2. Why would scientists want to study and understand great white sharks? List as many reasons as you can.

3. Diving with sharks is dangerous. How would you decide how much danger is acceptable during your own research? How do you decide how much risk and danger you will accept in your daily life?

For Further Reading About This Story

Arnold, Caroline. *Watch Out for Sharks!* New York: Clarion Books, 1991.
Behrens, June. *Sharks!* Chicago: Children's Press, 1990.
Berger, Gilda. *Sharks.* Garden City, NY: Doubleday, 1994.
Coupe, Sheena. *Sharks.* New York: Facts on File, 1990.
Langley, Andrew. *The World of Sharks.* New York: Bookwright Press, 1993.
Lawrence, R.D. *Shark!: Nature's Masterpiece.* Shelbury, VT: Chapter Publishers, 1994.

MacQuitty, Miranda. *Shark.* New York: Knopf, 1992.

Maestro, Betsy. *A Sea Full of Sharks.* New York: Scholastic, 1990.

Markle, Sandra. *Outside and Inside Sharks.* New York: Atheneum Books for Young Readers, 1996.

Perrine, Doug. *Sharks.* Stillwater, MN: Voyager Press, 1995.

Robson, Denny. *Sharks.* New York: Gloucester Press, 1992.

Romashko, Sandra. *Shark: Lord of the Sea.* Miami, FL: Windward Publications, 1994.

Wilson, Lynn. *Sharks!* New York: Platt and Munk, 1992.

Barbara Bond

Water Logged:　　　　　　Plant Biologist
A Science Adventure

Forests survive on sunlight and water. But how does a tree pump water up to its top branches? How much water does a large tree use? How much water does a forest require? Barbara Bond needed to find out—and she had to dangle 300 feet in the air in order to do it.

A Science Adventure in an Oregon Redwood Tree

A hot July sun filtered through towering redwoods to dribble splotchy light on the cool forest floor tucked at the 4,000-foot level of the Siskiyou Mountains along the California-Oregon border. A white van with orange and black letters, OSU, across both sides climbed over ruts and rocks struggling up this little-used logging trail. A trailer loaded with generator, gas cans, and camping equipment bounced behind in the choking dust.

Forty-three-year-old Oregon State University forestry professor, Barbara Bond, sat in the front seat this summer, 2000, afternoon poring over topographic maps. She pointed at an angle uphill. "Up through that small saddle."

The twenty-five year-old driver, graduate student Karen Gebhart, gunned the engine as the rear tires spun in the loose dirt and steered where her boss pointed.

Joseph Werner, a twenty-four-year-old graduate student, sat in the back. "Ow! Watch it!" he yelled as the vehicle lurched and he was tossed across the van stuffed with equipment and the rest of their camping supplies.

"It should be just ahead and to the left," Barbara announced.

She and Karen scanned the thick-trunked trees as the van inched forward.

"There. That one!" Barbara called, pointing at a massive red-wood, easily 300 feet tall and fifteen feet across at the base. "That's our tree."

She folded her maps and stretched. "Park in that clearing. Unload!"

"Right, chief!" Joseph called as he scrambled over piles of supplies and out the back doors of the van.

Barbara walked around her chosen tree, nodding with satisfaction. Deeply grooved reddish bark rose straight into the sky for over 100 feet before being interrupted by the first undersized branch. "Set up the generator and equipment here. We'll erect a canopy tent over it in case we get afternoon showers."

"We can set up camp on that level area beyond the van," Karen suggested.

The team's test equipment included a video monitor, power amplifiers, video recording equipment, coils of video cable, a power microscope, a tub of climbing gear, chemical monitors and sensors, medical imaging equipment, folding tables, probes and syringes laid out to look like operating room trays, shovels, axes, picks, and hand brushes like those used by umpires to dust off home plate.

"That's a lot of equipment just to look at a tree, chief," said Joseph, a last-minute addition to the team who was brought in because of his rock climbing experience. "What's the plan?"

Barbara glanced up from connecting equipment and power cords. "We do it all."

"Do it all?"

Karen Gebhart rolled her eyes and sighed. "That's what you get for bringing someone into the field who's never had a plant physiology class."

"Gimme a break! I'm an engineering student."

"What I mean," explained Barbara, "is that we will calculate a complete water budget for this one tree over three days. We'll measure xylem pressure at the roots and along the trunk, evaporation rates, photosynthesis rates, and water transport velocity and flow rate. We'll microscopically examine xylem walls and diameter to estimate friction. . . . "

"Whoa!" Joseph exclaimed, holding up his hands to stop her. "First, what's a xylum?"

"*Xylem.* They are the tiny pipes—like arteries—in the tree trunk that lift water up to the leaves. Most researchers think of them as inert pips. But I'm not sure that's correct."

"Do we care?"

"Of course we do. Plants are big water consumers. Pound-for-pound, a tree like this will drink up ten to fifteen times as much water as a human. You weigh . . . what . . . one hundred and fifty pounds? This tree weighs hundreds of tons. Do the math. That's a lot of water that has to be pumped up three hundred feet every day. And this tree has no heart, no power pumps to shove the water up to a great height. Trees have a lot to teach us."

"I've taken advanced classes in hydraulic engineering," Joseph said. "If I knew something about the friction in those xylem pipes, I could calculate how many horsepower you'd need to do the job. So how does a tree do it?"

"That's the question," Barbara answered, "These trees shouldn't be able to pump massive amounts of water three hundred feet into the air. But they do. There has been too much conjecture, theory, and simulation modeling of that process and not enough hard data. We're going to collect some data."

Karen asked, "Where do we start?"

"Root pressure," Barbara answered. "Shovels and trowels."

The trio split into a circle around the giant tree and began to dig in the sandy, powdery dirt. "Careful, Joseph," Barbara called. "Don't break any roots."

"Right, chief."

Once a digger exposed a main root—often as big around as a water pipe—they slowed their digging, carefully probing outward toward the maze of tiny rootlets that actually sucked water and nutrients from the earth.

"I've got a good system," Karen called, wiping sweat from her forehead.

"Good. Get a pressure probe."

Karen gently jammed the needle-sharp probe into a small root tributary. "Only one-and-a-half atmospheres." [One atmosphere equals the amount of pressure exerted by the atmosphere at sea level. It's 14.7 pounds per square inch unless a high-pressure or low-pressure weather system rolls in to slightly change it.]

"Try up higher," Barbara instructed.

Working her probe into a main root only six feet from the tree trunk, Karen glanced at the meter's dial. "Same reading here."

Barbara nodded. "'Bout what I expected. Junipers, pines, and conifers all seem to have low water pressure in their roots."

"So what does that mean?" Joseph asked.

"You should know that," scoffed Barbara. "It's basic engineering."

"I understand water pressure," Joseph replied. "I just don't understand trees."

Barbara explained, "It means the roots don't build up a powerful pressure that can force water up through the xylem. It means that the water has to be pulled up—sucked up—from above."

"A vacuum?" Joseph asked.

"Probably. Let's find out. That's where we're going next."

"Where?"

Barbara smiled and pointed up.

After three root probes had been inserted and cable connected to chart recorders, Barbara opened a large plastic tub.

"That looks like telephone pole climbing equipment," said Joseph.

"It is. Except for this harness belt."

Like telephone linemen, who use leather belts looped around the pole to keep them from falling, tree climbers looped this belt around a tree trunk. But this belt was sixty feet long and was really a twin belt. Two body harnesses were bolted in—one for each side of the tree. Two people climbed together. (One climber would never be able to maneuver the belts up the far side of a giant tree.)

"Why *two* belts?" Joseph asked.

Karen explained, "When you reach a branch, unbuckle one belt at a time and rebuckle it above the branch. You're always strapped in."

Barbara and Joseph strapped on crampons (spikes attached to climbers' boots) to grip the tree on the way up. Electric drills hung from their belts as did bags with a variety of probes.

"Take food and water," Barbara cautioned. "We're going to be up there a while." Once buckled into their climbing harnesses, the climbers couldn't see each other around the massive trunk. Karen, on the ground, called directions.

The pattern was simple. Lift one foot. Slam the spikes on that boot deep enough through the red bark so that it held the climber's weight. Step up. Finally, snap the belt to free it from the bark and hoist it up another foot.

Barbara's arms and shoulders began to burn from lifting and snapping the thick belt that seemed to delight in snagging on the rough bark. By the time they reached their first marker, sixty feet above the forest floor, she was panting.

Karen called, "Your plan calls for both pressure and video imaging probes at this height."

Barbara nodded and used specialty, extra-long drill bits to gouge two thin holes deep into the wood of the trunk. Into one she fed a needlelike pressure syringe and a second probe designed to detect ions (electrically charged atoms or molecules). Previously, scientists had had great difficulty accurately measuring pressure in xylem tubes in tree trunks. Barbara hoped her new medically based syringes would work better. Into the other hole she fed a slender video probe, the kind used for orthoscopic surgeries.

She attached both to a battery-powered radio transmitter that she nailed to the tree. "Getting anything?" she called down.

Karen clicked on the receiver and monitor. "Good video image coming in. . . . Excellent! I can see the boundary between two xylem tubes." She crossed to another monitor. "Not getting anything from the pressure probe. Try drilling a little deeper."

Barbara shoved the pressure syringe a small fraction of an inch forward.

"There! Getting a good negative pressure now. . . . Minus eight atmospheres."

Joe called, "What does *that* mean?"

From around the tree trunk Barbara answered. "If positive pressure in the roots *pushes* water up, negative pressure measures how hard the tree is sucking to *pull* water up."

Joseph asked, "How can a tree *suck?*"

"We think it starts in the leaves as water evaporates leaving an empty space behind. That space forms a vacuum that sucks water out of the veins in the leaf, which then have to suck water from the leaf stems, and so on." Barbara laughed. "But that's part of what we're here to find out. Keep climbing!"

They climbed higher. Ninety feet. One hundred feet. Barbara's arms and legs were beginning to cramp when they paused at 120 feet to work the belts around a gnarled branch.

Karen called, "Joe. Slow down. You're getting too far ahead of Barbara."

If one climber got ahead of the other, the belt would bind too tightly against the tree. Dangling high in the air, it became a dangerous struggle to free the belt.

With a sharp squeal, Barbara slipped when a chunk of bark broke away under her crampon spikes. She tumbled down, scraping across the tough bark until the belt snapped tight. Her left shirtsleeve was shredded by the bark. Welts and scrapes covered that arm. Blood oozed in trickles down her arm and hand to drip forty yards to the ground below.

Now both climbers were jammed tight against the tree, connected by the leather belts twisted at a steep angle between Barbara, dangling below, and Joseph above. Pressed tight against the tree, Joseph screamed, "What happened? What happened?"

Neither climber could see the other. The wind stirred, moaning through the forest branches, making it hard to hear Karen talk 120 feet below. Karen guided Joseph down the tree far enough to release the clamplike tension of the belt. Even with his climbing skills, it took a full ten minutes for him to wiggle lower and ease the grip of the belts.

In two hours the team had fixed three sets of probes into the trunk's xylem and had reached the top canopy at over 300 feet. Barbara ached all over. Her head still throbbed from being smashed against the tree and her left arm had grown stiff and tender.

Joseph's job was to estimate the size of the overall tree canopy while Barbara used hand-held meters to measure evaporation rates as well as oxygen (O_2) and carbon dioxide (CO_2) levels. From this lofty height, Barbara felt she had an eagle's view over the steep, rugged ridges of the Siskiyou Mountains.

She collected leaf samples and attached an evaporation meter to a small branch and connected that to the last of her radio transmitters. Now they would get a continuous reading of evaporation and photosynthesis rates.

"Why do you need more than a single reading?" Joseph asked.

"I believe that most tall trees close their pores in the hot afternoon to reduce water consumption rates. It also reduces photosynthesis, but keeps the tree from using more water than the xylem can deliver. It takes a series of measurements to create an accurate picture of it."

The rest of the afternoon was consumed in the descent. "Belt or no belt," Barbara said when they finally touched solid ground, "we were plenty high enough to kill ourselves if anything went wrong."

Early on the second morning, Barbara fired up the generator to power the monitor equipment. "Joseph, you'll climb about twenty feet up and drill two bores into the trunk. We'll study the xylem cells in those samples with the microscope."

"Right, chief."

"Karen, you inject tracer dye in a major root and we'll see how fast it moves up the trunk."

Sitting at the monitors thirty minutes later, Barbara said, "I'm detecting dye at the sixty-foot probe already. She checked her stopwatch and made several calculations. Water is rising at a rate of one hundred and fifty feet per hour!"

By noon Karen noticed the ion counter indicating a rapid ion buildup in the xylem. She shifted to the video monitor. "When ions build up, those membranes between xylem tubes swell. It increases water flow rates."

Two hours later, ion rates dropped dramatically. Membranes thinned. Flow rates slowed.

"Check evaporation rates," Barbara ordered.

Karen checked and reported. "Evaporation rates just fell way off."

Barbara flipped through the digital displays of their various probes and counters. "This tree seems to be a much more complex and sophisticated system than we thought. Water is sucked up through the xylem by negative pressure created by evaporation. But, look, as that pressure rose to a level that could collapse individual xylem tubes, the tree somehow increased the density of electrically charged ions to increase water flow rates and reduce the negative pressure back to safe levels. When that didn't work, the tree closed leaf pores to reduce evaporation and lower water demand."

Barbara tapped a pencil while she studied the screens and printouts. "This tree is very active in controlling water flow. We never gave them that much credit."

"So that proves it?" Joseph offered.

"Certainly not. Our data are for just one tree. We need detailed data for hundreds of trees from all across the country to prove anything. That will take decades."

After Words

The data Barbara Bond has collected on water flow through trees has become both a model for future data collections and a solid start toward the database needed to better manage the nation's forests and the interaction between forest and water.

* * *

Suggested Topics to Explore

This story deals with forestry and plant water consumption. Here are starting questions that will help you discuss and research both.

1. Why would scientists care about how much water a tree uses? To whom would that information be useful and valuable? Why would scientists want to know how a tree controls the flow of water from roots, through trunk and up to its leaves? How could scientists, forest managers, and urban managers use that information?

2. What do forest managers and foresters do? What does forest management mean? Research the history and practice of this field of science.

For Further Reading About This Story

Burnie, David. *Tree.* New York: Knopf, 1989.

Garfitt, J. E. *Natural Management of Woods.* New York: Wiley, 1995.

Greenaway, Theresa. *Trees.* New York: Houghton Mifflin, 1995.

Kohn, Kathryn. *Creating a Forestry for the 21st Century.* Raleigh, NC: Island Press, 1997.

Markle, Sandra. *Outside and Inside a Tree.* New York: Bradbury Press, 1993.

Page, Jake. *Forest.* New York: Time-Life Books, 1988.

Pascoe, Elaine. *Leaves and Trees.* Philadelphia, PA: Blackbuck Press, 2001.

Ann Bowles

"Sound" Advice: Bioacoustician
A Science Advenure

How can a scientist document the impact of human noise pollution on a desert species like a desert tortoise? Ann Bowles did it by crawling through the night desert with a microphone and a set of earphones, trying to avoid rattlesnakes, scorpions, and the razor-sharp cactus needles.

A Science Adventure in the California Desert

The afternoon heat peaked at a shimmering 112 degrees in the shade as thirty-eight-year-old animal linguist Ann Bowles and her assistant, Scott Eckett, stopped their trucks in the California desert forty miles southwest of Barstow. This grim, heat-soaked section of desert was their study site. On this afternoon of June 18, 1995, heat rose in waves and blurred the distant mountain peaks.

Ann Bowles was a bioacoustician with Hubbs-Sea World Park. For this project she had been hired to study the noise impact that proposed development would inflict on desert tortoises.

Ann climbed out of the cab of her truck and winced as the heat slammed into her. Scott pulled his truck to a stop beside her and groaned as the sweltering desert air flooded into his cab when he opened the door. "Now I know why I live along the coast in San Diego. Gawd, it's hot out here."

The two aquamarine trucks with red "Sea World" lettering on the side looked comically lost and out of place in the desert. Each truck pulled a trailer stuffed with sound equipment. One was set up as a portable sound studio.

Scott squinted as he gazed around the flat and barren landscape of dirt, bleached rocks, thorny scrub brush, and an occasional cactus. "So, where are the turtles?"

"Tortoises," Ann corrected.

"What's the difference?"

"What's the difference between a harbor seal and a sea lion?"

Scott shrugged, "Different species."

Ann nodded, "Uh-huh," and turned back to unlock her trailer and begin the process of unloading bulky, heavy sound equipment.

"Hey, I'm a *marine* biologist. I don't have to know about desert animals. We work for a *sea* park and study things that live in the *ocean*. So why come out to the desert?"

"Noise," Ann called from deep inside her trailer.

"I know *that*," he called after her. "But why did you accept the job? It's not marine."

Lugging out the first of the shade tents that would shelter their banks of equipment, Ann said, "It's about disrupting the natural rhythm and life of a part of nature." When she returned with her second armful of tent poles she added, "During the oral exam for my doctorate, one professor asked me why birds sing. I tried to give a scientific answer. He interrupted and said, 'No. Because they want to.' One of the first impacts of human encroachment into a new area is that human noise reduces birds' singing."

Scott shrugged, "So?"

"That has major impacts on their social structure, mating, and survival. But even more fundamentally, it negatively affects the quality of their lives."

Scott folded his arms and cocked his head. "But we're not here to study birds."

As the two began to assemble the pole frame and canvas cover of the first tent, Ann answered, "We're here to see if we can prevent new human noise from negatively affecting the lives of desert tortoises."

Sinking tent stakes into the soft desert soil, Scott repeated, "So, where are the *tortoises?*"

Ann smiled and wiped the sweat from her face, "Tortoises are nocturnal. We'll search for *signs* of tortoises during the day, and work at night when they're awake and active." She chuckled and pointed at the trailers. "First you have a lot of equipment to set up."

The sun set at 8:40 P.M. By 9:00, it was pitch black in the desert. Scott winced as he tripped over a campstool. "Oww! I can't see a thing out here in the dark. Turn on some lights."

Ann shook her head. "That might frighten away any nearby tortoises. Besides, we brought night vision goggles." She handed him a pair.

Scott adjusted the sensitivity dial on the side of the thick goggles. "Now everything is dull green."

"Better than not seeing at all."

Ann cocked her head, straining to hear any distant noises. "Stand still and record ambient background sound. Use both an omnidirectional mike and the shotgun mike. Slowly pan with the shot gun to see if you pick up any movement."

"It's so quiet out here," Scott answered, "I'm not sure I'll record anything."

He slipped on earphones and plugged in both mikes. The omnidirectional he placed on a mike stand, while he held the long shotgun mike, which only picked up sound from directly in front of it.

"Recording," Scott announced and began a slow steady turn with the shotgun mike. "End recording." He punched the stop button. "Want me to run it through the wave analyzer and see if we got anything?"

"We'll do that in the morning," Ann answered. "I saw fresh tracks of several tortoises just before sunset. I want to start by checking their hearing." She added, "Oh, and be careful when you look under things."

"Things?" Scott repeated.

"Rocks, fallen branches, bushes. Those are the kinds of places snakes and scorpions like to hide."

It took less than fifteen minutes for Ann and Scott to find two desert tortoises and carry them back to the sound studio trailer. The "studio" featured soundproof walls, and built-in recording and playback equipment. They placed the eighteen-inch-long tortoises on the padded floor. One stretched its neck and marched—like a drum major—around the walls, exploring. The other sat quietly in one corner, cautiously peering at the humans.

Ann sat on the floor, fascinated by these two charming animals and their distinct personalities. Their dry, wrinkled skin—warmed by the long day's sun—was soft to the touch.

"Look!" she whispered, "They like to be scratched." Both had repeatedly extended their necks after her light touch as if asking for more. "Their faces remind me of the village elders I met when I was a girl in Peru—so alive and full of character."

Scott finished checking the equipment, stooped low, and stuck his hand out to one of the tortoises.

"Owww!" He jerked back his hand and sucked on the deep red mark on his finger.

Ann chuckled, "Move slower and that won't happen. They can snap hard enough to break skin."

"But can they hear?" asked Scott.

Ann nodded toward the equipment controls. "Some reports I've read suggest that they don't hear well at summer temperatures. Let's see."

"Standard set of tones we'd use on marine mammals?" Scott asked.

"Let's start there and see what happens."

A series of tones varying in pitch played from a speaker in one corner of the room. "Watch for any reaction or movement. Start at a volume setting of minus two decibels. We'll increase from there if we need to."

At first the tortoises seemed not to acknowledge the noise in any way. They seemed not to be aware of it. Scott asked, "Should I increase volume?"

"Not yet," Ann answered, "Watch."

"Hey, look at that," Scott exclaimed. "They've both edged nearer to the back end of the trailer."

Ann nodded. "They've moved away from the noise. Shift the tones to a back speaker. Same volume."

In fifteen minutes, both tortoises had meandered a few feet nearer to the front.

Ann smiled. "So they *can* hear—even in summer temperatures."

"And at a fairly low volume," Scott added. "I'd call their hearing sensitive."

Then Ann frowned. "We need a more definite reaction than a two-foot meander. Hand me the smallest pair of earphones and a clamp-on monitor."

Ann clamped the heart monitor to one tortoise's shell. It would monitor heart and breathing rates. The earphones would allow her to feed exactly calibrated tones to the tortoise. "Getting a signal?" she asked.

Scott patched in an oscilloscope to the monitor's radio receiver. "Good blips for both heart and breathing."

Ann adjusted the earphones to fit the tortoise's small head. It blinked and mournfully looked up at her as if to ask, "What are you doing to me?"

"Start the tones," Ann ordered.

The tortoise sat still and blinked.

"Getting any reaction to the tones?" Ann asked.

"No change in breathing or heart rate," Scott answered from the control booth.

"Increase volume." Ann waited and watched. "Anything now?"

"Negative."

Soon the tortoise was being blasted by tones much louder than those they had seemed to react to over the speakers.

Ann sighed. "It's after midnight. We should let these tortoises go. Besides, I'm confused. Did they hear and react to our tones or not?"

Scott rubbed his face and scratched his head. "Well maybe . . . That is . . . I think . . . "

The next night the two researchers decided to test not in the sound booth—an unfamiliar, artificial environment for the tortoises—but in the desert itself. "We'll also use environmental sounds instead of standard tones," Ann decided.

They collected two new tortoises. One was docile and cautious. One was snappy and curious about the sound equipment, poking and pawing the portable speakers and bank of equipment tied by a long power cord to the trailers.

Ann connected the heart monitor to one of the tortoise's shell. "I'm convinced they physically hear very well. The question is: Do they *use* their physical hearing, or rely on other senses?"

She dug a set of digital tapes out of her tent. "I borrowed these tapes from the biology department of the natural sciences museum. You keep the tortoises in this clearing between the speakers. I'll play the tapes." She squinted through her night vision goggles to read the first label. "First up is a desert coyote."

The mournful howl of a coyote filled the clearing. Both tortoises froze. The bolder one twisted its head as if trying both to identify and locate the sound. Then it turned and sped toward the trailers. The other withdrew into its shell as a distant real coyote howled in chilling answer to the speaker.

Ann said, "No change in breathing. Slight elevation of heart rate. Next a rattlesnake."

Scott shivered and nervously glanced over his shoulders as the hiss and rattle of the ferocious snake played through one of the speakers. The reaction of the tortoises was much the same as before.

"See?" said Ann. "They are definitely making defensive decisions based on sound. They *do* use their hearing. Let's try some human sounds."

She played a jet aircraft flying low overhead as if coming in to land. Both tortoises froze, one of them in mid-stride. "Heart rate and breathing have both dipped slightly lower."

"Lower?" questioned Scott. "The jet noise calmed them down?"

"Let's try a dune buggy," said Ann. They waited twenty minutes for the tortoises to relax and move again before blaring the rumble and whine of a small dune buggy racing across the desert. Again both tortoises froze, standing stone still and unblinking. "Heart rate and breathing dropped again—just like before."

This time they had to wait a full hour before the tortoises began to move or walk.

"Wait!" Ann exclaimed. "*That* is their response. They freeze. Frightening, unaccustomed sounds make them freeze. They almost go into a catatonic state with depressed heart rate and breathing."

Scott nodded and agreed, "The sounds scare them and force them into this frozen response."

"But that's terrible," said Ann. "They're helpless for an hour or more every time a plane or truck passes by. One Jet Ski making one pass, racing along the shore of a nearby lake, could freeze dozens of tortoises for up to two hours. One jet taking off or landing could do the same. Then they're easy targets for any predator and susceptible to sun exposure during the day. They can't eat. Their whole lives will be disrupted. This could be disastrous!"

"Mystery solved. Mission accomplished," said Scott. "Now we can pack up and head back, right?"

Ann shook her head. "We have to test and verify this theory. We could be out here easily another week repeating the tests and varying sound and volume." She stretched and yawned. "But for now let's call it a night."

After Words

Ann Bowles's results helped change state and federal development policies in the southwestern deserts and protect greater land areas from noise encroachment. Her work with marine mammals continues up and down the Pacific coast and has been equally valuable to state and local government officials.

* * *

Suggested Topics to Explore

This story deals with noise pollution and desert tortoises. Here are starting questions that will help you discuss and research both.

1. What's the difference between a tortoise and a turtle? Research desert tortoises. Where do they live? How long do they live? Where do they fit within the structure of the desert ecosystem?

2. Why bother to study the language (oral communication) of birds and animals? What do scientists learn of value this way? Can you find any information in the library or on the Internet about bioacoustics?

3. What is noise pollution? When and how is noise harmful? Does noise pollution ever affect you? Make a list of all the unpleasant and harmful noises you hear in a day. Can you imagine what affect these noises might have on an animal that couldn't understand where they came from?

For Further Reading About This Story

Bailey, Donna. *Noise and Fumes.* New York: Franklin Watts, 1991.
Bare, Colleen. *The Durable Desert Tortoise.* New York: Dodd Mead, 1989.
Baskin-Salzberg, Anita. *Turtle.* New York: Franklin Watts, 1996.
Kavaler, Lucy. *Noise! The New Menace.* Chicago: John Day & Company, 1989.
Lehrer, John. *Turtles and Tortoises.* Stilwater, FL: Mallard Press, 1990
Obst, Fritz. *Turtles, Tortoises, and Terrapins.* New York: St. Martin's Press, 1992.

Rachel Fuller Brown

Bold Mold: Biochemist
A Science Adventure

Rachel Fuller Brown needed to find an antibiotic capable of killing a wide variety of disease-producing fungi. But the killer she found had to be gentle enough to not harm the human patients it was to be used on. To find this one miracle drug, she had to test eighty different antibiotics each on thousands of dangerous fungi and molds—both in laboratory dishes and in live test animals.

A Science Adventure in the Lab

As if she carried a grave secret, short, stocky Dr. Elizabeth Hazen held the door closed behind her for a moment as she entered the second-floor lab on this afternoon of October 10, 1948. "Rachel? Where are you? We have a problem."

It was an airy and spacious lab with stainless steel counters, tidy cupboards, shelves, and drawers for rows of chemical agents, glass beakers, test tubes, petri dishes, and other equipment. This lab belonged to the Division of Laboratories and Research of New York State Department of Health in Albany, New York, and was run by chemist Rachel Brown.

Draped in a white lab coat, fifty-year-old Rachel Brown poked her head out of a back office space and smiled. When Rachel smiled she looked like everybody's favorite grandmother with her short, styled, silver hair and wire-rimmed "granny" glasses. "What brings you down to the second floor, Elizabeth?"

Elizabeth glanced over both shoulders as if not wanting to be overheard. "Fungi and molds are becoming a serious problem."

Rachel perched on a stool and crossed her arms. "Molds?"

Sounding exasperated, as if this problem should need no explanation, Elizabeth said, "As the use of antibiotics to control *bacterial* disease increases, the prevalence of *fungal* disease has also increased!"

Rachel nodded, "I have read reports that ringworm and moniliasis [a fungus-produced soreness of the mouth] have risen sharply. And you think they are connected to antibacterial use?"

"Of course they are! Many common antibiotics kill the bacteria that control the spread of harmful fungi."

"I see," said Rachel. "And you think that this laboratory—me—should study the problem and search for effective anti-fungals?"

"Absolutely," answered Elizabeth with a stern nod.

Rachel drummed her fingers on a stainless steel work bench while she thought, "So . . . we are going to grow fungi and test them against various antibiotics. . . . and then test the successful antibiotics in laboratory animals. . . . But Elizabeth, there are over two hundred and fifty thousand kinds of fungi."

Fungi are plants that do not contain the green matter, chlorophyll, and so cannot use photosynthesis to produce their own nutrients. Ranging from mushrooms to molds, most are harmless, but a number can cause serious illness and a few can destroy living tissue and are deadly.

Rachel shrugged. "All right, let's grow some mushrooms."

Elizabeth arched her eyebrows. "This is no joking matter. Mold spores—some of them deadly—will infect this room unless we take adequate precautions."

Rachel chuckled as she walked to the far end of the lab and tapped the glass front of a metal cabinet. "Do you forget, Elizabeth, that this is a state-of-the-art lab? We'll grow any dangerous fungi in this partial vacuum cabinet to prevent the escape of any spores."

A week later, virtually ever surface of the lab was covered in metal trays—like those a baker might use to bake five or six loaves of bread at a time. On each tray sat rows of glass petri dishes. In each, Rachel spread a fortified mulch growth medium. On the front of each, she taped a label card. Like a careful gardener, Rachel and her assistants then planted a few spores of different fungi in each dish.

They grew fifty dishes of each fungus at a time so they could test each fungus against a wide variety of antibiotics. They grew 300 different fungi in this first batch, each in its own tray. Rachel's lab team tended these 15,000 cup-sized dishes of fungus, measuring and recording their growth and condition. The lab crew misted the fungi when they grew too dry. They moved them if the temperature was wrong for their ideal growth.

A week later, Rachel dialed Elizabeth Hazen's interoffice phone number. "Elizabeth, you might want to come down for this. I have collected thirty antibiotics used in medicine. We're ready to test our first batch of samples."

The team wore masks and long rubber gloves whenever handling the fungi in the partial vacuum cabinet. For handling the antibiotics, they also wore heavy protective lab coats. Using eyedroppers, they dripped one drop of an antibiotic solution into each petri dish. By the end of the day they had tested Rachel's thirty antibiotics on over 200 species of fungus—and found no successes.

"There were several of the chemical agents," Rachel offered, "that *seemed* to hamper a few of the fungi."

Dr. Hazen shook her head. "The effects were minor. None of these antibiotics destroyed any of the fungal colonies."

Rachel drummed her fingers as she thought. "We only grew three hundred kinds of mold for this test. We will, of course, have to grow and test many more. But I am surprised that our antibiotics did so poorly. I believe we must also search for different kinds of antibiotics."

Three days later, Elizabeth and Rachel met in the lab. Rachel's lab technicians were busy growing new samples of fungi to test. Elizabeth said, "I have thoroughly searched the literature and have found references to several effective anti-fungal agents. But almost all, themselves, are dangerous to humans."

"Let's test them anyway," Rachel answered. "I may be able to chemically alter any we find to be particularly effective and render them harmless to humans."

Elizabeth spoke as she walked along the rows of fungus incubation trays, inspecting their new crop of fungi. "I have scheduled meetings with botanists from the Department of Forestry, and with tribal healers from two local tribes of Native Americans. I am hoping to find additional natural anti-fungal compounds to test."

It took three weeks for Dr. Hazen to identify a dozen new anti-fungal agents and prepare liquid solutions of each. Three were naturally occurring compounds she had to isolate from dirt samples provided by Native American tribesmen. Four were groups of bacteria effective in treating tree molds.

For these tests, the women added goggles to their protective wear, not knowing what kind of reaction they might get. When these new killers were dropped into the petri dishes of mold, many of the fungi sizzled and withered. In several dishes, the fuzz of growing mold almost instantly vanished.

"Very good," Rachel sighed as she stretched her tired back. "I think we have achieved excellent results."

"For *preliminary* tests," Elizabeth corrected.

"To be sure," agreed Rachel. "We must refine and purify these fungicides and test them against a wider variety of fungi. Our testing has only begun. Still, I was impressed with the effectiveness of the agent in bottle number twelve. Which was that?"

Elizabeth scanned her notes. "That was the *streptomycetes* group of bacteria. I isolated them from dirt samples provided by a chief of the Seneca tribe."

Rachel nodded. "Let's keep our eye on that one."

Next day, Dr. Brown and her team began to grow the next batch of 300 fungi for testing. A rhythm and routine settled over the lab as they turned into a factory for growing, nurturing, testing, and killing their trays of fungi. They filled rows of notebooks with the results of their daily activity and tests.

Three months later they concluded their testing. Eighty potential fungicides had been tested on over 25,000 fungi. They had grown over 1.25 million dishes of fungi. The *streptomycetes* had clearly been the most consistent and effective killer of the tested fungi.

In her chemistry lab, Rachel began the process of chemically dissecting the *streptomycetes* they had used in their tests. Over the period of several weeks, she isolated the individual elements of this agent and found the one bacteria in the sample that attacked and destroyed the fungal cells. The women named this specific bacteria organism *Streptomycetes noursei.*

While reporting her findings to her lab team and to Dr. Hazen, Rachel said, "*Streptomycetes noursei* kills fungi very effectively in a glass dish. But will it also kill the animals it is intended to save?"

"On to phase two," Elizabeth agreed with a nod of her head.

They started with lab mice, giving each a daily dose of *Streptomycetes noursei* while charting their weight and growth against a control group that didn't receive the fungal antibiotic. After three months it was clear that the antibiotic did not harm the mice and even seemed to extend the mice's average life span.

Rachel concluded, "We have shown that *Streptomycetes noursei* will not harm lab animals. But will it kill harmful fungi as well inside an animal as it does in a laboratory dish?"

"On to phase three?" Elizabeth asked.

"I think so," Rachel answered. "We'll inject mice with various disease-producing fungi and see if *Streptomycetes noursei* is as effective in the mice as it is in the lab petri dishes." She added, "You do this part of the study, Elizabeth, while I try to isolate the exact chemical compound and chemical mechanism by which *Streptomycetes noursei* destroys fungi."

Elizabeth rubbed her hands together. "The ultimate test. So many seeming miracle drugs work wonders in controlled laboratory conditions and then fail miserably in live tests inside a complex living test animal." She slowly shook her head. "We've been working on this study over a year and now a group of laboratory mice and monkeys will decide if it has all been wasted."

Rachel chuckled. "I agree, Elizabeth. This is about as exciting as it gets for two old lab rats like us!" Then she added, "Good luck!"

"Good luck to us both," Elizabeth corrected.

Elizabeth infected thirty-two mice with eight dangerous fungal molds. Four mice received injections of each mold. Two of those four would be treated with *Streptomycetes noursei*. Two would not. Dr. Hazen tracked the progress of each mouse and its fungal-caused disease over the course of a month. Every mouse treated with *Streptomycetes noursei* recovered. Only one of the control group recovered.

Dr. Hazen repeated the experiment using monkeys and achieved the same impressive results. *Streptomycetes noursei* clearly worked. It consistently destroyed dangerous fungal molds and didn't harm the living patient.

During this same two months, Rachel Brown worked with her microscope and chemical agents to isolated the specific protein created by *Streptomycetes noursei* that destroyed fungal cell walls and thus killed the fungus. After identifying the chemical structure of that protein, she had to develop a process to chemically create and purify an artificial version of that protein in the lab. She was able to describe for state and medical authorities the physical, chemical, and biological properties of this compound that made it different from all other available antibiotics.

Finally the two women scientists repeated the live tests on mice and monkeys with Dr. Brown's synthetic protein to see if it worked as well as the naturally grown *Streptomycetes noursei* that Elizabeth had already used.

It did. The testing was over. The effort was a smashing success.

After Words

Drs. Brown's and Hazen's program consumed over two years of work. It involved over 3,000,000 individual tests and experiments, required them to grow almost 1.5 million dishes of fungi, and used over 60,000 person-hours of work. In the end, the two women had created a new synthetic protein they named Nystatin, after New York State, the funder of their research.

Since its introduction in 1950, Nystatin has been the most successful and widely prescribed anti-fungal agent ever developed. It has saved countless lives and opened the door for other researchers to explore for additional medicines in the natural environment.

* * *

Suggested Topics to Explore

This story deals with fungi and biological/medical research. Here are starting questions that will help you discuss and research both.

1. Research Rachel Fuller Brown. What other noteworthy research did she conduct? How did she get her start in biochemical sciences? What awards has she won?

2. What is a fungus? Are there funguses you use regularly? Eat regularly? Are some beneficial? Which are dangerous and cause diseases? Which diseases are fungally caused?

3. In this story, Rachel Fuller Brown conducts exhaustive trial-and-error research, testing as many possible fungicides on as many different fungi as possible. Is this process common in science research? How else could she approach her research?

For Further Reading About This Story

Coldrey, Jennifer. *Discovering Fungi.* Harrisburg, PA: Bookwrights Press, 1991.

Haber, Louis. *Women Pioneers of Science.* New York: Harcourt Brace, 1991.

Hudler, George. *Magical Mushrooms, Mischievous Molds.* Princeton, NJ: Princeton University Press, 1998.

Silverstein, Alvin. *Fungi.* New York: 21st Century Books, 1996.

Souza, Dorothy. *What is a Fungus?* New York: Franklin Watts, 2002.

Jocelyn Bell Burnell

The Stuff of "Scruff":　　Astronomer
A Science Adventure

It was only a few squiggles buried in miles of line-chart printouts—the same kind of line charts used to record earthquakes. However, these little squiggles came from deep space and looked like signals that might be somebody's attempt to communicate. Imagine being the first human to find those signals that look like radio transmissions sent by intelligent aliens. That's what happened to Jocelyn Bell.

A Science Adventure in Astronomy

It looked like a forest after a raging fire with all the leaves and branches burned from bare tree trunks. Or maybe it resembled rows of pilings to support some monstrous pier. In truth, it was a 4.5-acre radio antenna field strung across the English countryside.

Beginning in the fall of 1965, twenty-four-year-old graduate student Jocelyn Bell and three other students spent eighteen months digging postholes in Cambridge University Astronomy professor Antony Hewish's antenna field—1,200 postholes! Jocelyn's once delicate hands were now covered in blisters and calluses.

Bell broke through thin sheets of ice in the winter with an ax. The rest of the year, she hauled dribbling ooze and mud from her holes as she sank each one three-and-a-half feet into the English soil. Most days she tramped back from the field soaked, mud-covered, and too tired to study.

Professor Hewish was building this giant antenna to detect radio frequency transmissions from the farthest corners of distant space. He hoped this added receiver power would allow him to discover new deep-space phenomena and celestial secrets.

After digging 1,200 holes that were spaced across 4.5 acres, the students had to erect a twelve-foot, 200-pound pole in each and pack dirt tight around. Then they had to climb the poles like telephone workers to string a maze of wire.

Twelve hundred telephone poles supported a criss-crossing network of 120 miles of wire. The wire mesh would act as Hewish's radio telescope, detecting any radio waves (electromagnetic radiation in the frequency band used for radio transmissions) that came from objects in deep space. Extremely large radio antennas can be focused—like a telescope—to search for radio signals in a very narrow portion of distant space. This gargantuan maze of wire would be the most sensitive radio frequency receiver on Earth.

On July 11, 1967, the final cable connections between the building (which housed Hewish's equipment and computer) and the antenna field were completed. With a great fanfare from an applauding crowd of university onlookers, Hewish fired up his radio receiver. Colored lights blinked on the various panels of equipment. Motors and cooling fans hummed and whined. Chart paper with a series of squiggly lines began to steadily creep from a printer at the far end of the room.

With a flourish, Hewish ripped off the first few inches of paper and announced that this chart paper (produced at the rate of one hundred feet each day) would reveal the unknown secrets of the cosmos. He handed the paper to Jocelyn—as if reviewing squiggly lines were too tedious and mundane to be worthy of his lofty mind—and announced that his graduate assistant (Jocelyn) would study each day's chart and report any findings to him. As Hewish swept from the stuffy equipment room, and as the crowd appreciatively applauded, Jocelyn stared apprehensively at the paper, slowly snaking out of the printer with its set of squiggly lines she would have to analyze.

The radio telescope translated radio waves into a series of parallel squiggly lines made by pens moving across rolls of paper. Jocelyn spent hours each day comparing the chart's squiggly lines to the position of known stars and distant galaxies and nebulae. Then the graduate scientist student compared the known electromagnetic emissions of these bodies to the chart's squiggles and spikes in order to account for each mark on the chart. It often took her eight hours to complete a review of one day's worth of printout.

She couldn't keep up. Within six months her "in-basket" of charts needing to be reviewed stretched for over three-quarters of a mile. She worked long into the night until her eyes ached, and still the monster machine spit out paper charts faster than Jocelyn could analyze them.

Two months after the telescope started up, Bell noticed an unusual, tightly packed pattern of lines that she called a "bit of scruff"—a squiggling pattern she couldn't explain—when checking a chart for one narrow slice of the night sky. She marked it with a question mark and moved on.

Four nights later, she saw the same pattern. She circled the scruff and mentioned it to Hewish. With a quick shrug, he dismissed it as a random and unimportant anomaly. It didn't look like anything he was searching for. Still, the unexplained marks stuck in Jocelyn's mind like an irritating buzz that can't quite be identified and won't quite go away.

One month later, Jocelyn found the same pattern of scruff and recognized that the antenna was focused on the same small slice of sky. Instead of just circling it and placing a question mark, she took the extra time to expand and measure the squiggles. Whatever it was, this radio signal regularly pulsed every one-and-one-third seconds. No natural body in the known universe emitted regular signals like that.

Immediately, Bell notified Hewish of her find. Again, he dismissed it and told her it was meaningless radio noise. He scoffed that it was obviously man-made because it pulsed so regularly and rapidly. He scolded her for wasting time on meaningless human transmission.

Jocelyn asked, "Then how did our antenna receive the signal?"

Hewish shrugged as if this conversation was a waste of time. "Reflection off the moon, scatter off a nearby rooftop, interference from a sun spot. It could even be a flaw in the antenna field."

Jocelyn began to argue. With a wave of his hands, Hewish dismissed her back to her work.

But Jocelyn could not simply return to work. She would not ignore this signal. Over the next three weeks she doggedly disproved each of Hewish's explanations. No, it was not a reflection off the moon. The moon had been in the wrong position to reflect signals back to Hewish's antenna. No, it was not reflection off a nearby building. The geometry was all wrong. No, there had been no sunspots to create interference at the correct times. No, the signal was not man-made. It came from deep space.

When Jocelyn found the same signal a month later, Hewish finally took note. He finally admitted that it *might* be a deep space signal. But from what? Nothing astronomers had ever seen before created such a rapid and regular pulse.

They seriously discussed the possibility that the signal was being sent from extraterrestrials (which they dubbed LGM, Little Green Men). After all, radioastronomers believed that they would be the first ones to detect a signal from alien life forms, because almost any civilization produced signals in the radio wave band as soon as they began to develop as a technological society.

Before Hewish publicly announced their theory, Bell found another bit of scruff on chart printouts from a different part of the sky. The pulses of this second signal came 1.2 seconds apart and at almost the exact same frequency. Because it seemed unlikely that there would be two separate groups of Little Green Men simultaneously trying to contact Earth on the same frequency, they ruled out the possibility that extraterrestrials were sending the signal. But what was it?

Every theoretician at Cambridge was brought in to explain Jocelyn's scruff. Hewish chaired meetings and seminars on it. Jocelyn was never invited to attend. She was told to sit at her desk and continue to read charts.

After months of study and calculation the science team concluded that those little bits of "scruff" were being transmitted by rotating stars. Astronomers had mathematically theorized that when a huge star runs out of nuclear fuel, all matter in the star collapsed inward, creating a gigantic explosion, called a supernova.

What remained after the explosion became a hundred million million times denser than ordinary matter. They called this compressed star a neutron star. If the star naturally rotated, its magnetic and electric fields would broadcast beams of powerful radio waves. From Earth, a rapidly rotating neutron star would appear to pulse. Cambridge scientists decided that Joceyln had discovered rotating neutron stars and, because they pulsed, named them "pulsars."

After Words

Jocelyn's discovery of pulsars was hailed as the astronomical "find of the century." It advanced our understanding of the universe and deep space and earned the 1974 Nobel Prize for Antony Hewish. In accepting the Nobel, Hewish gave not one word of recognition or thanks to Jocelyn Bell, the person who actually made the discovery and forced him to study it.

* * *

Suggested Topics to Explore

This story deals with radio astronomy and pulsars. Here are some starting questions that will help you discuss and research each.

1. Pulsars are spinning neutron stars, which, themselves, are the remnants of supernova explosions of previously giant stars, many times bigger than our sun. Once collapsed into a neutron star, these stars are immensely dense.

   One cubic foot of a neutron star weighs as much as a hundred million million cubic feet of earth. How much earth is that? The state of California is about 900 miles long and 250 miles wide. If you scraped off the top fifteen feet from the entire length and width of California, that would be about one hundred million million cubic feet of earth. If you compressed that entire mass into one cubic foot of space, it would then be as dense as a neutron star. It's almost unimaginable! Find other ways to show how dense pulsars and neutron stars are.

2. How many pulsars and neutron stars have scientists found? How common are they?

3. Most astronomers use telescopes to peer into the distant heavens searching for visible light. Some, however, look for other bands in the electromagnetic spectrum. Radioastronomers search for radio waves coming from outer space. Research radio astronomy and make a list of the discoveries that have come from this branch of astronomy.

   Now search for other types of astronomy that use other bands of radiation in their search for knowledge about the universe. What radiation bands do they use? What do they search for? What do we call these types of astronomy?

For Further Reading About This Story

McGrayne, Sharon Bertsch. *Nobel Prize Women in Science: Their Lives, Struggles, and Momentous Discoveries.* New York: Carol Publishing Group, A Birch Lane Press Book, 1993.

Raymo, Chet. *365 Starry Nights: An Introduction to Astronomy for Every Night of the Year.* New York: Simon & Schuster, 1992.

Schaaf, Fred. *The Amateru Astronomer: Explorations and Investigations.* New York: Franklin Watts, 1994.

Stille, Darlene R. *Extraordinary Women Scientists.* Chicago, IL: Children's Press, 1995.

Eugenie Clark

Deadly Sample: Marine Biologist
A Science Adventure

Her assignment was to dive near coral reefs after poisonous fish, while fending off deadly sharks and moray eels. However, this dive was Eugenie Clark's first-ever job as an oceanographer and the experimental aqualung she used had never been tested by Americans.

A Science Adventure in the South Pacific Ocean

The sound of surging air roared in Eugenie Clark's ears each time she sucked on her aqualung mouthpiece, rhythmically disturbing the glorious silence of the ocean. As she descended, the white glare of the surface faded into undulating curtains of brilliant blue that shimmered through blue-green waters. Eugenie (Genie) felt that she could see for miles—maybe all the way from this tiny South Pacific island of Kwajalene back to America.

On this afternoon of June 24, 1949, twenty-three-year-old Genie made her first dive on Kwajalene. She dove alone through the sparkling waters and under a sky of billowing white clouds that drifted lazily to the north.

Genie's aqualung underwater breathing system was still experimental, having recently been invented by Jacques Cousteau in France. Genie had previously tried hardhat diving with bulky brass helmet and boa constrictor-like air hose she had to lug across the bottom. This was her first aqualung dive and it felt wonderful! Like she was free. Like she was *part* of the ocean instead of an alien observer.

Genie wanted to hover weightless in the water and soak in this magical moment so that she could remember it forever. But this was supposed to be a working dive, the first dive of her first independent job as a recently graduated oceanographer.

Eugenie Clark had been hired by the U.S. Navy to collect samples of South Pacific poisonous fish. Many sailors had been poisoned during World War II by eating fish in the South Pacific. The Navy wanted to study these species in a lab and find ways to protect their seamen.

Still, Genie couldn't force herself to concentrate on work. After each breath she watched her air bubbles wiggle their way toward the surface now fifty feet above her. She watched tight schools of brilliantly colored fish glide along the wall of Kwajalene's coral reef that rose from the shadowy depths. As if they were part of a choreographed dance, the fish turned as one and sped off.

Below her Genie saw the eerie shapes of three sunken Japanese destroyers rise out of the gloom, victims of the fierce Pacific fighting during World War II. Schools of damselfish glided through shattered bridge windows as if wanting to play captain. Rows of mussels and anemones clung to long, gray gun barrels, now pointing only toward the endless abyss of the deep ocean.

Genie's attention was drawn to a menacing tiger shark prowling the reef like a feudal lord. With a quick flick of its tail it drove toward Genie, as if to challenge and drive her off or devour her if she wouldn't flee. Dreaded tiger sharks were the most aggressive of all man-killing sharks. But to Genie that shark seemed not evil but sleek and graceful. Its flat black eyes seemed not cold and merciless but observant and curious. She hovered motionless while the shark completed three wide circles just below her and dashed off along the reef wall.

Twenty minutes later, Genie waded ashore thoroughly exhilarated by her dive. The local guide and assistant she had hired, eighteen-year-old fisherman Ramon Quenga, sat patiently waiting for her in the shade of a fluttering mango tree. "You catch plenty fishes, ma'am?" Ramon spoke the broken pidgin English common to many Pacific Islanders for whom English was not the native language.

Genie shrugged and held up her empty net bag. "It was so exciting, I forgot to collect at all."

Ramon sucked a breath through his teeth creating a shrill whistle and rolled his eyes. Then he shook a telegram cable message from the Navy Department at Genie. "The Navy man say you have to send samples plenty quick, an' you come back with empty bag? Was'a matta? No fishes?"

Genie bristled at this reprimand from a mere assistant. "I'll do better tomorrow, Ramon. I just need to get used to the water here."

He slowly shook has head. "Lady, you gonna' get us fired if you don't do betta'." The Navy pay rates offered Ramon more income in a day than he could normally make in two weeks—his paycheck meant a lot to him.

Ramon helped Genie strip off her dive tanks, fins, and weight belt. Then he paused and rubbed the wispy stubble on his chin. "Maybe there a betta' way catch fishes. My uncle, Uturo, got some plenty good stuff to knock 'em out."

"He poisons the water?" Genie gasped.

"Just a little in a tide pool. Fishes just float up. Then everything plenty betta' when tide comes back in."

"What poison does he use?" Genie demanded.

Ramon led her along a dirt trail through steamy jungle foliage. The thick undergrowth was filled with birdcalls, the cries of monkeys, and the constant rustle of leaves as unseen creatures scurried past. Genie passed several open areas, looking like festering open sores on the land. Trees were burned and uprooted. Grasses were scorched and withered—all ugly scars of World War II fighting on this island.

They reached a small cluster of houses. Most were grass-thatched roofs supported by poles and with open sides. Several were made of plywood with corrugated tin roofs—supplies left over from the war.

Ramon led her to a small storage shed behind a spacious grass house.

The shed door was padlocked. Genie tapped the lock and sighed. "Do you have a key?"

Ramon grinned. "No key. Lock is only for show." He pulled on the door and the entire locking latch pulled away from the shed with it. Inside Ramon proudly pointed at two U.S. Navy issue, five-gallon cans, both marked poison and labeled "Rotenone."

Genie struggled to remember her toxicology classes. Rotenone was a low-grade poison that, in low doses, would not harm plants, attached animals (clams, barnacles, etc.), or plankton, but would paralyze fish. With additional dilution from a new high tide, it would become harmless.

"I know a good tide pool," bragged Ramon. "Plenty fishes. Make Navy man happy."

Just before low tide next morning Genie and Ramon stood at the rocky edge of a wide tide pool. The crystal water showed a carpet of mussels, anemones, and plants clinging to the rocks twenty feet below the surface. Countless fish glided through the transparent pool, happy to linger in this sheltered cove until the next high tide rose over the coral wall connecting this pool with the bay.

Genie wondered, *How much rotenone should I use?* A cup seemed inadequate. A gallon, excessive. She measured out four cups of poison and spread them into the pool. Within five minutes, 300 fish bobbed to the surface. Genie and Ramon spent an hour raking them onto shore.

"See? You catch plenty fishes," said Ramon, swaggering proudly next to the fish pile.

Genie used a wheelbarrow to haul the fish to her tiny lab space at the Kwajalene Navy base. After a quick sort, Genie found she had over eighty species of tropical fish. With all windows wide open and two electric fans on high, she placed a specimen of each species into a bath of formalin, a foul-smelling preservative.

After two days in formalin, the samples were transferred to alcohol jars and boxed for shipment. That afternoon a cable arrived from the Navy Department. "Concentrate only on collection of poisonous species." The cable then listed a dozen suspected candidates for her to send back.

Genie looked puzzled as she read and reread the list. "We ate two of these species last night for dinner."

Ramon nodded. "Yes, ma'am."

"Then they're *not* poisonous," said Genie.

"Never this time of year."

"The same fish are poisonous in some seasons and not in other?" Genie asked. "Are any poisonous now?"

Ramon looked hurt. "I would never be serving poisonous fish to my lady boss." He tapped at the list. "You want poisonous, you wait 'til after monsoons."

Genie murmured, "Monsoon . . . heavy rain . . . fresh water runoff . . . slight change of water chemistry. . . . Of course! That would set up an algae bloom. A poisonous plankton bloom gets into the food chain and makes the fish poisonous to humans."

Some fish were always poisonous. Some became poisonous during an algae bloom. But some did not. It was a more complex problem than the Navy thought when they sent a lone woman to do their collecting.

Genie entered this new information in her project logs. Then she wrote a cable to the Navy promising to send samples of each species *now,* and again after the monsoons, when locals said many became poisonous. She would also collect algae samples after the next monsoon season.

The Navy lab would have to conduct extensive lab tests to determine what the poison was and how it worked its way through the food chain. Genie would need to supply a lot more samples than she had originally thought.

Eventually, Genie found it was easier to hunt the specific species she needed with a spear gun than by poisoning an entire tide pool. She hired a local expert, Siakong, to help her on her dives. Ramon always tagged along, waiting onshore to lug heavy diving gear and Genie's haul of new specimens.

During Genie's and Siakong's second dive together, they tracked an ugly, but always poisonous, scorpionfish as it darted in and out of the coral. Genie held onto a coral chunk with one hand and aimed her spear gun with the other.

Before she could shoot, Siakong knocked her hand away from the coral just as, like a deadly bear trap, the jaws of a giant clam slammed shut. It had looked like ordinary coral. Genie hadn't given it a second glance as she stretched out her hand to gain balance. One second longer and her hand and forearm would have been crushed in the deadly grip of the three-foot-diameter, coral encrusted clam that was fully capable of holding her there until she drowned.

The scorpionfish was gone. Genie hardly noticed. She stared at her hand and shuddered. So easily she could have lost it—or her life.

Siakong pointed at a gap in the fanlike coral. Genie could see the snout of a moray eel. One species of moray was believed to be poisonous. The Navy wanted samples. Siakong motioned for her to go get him. Then he pointed again, and Genie saw the eel's angry looking face and razor teeth.

Genie gulped. Her heart pounded. Morays were shy but also moody and vicious. On the wrong day they were fully capable of snapping off fingers and hands just because they were grumpy. She had studied morays before but had never had to catch a live one in the open ocean.

Timidly Genie reached a gloved hand toward the eel. Siakong pulled her arm back and seemed to laugh behind his mask. He roughly prodded the eel with the tip of his bamboo spear until it lashed out and locked its jaws on the thick bamboo. With a quick wrist twist, Siakong dragged the moray out of its hole and grabbed it behind the head with his free hand. The eel thrashed and twisted, snapping its razor jaws.

With a soft shrug, Siakong released the eel. It hadn't been the poisonous kind after all. Genie sighed, and the eel slithered back into its hole, snapping angrily toward the humans to signal its anger at being disturbed.

Twenty minutes later, with full sacks of samples for the Navy lab and nearly empty air tanks, Genie and Siakong headed back to shore. Seemingly from nowhere, a twelve-foot Mako shark glided in behind the divers. Siakong instantly dropped his bag and fled, a look of terror on his face. He had seen too many of his villagers die after being mauled during shark attacks.

However, Genie hesitated, hanging still in the water, unwilling to drop her valuable samples. She hovered, watching the shark as the beast first gulped Siakong's bag as it slowly fell, and then sized up Genie and her bag for its next bite.

The shark drove forward with almost blinding speed. But Genie calmly slammed it on the nose with the butt of her spear gun. The shark backed up, circled twice below Genie, and swam off along the wall of the coral reef.

Back on shore, Siakong felt humbled as he expressed his new-found respect for this lady diver. He had watched from the safety of coral rocks and was sure that Eugenie would die. Ramon bragged, "Ma'am is a fine, brave lady! I taught her."

After Words

Within six months, Eugenie Clark had a world-class collection of triggerfish, ugly scorpionfish, lionfish, stonefish, sea urchins, jelly fish, surgeon fish, sea snakes, even the elusive cowfish—a menagerie of deadly oceanic poison. She had also collected samples of virtually every edible fish in the region both before and after the monsoon rains. Each sample was labeled, documented, and on its way to the Navy's research lab, and Eugenie Clark boarded a sea-plane to head toward her next ocean adventure.

After a dozen years of small oceanographic jobs, Genie was hired as the director of the Cape Haze Marine Laboratory in 1955. There she became famous for her research on shark intelligence. Her data and methods revolutionized shark research worldwide and led marine biologists to rethink their basic approach to behavior and intelligence research for many other marine species. She taught and continued her research until her retirement in 1995 at the age of seventy-four.

* * *

Suggested Topics to Explore

This story deals with marine biology and poisonous fish. Here are some starting questions that will help you discuss and research each.

1. This story talks about tide pools. What is a tide pool? Why are they special and important? What lives in a tide pool?

2. What is an algae bloom? Where and when do they happen? Are their different kinds of algae blooms in the ocean? Do they only happen in the ocean?

3. Research poisonous things in the ocean. Which fishes and marine mammals are poisonous? Which plants are? Which ones are poisonous part of the time? What makes them poisonous?

4. Research Eugenie Clark. What other adventures did she have? What research is she famous for?

For Further Reading About This Story

Clark, Eugenie. *Lady with a Spear.* New York: Harpers Publishing Co., 1953.

Emberlin, Diane. *Contributions of Women to Science.* Minneapolis, MN: Dillion Press, Inc., 1992.

Halstead, Bruce. *Poisonous and Venomous Marine Animals of the World.* Washington, DC: U.S. Government Printing Office, 1980.

McGovern, Ann. *Shark Lady: True Adventures of Eugenie Clark.* New York: Four Winds Press, 1994.

Yount, Lisa. *Contemporary Women Scientists.* New York: Facts on File, 1994.

Marie Curie

Death Glow: Physicist
A Science Adventure

Imagine holding a test tube of deadly radioactive poison in your hand. Marie Curie did—long before the dangers of radioactivity were known. She stirred, sifted, and handled radioactive dirt day after day for years without any protection at all, but her discovery revolutionized science.

A Science Adventure with Radioactivity

As the gray Paris afternoon faded into twilight on a damp day in February 1901, a growing line of eager university professors and students snaked across the frozen campus grass. Was it dark enough yet? Could the daily tour begin?

At the head of this expectant line stood a dilapidated shack. For three years it had been the laboratory of graduate student Marie Curie and her professor husband, Pierre. Marie had found some new metal. And this metal glowed—all on its own—even at night, with a soft, ethereal, fairylike glow. Marie had hung test tubes of the stuff from the ceiling of her shack to brighten it up.

As darkness fell each evening, visitors marched through the shack, faces and hands bathed in warm pastel glows from the radium and polonium salts. Yellow from one test tube, a faint pink from the next, luminescent green from a third. Each night this dilapidated shack was transformed into an enchanted, glowing fairyland. Gasps of wonder and delight rose from each person. No one knew that the glowing light Marie had found was concentrated, deadly radioactivity.

"How incredible!" gasped a biology professor and his wife, as they peered closely into the test tubes. Marie thought back to the afternoon three years before when she, herself, had first uttered those two fateful words. "How incredible!"

On that afternoon (in 1898), a friend had shown Marie and Pierre a developed photographic plate with streaks of white smeared across it. The light had come from a sealed chunk of uranium. "How incredible," Marie murmured, wondering what could possibly have spilled out of a chunk of rock to expose a photograph.

At age twenty-nine and still a graduate student at the university, Marie decided to drop her other studies and concentrate on this amazing natural activity, or "radioactivity" as she called it. It was new. It was exciting. It was something no one had ever seen or studied before.

Because the Curies had had no money of their own to pay for her research, and because the university refused to fund a woman's graduate-level physics research, Marie scrounged for free lab space. She found an abandoned shed that had been used by the Biology Department to hold cadavers. But its sagging roof, dirt floor, and leaky walls had made it unsuitable for the department's needs.

Over the next six months Marie and her husband, Pierre, examined each of the seventy-eight known chemical elements to see if these mysterious radioactive rays flowed from any other substance besides uranium. Most of their time was spent begging for tiny samples of the many elements they could not afford to buy. Their long search uncovered only two elements that possessed this amazing natural radioactivity: uranium and thorium.

Near the end of their search Marie was given a ton of pitchblend to test. Pitchblend is a weak ore of uranium found in western Czechoslovakia. She saw little reason to be interested in pitchblend but included samples of it with a group she was testing.

But what was this? Her wild readings when she measured radioactivity convinced her she must have made a mistake. The amount of radioactivity she measured in this pitchblend couldn't be right. Chemically she recalculated to within a one hundredth of a percent the amount of uranium in the sample. With an electrometer (a very early Geiger counter) she remeasured its radioactivity.

"This can't be right!" she sighed. Again she thought she must have made a mistake. But where?

Six times Marie tested the pitchblend. Six times she got the same result that she could not believe. There was hardly any uranium, and no thorium in this pitchblend. But she measured massive radioactivity. Something was very wrong.

During dinner discussions with Pierre that night, the truth finally hit Marie like a sledgehammer. There must be something *else* in the pitchblend that was the source of this massive extra radioactivity! That "something" had to be a new, undiscovered element. Marie had stumbled on the greatest scientific prize of all: the discovery of a new chemical element in the makeup of the Earth.

Her plan was simple. First, she would use a long series of chemical agents to separate every known metal in the pitchblend and measure its radioactivity. When she finally separated out every metallic element, whatever was left should be her new mystery element.

It sounded easy. But doing it would take months of backbreaking work.

Marie borrowed a large iron cauldron to boil her solutions of pitchblend during the many phases of the chemical separation process. She placed the cauldron fire outside—summer or winter, heat, rain, or snow—because she had no other way to vent the noxious fumes that rose from her bubbling solutions.

Using a long iron rod almost as tall as she was, Marie mixed and stirred her boiling mass until her arms felt more leaden than the stir rod. Day after day she mixed, measured, hauled, and stirred over the noxious fumes of her cauldron. Between aching groans she often smiled at how she must look like a fairytale witch, hunched over a foul-smelling bubbling cauldron.

Pierre chopped and hauled tons of firewood. They both stoked and tended the crude fire.

Slowly, through 1898 and 1899, Marie sifted through her donated dirt searching for the few grains of some new radioactive metal. Often the chemical reactions Marie performed inside the shed were contaminated and ruined by leaking rainwater, or by leaves, dirt, and dust that swirled in through the cracks in her shed walls. Hours of work would be wasted and she would have to start over with a new batch of pitchblend.

What should have taken weeks dragged into long months because of their dismal working conditions. Still, by late 1900, Marie knew she was getting close. Feverishly she worked through freezing rains and bitter cold, sifting, sorting, boiling, hauling, mixing, and testing that ton of pitchblend over and over again.

In March 1901, the pitchblend finally gave up its secrets. Marie had found not one but *two* new radioactive elements: polonium (named after Marie's native Poland) and radium (so named because it was by far the most radioactive element yet discovered). After three years of work, she had produced a tiny sample of pure radium salt. It weighed .0035 ounces—less than the weight of a potato chip—but it was a million times more radioactive than uranium.

The radioactive salt compounds of those two elements shimmered and glowed in Marie's darkened shed. They shone like fairy lights, like nothing the world had ever seen. Marie—not realizing the terrible danger of radioactivity—isolated more of these two deadly, radioactive metals. She began to hang test tubes of radium salts around the shed to cheer up the place and make it look bright for the long evenings of work.

Soon the lines and tours began. Everyone demanded a peek at the bewitching glow spilling out of the Curie's shed.

After Words

For a time, Marie Curie's incredible discoveries were lost in the magical glow of her radioactive lanterns. Everyone thought she had discovered only a pretty—but eerie—light source. However, the scientific world soon realized that, with that one ton of pitchblend, Marie Curie made two monumental discoveries. First, she found two new radioactive elements. Second, by proving that an atom was not the smallest particle of matter and that something came out from inside an atom as radioactivity, she opened the door to our atomic age. Marie Curie changed the world of physics forever, and she won two Nobel Prizes (one for physics, one for chemistry).

Because the dangers of radiation were not yet known, Marie and Pierre were plagued with health troubles—aches and pains, ulcer-covered hands, continuous bouts of pneumonia, and never-ending exhaustion. Finally, in 1934, radiation poisoning killed Marie. Indeed, for many years after her death, her notebooks and desk were still too radioactive to touch.

* * *

Suggested Topics to Explore

This story deals with radioactivity and chemical exploration. Here are some starting questions that will help you discuss and research both.

1. What is radioactivity? What comes out of a radioactive atom? What happens inside the atom to release this radioactivity?

2. Is all radioactivity man-made? What are natural sources of radioactivity?

3. What is the smallest unit of matter? Once it was thought to be a molecule. Then atoms were discovered. Then Marie Curie opened the atom and scientists discovered electrons, protons, and neutrons. Now scientists have opened protons and neutrons and found quarks inside. Is there anything smaller than a quark? What is a quark? What does it look like and act like?

4. Marie Curie suffered greatly because of her willingness to explore the unknown. Is exploration of the unknown always risky for scientists? Do they still face such risks today? Have they always faced grave risks? Can you find other examples?

For Further Reading About This Story

Boorse, Henry, and Lloyd Motz. *The Atomic Scientist, A Biographical History.* New York: John Wiley & Sons, 1989.

Born, Max. *Atomic Physics.* New York: Dover Publications, Inc., 1979.

Dunn, Andrew. *Pioneers of Science, Marie Curie.* New York: The Bookwright Press, 1991.

Keller, Mollie. *Marie Curie, An Impact Biography.* New York: Franklin Watts, 1992.

McGrayne, Sharon Bertsch. *Nobel Prize Women in Science: Their Lives, Struggles, and Momentous Discoveries.* New York: Carol Publishing Group, A Birch Lane Press Book, 1993.

McKown, Robin. *Marie Curie.* New York: G.P. Putnam's Sons, 1991.

Parker, Steve. *Science Discoveries: Marie Curie and Radium.* New York: HarperCollins Publishers, 1992.

Sylvia Earle

Dangerous Depth Dive:
A Science Adventure

Marine
Biologist

Scuba divers can reach depths of 175 to 200 feet. But that depth is nothing compared to what's needed for deep ocean dives. Sylvia Earle wanted to walk on the deep ocean floor—1,255 feet below the surface. There she came face to face with menacing sharks, slithery eels, and giant corals. If anything went wrong—anything—she'd be done for.

A Science Adventure

"Aren't you even a little bit worried?" scowled William Blake.

"Yes, I am," answered Sylvia Earle, flashing her broad and famous smile. "There might be a problem with the submarine."

Blake slammed his fist on the ship's rail. They stood on the rear deck of a 250-foot research ship two miles off the southern coast of Oahu, Hawaii, on a sunny March morning just after dawn in 1979.

"That submarine has made over fifty deep dives. It's reinforced steel. It has a three-man crew tucked safely inside. It'll be fine. You'll be on your own riding outside the sub and you *should* be worried about that flimsy JIM suit you're going to wear."

"The JIM suit is solid," insisted Dr. Earle. "I'll be fine."

"But no one has ever free dived anywhere near 1,250 feet. If anything goes wrong—*anything*—it will be fatal."

This dive by Sylvia Earle would be the first deep, free dive in a JIM suit. It would also be the deepest free dive in history. Sylvia needed to find out if the JIM suit could withstand the pressures of deep ocean work and allow a diver to function where no diver had ever been able to survive before.

The hard-framed JIM suit (named after a hardhat diving pioneer of the 1930s) looked like a bulky robot from a 1950s space science-fiction movie. There was enough room inside for Sylvia to pull her arms out of the sleeves to write notes. In this suit with its re-circulating, pressurized breathing system, she planned to dive to a depth of 1,250 feet. There she would walk along the ocean bottom for two hours before returning to the surface. A small, three-man submarine would carry her down and back.

Sylvia Earle shook her head and smiled as she climbed into the suit. "Nothing will go wrong," she repeated.

"You've said that before," Blake grumbled.

"You mean that lionfish bite?"

"You almost died! Don't you remember?"

How could Sylvia forget? Two years before she had helped photographer Al Giddings capture images of a beautiful but deadly lionfish along the wall of a South Pacific coral reef. Instead of trying to position the fish with a long-handled net, Sylvia used her hands to push and prod the fish to get it to turn and move toward the camera.

The fish stabbed her with its potent poison.

Her hand exploded in burning pain. She felt that her fingers were literally on fire. The hand began to swell. The pain and swelling inched up her wrist and arm. Her head throbbed and her breath came in ragged gasps. She wanted to scream. She feared she might pass out from the waves of searing pain.

Sylvia couldn't bolt to the surface for medical help. She had been down below eighty feet, and for too long. She would have to stop along the way for an hour of decompression to avoid the formation of potentially deadly nitrogen bubbles in her blood.

But a lionfish's poison can kill within an hour or two. If she waited through decompression, the poison might kill her. If she kicked straight to the surface, the bends might kill her. Which should she do? And all she could think about was the excruciating pain that ripped through her hand and burned up her arm.

Every minute of the wait through decompression felt like a never-ending torment. It seemed that she waited through days, not minutes, of screaming pain before she could kick to the surface. Then she had spent three weeks in the hospital in fevered delirium while the poison slowly drained from her body.

That had been at a depth of eighty feet and Blake was right. She had almost died. This would be 1,250 feet. There would be no recovery from a mistake this time.

William suggested, "Why not send the suit down without a diver, to test it before you try a dive?"

Sylvia shook her head. "We'd waste a whole day to learn what? That the suit doesn't leak?"

"That would be *something,*" William muttered.

She adjusted the padded harness on the JIM suit to fit her arms. "Science always involves risks, whether it's working with lionfish or testing new equipment. I need to know if I can depend on this suit during a typical dive and there's only one way to find out."

As the dive crew lifted the bulky JIM suit helmet, William again grumbled that the JIM suit hadn't been properly tested. But Sylvia didn't hear as her dive helmet was locked against the metal collar of her suit.

Earle believed in direct, firsthand observation. How could she claim to know about deep-sea life until she had watched it in its own environment—not for a minute or two, but for hours at a time, day after day? So she had volunteered to be the human guinea pig to text the JIM suit. If it worked, it would allow her to dive quickly and deeply without having to endure days—or weeks—of difficult and costly decompression after each dive. It would open a whole new world of ocean exploration for marine biologists.

Now her heart raced, both from excitement and from the sheer drama of the moment as she stepped onto, and was clamped to, a small platform welded to the nose of the diving submarine. Onboard cranes dangled the thirty-foot sub (with her strapped to it) over the ship's stern and above the calm, blue Pacific.

Early morning sun streamed golden light onto her helmet visor. Her shadow stretched far off to the west across the ocean. Sylvia mused that if even the slightest thing went wrong on this dive, she would never see these sights again.

The intercom's squawk interrupted her thoughts. "This is dive control. Com check. Over."

"This is Dive 1. Read you loud and clear." Dive 1 was the three-man sub.

Sylvia pressed the talk button strapped to the waist of her three-eighths-inch wetsuit. (The JIM suit would protect her from the crushing pressure of the deep but not from its cold.) "This is Dive Mobile," she spoke into the microphone built into her helmet. "You're loud and clear."

"Roger. We are 'go' for launch."

The ship's crane lowered the sub until it gently settled into the ocean. With a grating clang, the crane's clamps released the sub. It bobbed quietly in the calm water.

Two teams of scuba divers with grappling hooks hovered near the sub's nose. Each team dragged an inflatable rubber raft. Their job was to hook the JIM suit if anything went wrong during the launch. If Sylvia slipped off her tie-downs on the sub's nose she would literally fall 1,250 feet to the ocean floor. There was no way for her to swim to the surface with the bulky suit on. It weighed far too much.

"This is Dive Control. Dive 1, are you 'go' for dive?"

"Control board is all green. We're 'go' here."

"Dive Mobile. Are you 'go' for dive?"

Sylvia pressed her talk button. "Ready—and tired of talking. Let's get this show going."

There was a pause before Sylvia heard. "This is Dive Control. We are 'go' for dive. Good luck and happy exploring."

"Yes!" cheered Sylvia without pushing the button to broadcast her joy over the intercom.

"This is Dive 1. Dive Mobile, we are going down. We'll call out depth every 500 feet."

"Thank you, Dive 1."

Blue ocean water closed over Sylvia's head. The water's color changed from pale, baby blue to brilliant royal blue with curtains of light undulating through it, then to deep indigo as the sub slowly drove toward the bottom with its electric motor purring. Sylvia could hear the rush of air through her regulator as she breathed and the soft hum of the sub's motor.

At 600 feet Sylvia could no longer see any color in the water. It had darkened to a never-ending black. The only light came from the green glow of the sub's control panels shining through the pilot's porthole. It felt eerie—even creepy—descending through the blackness with no walls of steel to protect her. A shark, a giant squid—anything—could be only a few feet away and she would never see them coming!

"Dive Mobile, this is Dive 1. We're nearing the bottom at 1,255 feet. Prepare to release tie-down clamps."

"Roger Dive 1. Ready on your mark."

It had been a quiet and uneventful decent. Sylvia had seen virtually no sign of life as she rode the leisurely twenty-minute dive into the depths.

The sub settled into the Pacific bottom silt so softly that Sylvia never felt the landing. "Dive Mobile. You are cleared to release and explore. We'll track you on radar and will initiate com check every five minutes. Happy exploring."

"Thank you, Dive 1."

Sylvia clicked on the JIM suit's twin lights. Twin beams stabbed out like lighthouse beacons across the waving sand. She released her tie-down clamps and stepped off the sub's nose. The only word she could think of was "incredible." It felt like she was stepping onto the surface of an alien moon.

The difference was that this underwater alien world pulsed with life. It was anything but the barren desert she had expected to find. A green-eyed shark cruised by, circled twice around Sylvia and eyed her suspiciously before darting off. A pair of eels slithered past. One, with an oversized jaw and spikes for teeth, brushed against her leg. It recoiled and glared at the intruder, opened mouth, fangs gleaming.

Sylvia was mesmerized by the abundance of life in this forever black and silent world. She loped past giant spirals of bamboo coral resembling a field of giant bedsprings. Giant sea fans with bright pink polyps reminded her of fruit trees in full bloom. She touched one and it glowed with a blue, luminous light.

Sylvia regularly paused to pull in her arms and scribble hasty notes and research questions. She found herself in a wonderland instead of a wasteland. Scientists did not believe that complete ecosystems could exist at depths where no light penetrated.

"Dive Mobile, your bottom time is up. Return to the take-out point."

"You're kidding," scoffed Sylvia. "I've only been down here a few minutes."

"You've been on the bottom for two hours and ten minutes, Dr. Earle."

Stunned, Sylvia could only repeat, "You're kidding."

Reattached to her platform on the nose of the sub, Sylvia began her ascent into the growing light nearer the surface. It was a tremendous struggle for her to believe that she had really walked on the bottom of an ocean and would make it back to the surface for lunch. If she had scuba dived at that depth, she would have had to spend a week in decompression before she could step out into the sunshine. The JIM suit's hard shell had protected her from the 600 pounds-per-square-inch pressures of the deep. She had risked her life to test and prove the JIM suit. It had performed splendidly and now she ascended in triumph.

After Words

Sylvia Earle's dive marked the beginning of a whole new generation of ocean exploration and research. In her lengthy career, Dr. Earle has swum with whales, punched sharks, captured sea snakes whose poison is far deadlier than a cobra's, and explored and studied every ocean on earth. Her groundbreaking work has benefited whole generations of other marine researchers.

✳ ✳ ✳

Suggested Topics to Explore

This story deals with deep-ocean exploration and marine biology. Here are some starting questions that will help you discuss and research both.

1. Research the history of ocean diving. Scuba gear was invented in the late 1940s. What did divers use before that time? How well did it work? When were the first deep dives ever made? By whom?

2. Do you envision the deep ocean floor as a lightless desert of rolling sand? Most people do. How can anything live where there is no sunlight? Research deep ocean ecosystems, especially those around mid-ocean ridge vents.

3. Why do divers need high-pressure tanks to breathe under water?

For Further Reading About This Story

Baker, Beth. *Sylvia Earle, Guardian of the Sea.* New York: Lerner Publications, 2001.

Conley, Andres. *Window on the Deep.* New York: Franklin Watts, 1991.

Earle, Sylvia. *Dive: My Adventures in the Deep Frontier.* Washington, DC: National Geographic Society, 1998.

Gleasner, Diana. *Breakthrough Women in Science.* New York: Walker & Company, 1993.

Haber, Louis. *Women Pioneers of Science.* New York: Harcourt Brace, 1991.

Hall, Michelle. *Secrets of the Ocean Realm.* New York: Carroll & Graf, 1997.

McElroy, Lisa. *Meet My Grandmother: She's a Deep Sea Explorer.* Brookfield, CT: Millbrook Press, 2000.

Van Dover, Cindy. *The Octopus's Garden.* New York: Addison Wesley, 1996.

Dian Fossey

The Great EscAPE: Primatologist
A Science Adventure

What would you do if you found yourself standing face-to-face with a roaring, 800-pound silverback gorilla, who could easily snap every bone in your body; who hates all intruders in its mountain jungle domain—especially humans? Dian Fossey searched the jungle for weeks—alone and unarmed—hoping for that very meeting.

A Science Adventure in the African Jungle

Distant thunder rumbled up each crag and gully of the rugged mountainside. Rain was coming. But then, it rained almost every day during the African wet season. Thirty-five-year-old Dian Fossey sat hunched on a rounded boulder near the two tents she had called home these first two months of 1967.

Above her, lost in the swirling clouds loomed the peaks of the Virungas Mountains along Rwanda's border with Zaire. Stretched out far below lay the terraced farmlands of Rwanda—farmlands that crept higher up the mountain each year, gobbling precious acres of high mountain rain forest habitat.

Dian had survived on her own in this lush mountain rain forest for four months trying to observe and study wild mountain gorillas—and had not once seen a gorilla up close. For the last two months, she had camped on this small meadow with a stream racing through and surrounded by tall trees and rocky gulches that cut into the steep mountainside. Bamboo and stinging nettles crowded around the skirts of her meadow. Each day she hiked the rugged trails and felt lucky to glimpse a far-off gorilla through high-powered binoculars, or to hear a distant call.

Dian sat on the boulder lost in a desperate internal debate. Traditional science doctrine argued on one side. Her months of frustrated failure argued on the other. The rules for field observation said, "Don't interact with the subject species. Don't touch them. Don't do anything to affect or change the subjects' life patterns and habits." If you did these things, your study would be invalid and worthless.

But mountain gorillas were painfully shy and they distrusted strangers. They lived in an exceedingly dense and lush rain forest. Dian hadn't been able to get close enough to make any observations about community and family structure, about diet, or about lifestyle. She scoffed, "*Interact* with them? I can't even *see* them!"

She knew that she wasn't a trained, degreed scientist. She was a children's hospital physical therapist. Maybe that's why she wasn't getting anywhere. But she *was* here, and she had to try. Famed anthropologist Louis Leakey had believed in her and sent her after the gorillas. She was supposed to collect much-needed observational data before Rwandan farmers plowed under the last of the gorillas' habitat for more terraced farms. Deep and bitter frustration welled up inside her. Her study wasn't working.

"I know that it may invalidate my observations if I interact with the gorillas," she muttered. "But at least then I would *have* some observations."

Dian sighed and tucked her arms around her knees and thick khaki hiking pants. She was tired of watching for brief glimpses of distant gorillas from a concealed blind. She was tired of never getting close enough to hear or smell them. She was wasting what precious little time and chance the gorillas still had for survival.

She slid off the rock and jammed her fists into her hips. Fine! Maybe she wouldn't be a great scientist. But she *would* collect her data!

She was going to get close to the gorillas, close enough to touch them, close enough to be like one of the family.

But how? No one got close to mountain gorillas unless they were accepted by the gorillas. To be accepted, she would have to think like and act like a gorilla. She would have to stop being a human and start being a gorilla.

Dian nodded hard to herself. The debate was over. Let trained scientists laugh. Let them dismiss her as a crazy amateur. She didn't care any more what the scientific community thought of her work.

Dian began weeks of gorilla practice. She learned to walk sloped shouldered and bent forward so that her knuckles could drag along the ground. She practiced the gorilla hoots, cries, and calls that had been recorded by other researchers. For a week her throat was raw from the effort. Then she found she could sound "very much like a gorilla."

She spent hours trying to imitate the deep "pok, pok" sound of gorillas' chest thumping. The closest she could come was by slapping her hands, slightly cupped, against her thighs. She practiced like a dedicated drummer until she could match the rhythms, patterns, and rising and falling intensity of tape-recorded gorilla chest thumps.

She learned to scratch like a gorilla and to groom like a gorilla. She even learned how to convincingly pretend to eat the gorilla's favorite foods.

It was time to test *her* way of conducting field research to see if it would earn her better results than had the methods of traditional science.

Dian loped out of her clearing, along steep forest trails, past her observation blind, and toward the area—dense with bamboo and ferns—where she had, on several occasions, detected signs of gorillas.

She paused to examine an area of broken bamboo shoots. She sniffed the flattened grass and guessed that gorillas had been here less than a day ago. She pushed through thick nettles as a misty rain fell, flattening her hair against her head.

Dian stopped and sniffed the air. She detected a faint musky, musty barnyard smell, a damp smell, like opening a trunk from a mildewed corner of a cellar. Gorillas! Local guides said that the sound of gorillas precedes sight and that their smell precedes sound.

Dian pushed slowly forward through bamboo and ferns. Even though she couldn't see them, Dian knew she was closer than she had ever been to wild gorillas. The smell grew stronger—overpowering, yet comfortable. Then she heard the sound—a murmur—deep and throaty.

A high-pitched series of screams seemed to rip through the air. Dian froze, her heart pounding, her eyes lowered timidly to the ground. When she looked up, there stood a silverback, a massive male—easily 800 pounds of bone-crushing power—no more than twenty feet from her.

Dian tried to hoot passively but her throat was too dry to make any sound.

The silverback roared and glared at her. He pounded his chest, the rapid, deep pok-pok sound. Being this close, Dian could actually feel the vibrations rumble through her chest. He rose taller, swaggering as he stepped slowly forward and back. Then he roared and charged toward her.

Dian felt overwhelming terror as the ground shook. She knew that the silverback was using intimidation tactics. And they were working! She felt a powerful urge to turn and run. Too afraid to look, she still managed to faintly grunt several of the calls she had practiced.

The silverback stopped and pounded his chest again, pok-pok-pok—but softer and less intimidating this time.

Dian imitated several more hoots. She heard the reply hoots of other gorillas hidden in the foliage. She rocked forward and slapped her thighs to imitate chest slaps. The silverback cocked his head, glaring at her through knowing but suspicious eyes.

Dian hooted again. Her call was answered by echoing hoots as other gorilla heads popped out of the ferns and bushes. Dian had the feeling that she was deep in a conversation for which she had learned how to pronounce the words but had no idea what they meant.

Was she saying, "Hi, how are you?" or "Go eat a tree stump." She had no idea.

The silverback grunted, snorted, and turned to amble back toward a stand of bamboo where he had been nibbling before Dian's intrusion. Suddenly, she was being ignored. The gorillas stepped out of hiding to continue their morning as if Dian wasn't there. Besides the silverback, this family included three females, each with an infant, and two young males.

Dian realized she was holding her breath and forced herself to exhale. Still she shook with excitement. She was standing in the midst of a gorilla family—and they didn't mind. They did still glance at her warily, cautiously. But they didn't run.

Dian's practiced plan of action flooded back to her. She hooted and scratched, then plopped down, imitating two of the females, and began to groom herself. With slight nods—that looked like nods of understanding and acceptance—the females hooted and groomed in a tight circle, looking very much like three human friends chatting over cups of coffee.

The two young males resumed their wrestling match, rolling across the forest floor, locking each other in restrained bites. They'd pant, roar, and then burst into hooting laughter as their play turned from wrestling to tickling.

They stopped and momentarily wandered apart, panting to catch their breaths. Soon one would pound his chest and launch himself at the other. The rolling, wrestling, tickling, and hooting began all over again.

During a brief break, one of these males plopped down next to Dian. He sat, chest heaving, and stared at this strange-looking creature. Leaning forward, glaring at her as if trying to understand her odd facial shape, he stared from less than an arm's length away. Again Dian held her breath, staring back into eyes so expressive she almost wanted to cry. Gorilla eyes, up close, seemed so much wiser than a lowly human's. It was a profound and unexpected sensation to feel inferior to these gorillas she had come to study.

Then the two males sprang into the air, collided with a great thud, and rolled back across the ground.

Dian stood, leaning forward on her knuckles, shaken to her very core and overjoyed beyond her wildest hopes. She had won! She sat in the midst of a gorilla family! Her first few minutes of observation had already given her insights and impressions no other research had been able to collect. She had broken all the rules for conducting wildlife studies. But she had gained the rare chance to directly observe the life of the wild mountain gorilla.

Dian felt giddy and lightheaded. She felt deeply torn between staying with this gorilla family and rushing back to her tents to record her success and her initial observations of family structure. It was long after midnight when, jubilant and exhausted, Dian flopped onto her cot to sleep. First contact was over. Her adventure and work were just beginning.

After Words

Dian's was lonely work, often filled with great personal discomfort. Still, she amassed huge quantities of information about the gorillas and their behavior that had never been observed before. Fossey recorded her study of the gorillas in the autobiographical book, *Gorillas in the Mist,* which included scientific analyses (autopsy reports, dung analyses, kinship studies, spectrographic charts, etc.) along with her personal accounts.

As she fought to protect her gorillas, a fierce tension grew between her and the locals until, on December 27, 1985, she was murdered in her camp. According to her wishes, she was buried in the cemetery she had established for gorillas killed by poachers. She left behind a rickety cabin, a few personal affects, and a mountain of compelling, detailed information on the most misunderstood and endangered of all the great apes.

* * *

Suggested Topics to Explore

This story deals with biological field research and wild mountain gorillas. Here are starting questions that will help you discuss and research both.

1. Are gorillas different than chimpanzees? How? Research both species and compare these two members of the ape family.

2. Why study endangered species? Why not study those that are most plentiful on Earth instead of those about to disappear?

3. Why do you think it takes so long to build up a complete picture of the life and social structure of an animal species? Does it take this long with all species?

For Further Reading About This Story

Clutton-Brock, T. H., ed. *Primate Ecology: Studies of Feeding and Ranging Behavior in Lemurs, Monkeys, and Apes.* London: Academic Press, 1987.

Fossey, Dian. *Gorillas in the Mist.* Boston, MA: Houghton Mifflin, 1984.

Graham, C. E., ed. *Reproductive Biology of the Great Apes.* New York: Academic Press, 1988.

Roberts, Jack. *The Importance of Dian Fossey.* San Diego, CA: Lucent Books, 1995.

Rosalind Franklin

"X" Communicated   X-Ray
                    Crystallographer

Rosalind Franklin spent years painstakingly unraveling one of the greatest mysteries of the century—the structure of a DNA molecule. She had to create new techniques and devise new equipment and tests. Just as she neared final triumph, her results were stolen by a competitor, who then claimed all the credit for the discovery.

A Science Adventure in the Lab

"I can't work for you any more." King's Medical College of London graduate student Raymond Gosling stood in thirty-three-year-old Rosalind Franklin's office doorway. Long sheets of X-ray film were strewn across her desk and worktable.

Rosalind slammed down her pencil and glasses. "What?! I need you now more than ever!"

"I know."

"There are four groups closing in on the shape of the DNA molecule. It's a great race, and I can't win it without your help."

Raymond grimaced and reddened, his gaze fixed on the wooden floor of this centuries-old London, England, school building. "Maurice Wilkins pulled my funding." He raised his eyes to meet Rosalind's intense glare. "I don't *want* to go. But Wilkins originally hired me and if I don't shift when he tells me to, I'll never be able to finish grad school."

Rosalind sighed and leaned back in her swivel chair. "I don't blame *you*. This is between me and Maurice." She smiled. "Oh, and Merry Christmas."

The date was December 17, 1952. Rosalind had been hired by Dr. Sir John Randall to develop a procedure for using X-ray diffraction to unravel the mysterious—and frustrating—structure of the giant DNA molecule. Although DNA was enormous for a molecule, it was still a microscopic molecule housed deep inside every living cell, the one molecule that carried the blueprint and commands for every detail of life and growth.

Franklin's assignment was difficult, but straightforward and clear. However, Randall never clarified the relationship between Franklin and Maurice Wilkins, the deputy director for Randall's Biophysics Unit. Wilkins was also working on DNA structure. He believed that Franklin should be working for him as his high-priced technical assistant. Rosalind both disagreed and refused. Friction and jealous competition ran rampant between the two researchers.

Tensions heightened when Randall gave graduate assistant Raymond Gosling—who had been hired by Wilkins—to Franklin. Now, when she had almost solved the mystery of DNA's structure— almost—Wilkins pulled her only assistant, undermining any chance she had to win the race to success.

Rosalind stormed into Wilkin's office, shaking an angry finger at him. "How dare you?"

Wilkins leered back. "You're not producing enough results to justify both your salary and that of an assistant."

Rosalind was thunderstruck. "I've discovered more about DNA's structure than anyone. With my improved X-ray techniques *I* proved that the DNA's molecular backbone is a chain of phosphate groups that lay on the outside of the molecule with bases tucked on the inside."

Her voice edged toward a screech. "*I* proved that A and B forms of the DNA molecule exist and that the molecule shifts from one to the other as a function of humidity. *I* discovered that that shift was best controlled using a saltwater solution."

Wilkins shrugged and waved the back of his hand as if to shoo her away. "Old hat. Crick and Watson at Cambridge, now *they* are getting close. They're already building test models . . . "

"Which are *wrong*," Rosalind interrupted. "And *I* am the one who showed them where their model theory was wrong."

"And they were quite angry at being corrected by . . . *you*."

"Just because they're men doesn't make their science right."

"Science is a man's field. Women don't have the capacity to understand."

Rosalind's face tightened into a fierce scowl. "Are you saying I'm not capable of doing valuable science?"

Now Wilkins jabbed a thick forefinger at Rosalind. "All you do is shoot up expensive X-ray film and waste too much of this department's budget." He dismissed her with a final wave of his hand and returned to his reading.

Rosalind stormed back to her office convinced that politics, not science, would determine who first discovered the shape of the DNA molecule.

All through the Christmas holidays, she sat at her desk glaring at her X-ray photographs and notes. Somehow she knew all the necessary clues were scattered across the table before her—if only she could put them together correctly. They were the best, most advanced, X-ray molecular photographs in the world—reasonable clear 10″ by 24″ photographs of a molecule less than 1/10,000th of a millimeter long. Rosalind had developed the techniques for shooting them. And still she couldn't make the final leap to interpret the shape of the convoluted molecule that showed as patterns of fuzzy blobs on her X-rays.

Outside, sleet and freezing rain swirled through London, matching her dark, glum mood. A soft knock on her the wood frame of her office door made Franklin turn her head. Raymond nervously rocked back and forth in the doorway. "If it's alright, I can work with you now. College is on Christmas break. So I don't have to be anywhere else."

Rosalind smiled, her angry tension dissolved, and she slid out a chair. "Help me go over this. I have to be missing something. She plopped down the pages that showed the various conclusions of their experiments as she talked. "Crystalline A pattern of a DNA molecule forms at seventy-five percent humidity; Crystalline B at ninety-five percent. The two strands of a DNA molecule are held together by an electrostatic charge between O^- (oxygen) and Na^+ (sodium) atoms."

Raymond tapped his finger on another set of X-ray film. "And you showed . . . "

"*We* showed," interrupted Rosalind.

Raymond blushed. "We showed that some hydrogen bonding exists between amino acids and base groups."

Rosalind nodded. "Yes, certainly." She plopped down a thick bundle of photos and calculations. "And we have shown that—whatever the shape of this molecule is—it structurally repeats itself at half the height of the unit cell." She sighed and flopped her hands into her lap. "So what does all that mean? Why doesn't that tell us the shape of two strands that make up a DNA molecule?"

Raymond suggested, "Maybe we should confer with someone else. What about Watson and Crick at Cambridge?"

Rosalind shook her head. "I can't. They won't talk to me since I publicly corrected their error."

"What about Wilkins? He's working on DNA structure."

Rosalind snorted. "Not a chance in the world he'd help." She spread out the key X-ray photographs into a grand collage. "I think that our work suggests a cylinder shape, or diagonal linked pairs, or even pairs back-to-back." She sighed and pushed back from the table. "It's right here in front of me in these pictures. . . . But I can't see it."

Rosalind rolled her chair over to a bookshelf and slid her finger along the titles. "Ah, here." She pulled out a binder stuffed with notes from a project on carbon structure in coal she had completed four years before. She flipped through the pages, then stopped and hastily read. "Patterson functions! We'll inductively solve the shape of the DNA molecule using Patterson functions."

Raymond knitted his brow as he thought. "Won't we need new X-ray photographs to create the data points we'll need?"

Rosalind closed her eyes, visualizing the mathematical shape of a Patterson function. "We actually need to see more clearly *between* the strands of the DNA."

"Our cameras won't do that," Raymond answered.

Rosalind drummed her fingers on the desk as she thought, eyes still closed. "We need to build a new tilting camera to shoot at the right angle."

By mid-January the redesigned camera was ready. Rosalind shot new film of both A and B forms of DNA by altering the saline solution content of her samples. The next day they began to analyze their results.

One of those X-rays showed the now famous "X" shape. Rosalind tapped the X-ray. "What does that shape suggest to you?"

Raymond shrugged, "Twisting? Maybe it's a helix."

"I've already ruled out a helix shape," Rosalind answered, "Though I admit, that's what this image suggests to me, too."

Desperate for a new perspective, Rosalind cabled Linus Pauling in California, the one American working on the structure of DNA. She summarized her findings, asked his advice and suggested a collaboration. Perhaps American researchers would take a woman scientist more seriously than did the English.

Pauling never wrote back. Instead, he contacted Crick and Watson at Cambridge and told them that Dr. Franklin at King's College had some new data they should see. Crick and Watson contacted Wilkins.

On about January 20, in what amounted to industrial espionage, Wilkins sneaked Francis Crick into Rosalind's office and showed him all of Rosalind's recent work—including the "X" shaped X-ray with the new tilting camera.

This stolen insight finally put Crick and Watson ahead of Rosalind in the race to solve the structure of DNA. By mid-February they had constructed the first complete physical model of a DNA molecule, using the now-familiar double helix shape.

When Rosalind heard that Crick and Watson had won the race— and that they had stolen her work to do it—she sat alone and quiet in her office, feeling like an unwanted outsider in the world of science. What could she do? What would you do?

After Words

Indeed, without using Franklin's work, it is clear that Watson and Crick could not have made their momentous discovery. Worse yet, when they received the 1962 Nobel Prize for their discovery, they dismissed Rosalind's contribution as unimportant and trivial.

Shortly after Crick and Watson announced their "discovery," Rosalind Franklin left her position at King's College, abandoned research, and took a teaching post at Birkbeck College. There she taught and lived quietly until she died of ovarian cancer five years later.

Once the structure of DNA was understood, the field of molecular biology exploded, becoming probably the most important and rapidly developing field of the late twentieth century. Bioengineering is likely to be a most important technology of the twenty-first century. Rosalind Franklin helped get us there.

* * *

Suggested Topics to Explore

This story deals with X-ray crystallography and the structure of DNA. Here are starting questions that will help you discuss and research both.

1. What is DNA? Why was it important to figure out what the DNA molecule looks like?

2. Why was it easier to figure out what was in a DNA molecule by working with crystals? What is a crystal? Research crystals and name a dozen crystals you commonly use.

3. Why don't all scientists cooperate with each other and share information? What's the difference between competition and cooperation?

4. Have women always worked in science? Research women in science. Who were the real women pioneers in the various fields of science?

For Further Reading About This Story

Bloss, Donald F. *Crystallography & Crystal Chemistry: An Introduction.* Columbus, OH: Ceramic Books & Literature, 1989.

McGrayne, Sharon Bertsch. *Nobel Prize Women in Science: Their Lives, Struggles, and Momentous Discoveries.* New York: Carol Publishing Group, A Birch Lane Press Book, 1993.

Sayre, Anne. *Rosalind Franklin and DNA.* New York: Norton, 1991.

Stille, Darlene R. *Extraordinary Women Scientists.* Chicago, IL: Children's Press, 1995.

Wood, Elizabeth A. *Crystals & Light: An Introduction to Optical Crystallography.* Mineola, NY: Dover Publications, 1977.

Jane Goodall

Monkey Business: Biologist
A Science Adventure

Jane Goodall hiked steep, rugged jungle mountains every day for five months, searching for the chimpanzees she was supposed to study without ever getting close to one. Bitter and frustrated, Jane was ready to quit, to give up, when, in one glorious—and frightening— moment, the chimps came to her.

A Science Adventure in the African Jungle

The air swirled fiercely hot and dry around her. The thick trees and ferns seemed to beg for a hint of breeze. On this sweltering day in early 1961, Jane Goodall sat brooding on an abrupt rock outcropping she had named "the Peak." Perched 1,000 feet above Lake Tanganyika, the Peak provided an unobstructed view of the Gombe Jungle's long ridgelines facing out over the slopes and valleys of the African country of Tanzania below.

After five months of careful, patient work, Jane Goodall felt like a complete failure. Yes, she had become as sure-footed as a baboon climbing the smooth, exposed roots up the rugged hills. She had learned the patterns and rhythms of the jungle. But none of that mattered. She had failed to get within 300 yards of even one chimpanzee. And chimpanzees were her reason for being here.

With her twelve-power binoculars, Goodall could routinely observe distant chimps in the forest far below. But distant glimpses were a cruel tease. Researchers had warned Goodall that no one could get close to chimpanzees in the wild. Five months ago she had laughed. Now the distance—so close and yet so far—tormented her.

Jane tucked her knees under her chin and wrapped her arms tight around her legs. She was on her own here in the African jungle. And she was failing. A slender woman of twenty-six, Jane had a delicate, compassionate look and soft face. But her look, her skin, and her muscles had been roughed up and hardened by the long days of strenuous scrambling up and down these slopes.

Goodall had been sent into the jungle five months before by Dr. Louis Leakey, the famed anthropologist. Leakey believed that beyond the earliest humanoids lay chimpanzees, our closest evolutionary relative. If we knew how chimps acted in the wild, we might gain some insights into early human behavior. But modern farms, roads, hunters, and human diseases daily cut deeper and deeper into chimp habitat. Leakey needed a brave volunteer to live with the chimps and catalog their lives and behaviors.

Over these past five months Jane had often sat face to face with the jungle's silver and blue monkeys, with red colobus monkeys, and with baboons. Why did the chimps still dash away? She often heard their loud hooting calls. She called it a "pant-hoot," because the series of sharp hoots was always punctuated by loud, deep breaths. But she had not once come close enough to a chimp to directly see, smell, or touch these marvelous creatures.

With a long sigh, Jane raised her binoculars to her eyes and wearily scanned the slopes and craggy ridges around her. Her gaze drifted to the far-off mountains, whose green sides looked as smooth as carpet at this distance.

A soft noise, like a light rustling behind her caused her head to snap around and the binoculars to drop from her hands. At first she couldn't tell where the noise came from. Then she heard it again.

Jane's eyes widened. Her shoulders straightened and a chill knifed down her back. Her breath came in squeaky excited gasps.

Less than fifty feet away across the narrow clearing leading up the ridge line, quietly studying her, stood two male chimps! The larger, almost five feet tall and weighing over one hundred pounds, leaned forward on his knuckles staring at her, his eyebrows furrowed with intense concentration.

The smaller one squatted, with one forearm wrapped around his bent legs, the other softly fingering one corner of his lower lip as if lost deep in thought. His eyes were locked on her face as if trying to decide what should be done with this odd-looking intruder. Both chimp faces were astonishingly expressive and filled with unique personality.

The sight of these two chimps hit Jane with the power of a tidal wave. She felt lightheaded with the elation of this first direct contact. She felt flustered and a bit embarrassed by the intensity and knowing thoughtfulness of the chimp's gaze. She felt vindicated, joyful, and triumphant, as if this moment proved that all her time and struggles had been worthwhile. Glancing at the size and raw power of these apes, she also felt a twinge of fear.

Jane was too stunned to move, overwhelmed by the wonder of the moment. She tried to breathe regularly and softly so as not to frighten the chimps. She tried to get her brain to click into scientific gear and make rational observations. But her mind was too preoccupied with one glorious thought to function in a rational way. "Chimps at last! They're magnificent!"

After a long minute of silent staring that felt like a lifetime, the two chimps turned to look at each other. The smaller one seemed to shrug. The larger one turned back to Jane.

Then both chimps screamed and charged. They bounded into a tree near Jane, grabbed branches, and shook them. Twigs, leaves, and debris rained down on her head. The larger chimp uttered an eerie alarm call. Other chimps emerged from the underbrush, surrounded her, and took up the call. They also began to shake the vegetation. Jane later wrote in *The Chimpanzees of Gombe,* "All around me branches were swayed and shaken, and there was a sound of thudding feet and crashing vegetation. My instincts urged me to run; my scientific interest, my pride, and an intuitive feeling that the whole intimidating performance was a bluff kept me where I was" (Replica Books, 1977, p. 1).

She pretended not to notice the chimps, and then pretended to chew on leaves and stems. The chimps ceased their cries and melted back into the forest. Jane rose and walked slowly across the clearing. No sign remained of the chimps. They had vanished as suddenly as they had appeared.

Jane couldn't think of anything to do except wait and see if they'd return. She waited, her mind whirring with excitement. Fifteen minutes dragged by. Thirty minutes. One hour. Two hours.

Was that it? Was that one tiny taste all she'd get? Her spirits began to sag and she thought of heading back down the slope to camp.

Then she again heard a soft rustling sound. She looked up to see a group of chimps cautiously edge out of the underbrush and start down the clearing toward her. Two large males led the family group of fifteen chimps. Females either carried or closely herded the children and babies. Several chimps stepped out of line to stare momentarily at Jane with a surprised and slightly frightened look. Then they'd hoot and dash back in line, having reached the limit of their bravery.

Within a minute the whole family passed around Jane and noisily attacked ripe fruit in a group of fig trees part way down the slope.

Jane's knees wobbled and she felt faint. Her heart pounded. She sat for several minutes staring at the now-empty trail before she dared to stand. Another minute passed before her head cleared enough for her to decide that she should follow the chimps down to the fig trees. It meant she'd risk scaring the chimps away. But at least she'd find out how close they'd let her come.

Before she could scramble down from the peak, a second, larger group broke from the underbrush and passed through the clearing toward the fig trees below. Again, many paused to stare—or glare—and hoot at her before rushing back into line.

One male with a thick gray streak through the hair over his head and face stepped out of line and thoughtfully played with the corner of his lip. He eased forward, cocked his head, and reached out one finger to touch Jane's leg before bounding back. He hooted at Jane with two friends from the safety of a dozen feet and fell back into line.

Were the hoots a warning or friendly greetings to a now-accepted jungle neighbor? Jane couldn't tell and, at the time, was too overjoyed to care.

She knew a great corner had been turned and she could finally begin the study she had been sent to do. That night she wrote in her diary, "Without a doubt, this was the proudest moment I have ever known."

After Words

Jane stayed on, first for one year and then for a second. Then the second melted into a third while she mapped the life history of new chimps. Instead of living with the Gombe chimps for a few years, Jane Goodall lived among them for thirty-four years. The detailed mosaic she has been able to create of chimp life has shocked many scientists, and thrilled others. Her study and findings have been more detailed, comprehensive, and personal than those for any other study ever conducted in the wild.

Jane Goodall revolutionized long-term field biological studies by directly interacting with the subjects of her study, chimpanzees in the Gombe Stream Game Preserve in Africa. She communicated with them, played with them, and virtually lived with them, and thereby obtained access to their daily lives in a way no other researcher had been able to do. Her studies completely rewrote the manual for the successful conduct of biological field studies.

* * *

Suggested Topics to Explore

This story deals with chimpanzees and field biology. Here are starting questions that will help you discuss and research both.

1. Could you study four-year-old human boys in a laboratory and expect to understand how they think and act? What might you be able to learn in a lab? Where else would you have to go to understand them? What extra problems might you find in this new location? Can you find reports of studies on human behavior? Where? Where would you look to find reports on animal behavior?

2. Jane Goodall wasn't trained in science or scientific methods before she began her study. Is it important to get a degree in science before beginning to work in one of the sciences? What could you learn in school that you wouldn't learn on the job? What could you learn on the job that you wouldn't learn in school?

3. Research Jane Goodall and other researchers who have spent long years in the field conducting animal studies. How many did you find? What species did they study?

For Further Reading About This Story

Fromer, Julie. *Jane Goodall: Living with the Chimps.* Frederick, MD: 21st Century Books, 1992.

Goodall, Jane. *The Chimpanzees of Gombe: Patterns of Behavior.* Bridgewater, CT: Replica Books, 1997.

―――. *In the Shadow of Man.* New York: Houghton Mifflin Co., 1971.

―――. *Through a Window: My Thirty Years with the Chimpanzees of Gombe.* Boston: Houghton Mifflin Co., 1990.

Montgomery, Sy. *Walking with the Great Apes: Jane Goodall, Dian Fossey, and Birute Galdikas.* Boston: Houghton Mifflin Co., 1992.

Senn, J. A. *Jane Goodall.* Woodbridge, CT: Blackbirch Press, 1993.

Alice Hamilton

Deadly Detection: Industrial
A Science Adventure   Medicine Pioneer

Imagine crawling along rickety catwalks above vats of boiling acid, and facing waves of blast-furnace heat from the inferno fires of steel plants—all in a swishing floor-length, high-collar dress! That's what Alice Hamilton did for almost twenty years to uncover the dark and dirty health secrets of early American industrial plants.

A Science Adventure in Chicago Factories

"Lead poison . . . It had to be lead poisoning." Forty-one-year-old Dr. Alice Hamilton repeated it to herself as she trudged home through the Chicago heat on an early September evening in 1910. A slender, short woman wearing her typical tweed, ankle-length dress, Dr. Hamilton was returning from her inspection of a bathtub-enameling factory, where she had expected to find lead-based products and lead dust. Documenting industrial poisons was her job. Hamilton was the director of the new Illinois State Occupational Disease Commission, the first industrial health commission in the United States.

True, enameling plants were a new industry for her to investigate. But what she had found at this plant didn't add up, not at all.

Alice had examined three disabled workers earlier in the week at the free clinic she ran. Each showed every sign of severe lead poisoning. They would probably die within the year from the disease. All three had worked at this enameling plant. But she found no evidence of lead at the plant. Something didn't add up.

Alice had often seen the signs of lead poisoning over the past four months as she inspected different lead-based factories and examined workers in those plants who suffered from palsy, body tremors, arms that couldn't be raised, paralysis, mental breakdown (insanity), coma, and convulsions (called lead fits)—the typical symptoms of lead poisoning. Yet this enameling factory seemed clean and free of lead. The workers she examined on the factory floor showed no sign of lead poisoning.

Alice Hamilton's well baby and worker health clinics were part of Hull House, a Chicago estate converted by Jane Addams into a residence community service center. Each resident volunteered services to the poor.

"You were successful?" Jane asked from a front porch chair.

Mounting the wide stone stairs, Alice answered, "No. And it is most troubling."

"The factory refused you entry?"

"Quite the contrary. The manager was most cooperative. Showed me the plant and even their medical records. But I found no sign of lead dust as I have in factories from felt making to paint, to smelters, to coffin manufacturing."

"Odd . . . " Jane replied.

Alice reached the Hull House front door. "Most odd. But I am due downstairs in the clinic. We'll have to talk later."

After examining and treating two babies and showing the mothers proper baby bathing techniques, Alice greeted a young, nervous looking woman. "They knew you was coming. We all did."

Confused, Alice asked, "*Who* knew?"

"The factory. They been cleaning something fierce. All the sick men got told to keep to home. They brung in a dozen new ones for you to examine that ain't never worked there at all."

"The enameling plant?" Alice stammered. "They did that?"

"My husband was one of them ordered to keep to home. 'Sides, you only saw the touch-up room. You ain't seen the enameling and sandblasting rooms. They tricked you."

"Really?" Alice repeated, her anger beginning to boil. "They intentionally deceived an official state commissioner?"

"Just don't say I told," begged the woman.

"I most certainly will," Alice announced. "I'll confront them first thing tomorrow."

"My husband'll get fired. We can't live without the money."

Alice thanked the woman and promised both to treat her husband and to not mention the woman's visit. Then Alice spent the night in frenzied debate. She hated confrontations. They rarely produced progress. But this was inexcusable.

Next morning, Alice was blocked at the factory office front door by the manager flanked by two burly assistants. "You have already inspected our factory, Dr. Hamilton. What brings you back?"

Alice breathed deeply to compose herself and tried to seem more imposing than her trim size allowed. "First, you only showed me the touch-up room. Second, you hired men off the street to pose as employees. Third, you showed me false medical records. I *demand* to inspect this factory and its real employees."

"No."

Alice momentarily closed her eyes, trying to gain strength from the desperate look in the woman's eyes last night. "You are responsible for the health—and sickness—of the men who work in your factory and the governor has empowered me to openly inspect every factory in the state."

The manager scoffed, "I'm not responsible if they get sick. That's their own business. I give them jobs. I *pay* them. I make it possible for them to support their families. I even provide a doctor for their medical needs."

"Who falsifies his records so it won't appear that anything dangerous happens here," Alice interrupted.

"Besides," bellowed the manager, "I told you we don't use lead. The men you examined probably got sick from getting drunk every night."

Alice replied, "If you protect your employees' health, they'll live longer and you won't need to hire and train as many new workers. And if you use no lead, you certainly won't mind if I inspect your factory for signs of lead dust and lead poisoning."

The manager slowly ground his jaw as he thought. "Very well. Show Miss Hamilton the rest of the plant."

"All of it, boss?" asked one of the thugs.

"Anything she *asks* to see."

"I would like to start," Alice announced, "with the enameling and sandblasting rooms."

As Dr. Hamilton entered the dingy enameling room heat billowed from a row of giant furnaces. Two men stood in front of each furnace. Thick dust swirled through the stifling heat, making Alice gag and choke.

One furnace door swung open. Waves of searing heat rolled across the expansive room knocking the breath from her. A mechanical arm swung a red-hot iron bathtub out of the furnace and set it on a metal turntable. The tub glowed and pulsed with shimmering heat.

The enameller, as quickly as possible, dredged powdered enamel over the hot tub surface, where it melted and flowed to form an even coating of enamel glaze. An assistant slowly spun the turntable to expose all parts of the tub to the enameller. Both men panted in the swirling enamel dust because of the exertion and extreme heat.

Once the enamel coat was applied, the tub swung back into the furnace. The men had a few minutes to relax. Their face, hair, and hands were coated thick with enamel dust. Trickles of sweat left streaks through the grime on their cheeks and necks. Usually, the men walked to one of the two windows to breathe fresh air or to eat. Because they weren't allowed a formal break during their ten-hour shift, they had to eat with dust-covered hands in a dust-thick environment.

Instantly Alice saw that ventilation was substandard and that the dust itself was a health hazard. But was there any lead in the enamel dust? Alice collected dust samples in a glass jar. She examined six of the enamellers. Each showed a thick, black lead line, a deposit of lead sulfide in the cells of the mouth, and most visible in the gums along the margin of the front teeth. It was the first sure sign of serious lead poisoning.

Back in the office, Alice demanded to see the men's medical records.

"You saw them yesterday."

"The *real* records," she insisted.

The manager scowled and said to his two brute assistants, "I believe Dr. Hamilton is ready to leave."

"I most certainly am not."

The manager glared at Alice. "Make sure she leaves. And make sure she never sets foot on our property again."

Alice was roughly hustled out the door and shoved through a gate onto the street. But she believed she had found enough. She had seen the signs of lead poisoning and she had a dust sample.

Back in her Hull House laboratory, she conducted a chemical analysis on the dust. It only took an hour to isolate the major chemical components of enamel paint. Lead was the biggest single component. Ten hours a day, six days a week, enamel workers breathed thick lead dust. It settled on their food, swirled in their mouths, and collected on their teeth and exposed skin. They couldn't work in that room and *not* get lead poisoning.

Dr. Hamilton tried to interview workers outside the gate as they left their shift. Most were afraid to talk to her, especially within sight of the factory. She had to follow them to their homes and hangouts before she could coax them to talk at all. She found no one who had worked in the enameling factory longer than three years. By that time, the effects of lead poisoning left the men too weak to work. They either quit, died, were hospitalized, or were fired.

But what to do about it? First, of course, was to properly vent enameling factories with exhaust fans. Some factories would voluntarily install them to protect workers. Some would not. American industrialists had adopted a sort of joyous ruthlessness. A manufacturing process that was deadly took on a certain kind of charm, a glamour. These factories would have to be forced to change with strict state laws.

Second was to eliminate lead from powdered enamel paint. Alice spent a month touring paint factories, learning the chemistry of their production process, crawling on narrow catwalks over bubbling vats of acids to collect samples of dangerous fumes that wafted up to seep into upper floors and scar the lungs of workers. She helped create lab space and equipment for testing nonlethal alternatives to lead in the production of paint and enamel. She hunted through hospitals and banged door to door through slum neighborhoods, union halls, ethnic social clubs, and dingy bars to find men now too sick to work, but who had once worked in the factories she studied. She carefully examined each man to document the hazards of industrial lead. When Alice Hamilton finished her studies and examinations, she turned in her report.

After Words

Alice Hamilton's report back to the Illinois governor resulted in the first law in America to reduce and control industrial toxins. Her methods and findings revolutionized working conditions throughout the country.

Over the next twenty-five years, Alice investigated a dozen industries from match making, to refineries, to explosive manufacturing. During this time Dr. Hamilton worked for fifteen states, for the national government, and for four foreign countries. Almost single-handedly, Dr. Alice Hamilton created the field of industrial medicine in America and brought the national tragedy of industrial poisoning to the attention of both the public and the government.

* * *

Suggested Topics to Explore

This story deals with lead toxicity (poisoning) and industrial medicine. Here are starting questions that will help you discuss and research both.

1. How can business managers know that a new industrial process will be, or might be, harmful to workers? If the products of that process will benefit the public, shouldn't they get their plant built and working as soon as possible?

2. Research Alice Hamilton and her remarkable life. What industries did she investigate? How did she get started in that dangerous work?

3. Who should be responsible for the health problems in workers created by industrial toxins? What about problems created in people who live nearby—or downwind, or downriver from an industrial plant?

4. What are the most dangerous industrial jobs today? Make a list of these dangerous jobs and their health and safety risks. Can you think of any way to reduce those risks? What are the health dangers of other types of jobs today?

For Further Reading About This Story

Brodeur, Paul. *Expendable Americans.* New York: Viking Press, 1986.

Grant, Madeline. *Alice Hamilton: Pioneer Doctor in Industrial Medicine.* New York: Abelard-Schuman, 1987.

Haber, Louis. *Women Pioneers of Science.* New York: Harcourt Brace, 1991.

McPherson, Stephanie. *The Worker's Detective.* Minneapolis, MN: Carolrhoda Books, 1992.

Sickerman, Barbara. *Alice Hamilton.* Cambridge, MA: Harvard University Press, 1988.

Wax, Nina. *Occupational Health.* New York: Chelsea House, 1994.

Janet Harrington

Shall We Dance?   Insect Biologist
A Science Adventure

When Janet Harrington stands in a field with bees swarming around her head and crawling across her neck, arms, and face, she hardly notices. It's just another typical workday for her.

A Science Adventure in an Indiana Field

A tan three-quarter-ton pickup truck with university markings lurches across a wide, tree-lined Indiana field. Thirty-eight-year-old Janet Harrington walks ahead guiding the truck with her arms. Bees buzz from blossom to blossom. A few light on Janet's arms, legs, and shoulders only to buzz off moments later in search of sweeter treats.

Janet has traveled 10,000 miles to this Indiana field to watch these honeybees zigzag above the clover and soft summer grass. The bees seem not to care that her theory, her position, and her reputation ride on their every move.

A hazy, pale blue sky this afternoon of July 12, 2001, almost drips with steamy humidity. Thunderheads are building far off in the west. Janet signals for the truck to stop. Two graduate students pile out of the cab.

One of them, summer intern Charles Wilcock, grimaces and swats the air in front of his face. "There're too many bees here! Let's unload somewhere else."

Janet answers, "The bees are why we're here." Then she adds, "They won't sting if you don't make them angry."

"Yes they will! I *always* get stung."

Dodging bees, the trio unloads fake and potted bushes and a half-dozen papier-mâché boulders from the truck's bed.

"Seems strange to put fake rocks and bushes in a field," says Charles.

"We're creating additional visual landmarks between a feeding station and the hive," Janet replies. Her answer generates only blank stares from the grad students. So she adds, "To see if extra landmarks change a returning bee's dance."

Janet took this summer of 2001 off from her teaching duties at Australian National University in Canberra to join University of Notre Dame professor Harold Esch. She planned to test (and hopefully prove) their theory for how honeybees communicate. The problem was that their theory meant that honeybees had to be far more intelligent than other scientists believed possible.

In the 1940s, Nobel Laureate Karl von Frisch discovered that bees perform a dance to direct hive mates to a food source. But *how* do they transmit the information? Some said it was by scent. Some said the dance indicated direction and flying time. Others claimed the dance communicated direction and distance.

Janet Harrington and Harold Esch believed that returning bees created a visual two-dimensional map of landmarks in their mind, and communicated that visual map to others during their dance. Others scoffed at their idea, saying bees were not smart enough to either create or understand a multidimensional spatial map.

Janet had already released several test bees at a feeding station (a cup of sugar water) and watched them fly back to the hive. Cameras mounted into the wooden walls of the hive had recorded the dance of each returning bee. While watching the video in a university lab, Janet had timed each dance and recorded the number and direction of turns the dancing bee made. If honeybees used visual cueing in their dance, additional landmarks along this same thirty-five-yard path from feeding station to hive should translate into the bees performing a longer and more complex dance for other bees.

With a dozen new landmarks now scattered along the bees' path, Janet announces, "We need to check the cameras."

"Not me!" squeals Charles. "I'm not walking up to a bee hive!" He leaps into the truck, then screams and rolls out, having discovered three bees in the cab.

Janet chuckles and shakes her head. "Graduate students . . . " she mutters and walks her thirty-five-yard long obstacle course to the white wooden hive the university had built around mounted video cameras. Occasionally the lenses became smeared with wax that obscured their view of a test bee's dance. Someone has to physically check each camera before they are used.

Janet unbolts the first camera. Bees swarm out this new hole in their hive, a thick cloud of black, orange, and yellow. Instinctively Janet ducks, squeezing her eyes shut, her heart pounding at the fierce chainsawlike whine of bees that surrounds her. She can feel a hundred tiny bee legs crawling across her arms, neck, and face—across her lips, eyes, and nose. She can even feel the wind created by their beating wings. She must consciously force herself to breathe slowly and evenly through her nose.

Part of her wants to scream and run. Her mind knows that would upset the bees and lead to deadly disaster. Her body is not so sure. It takes all of her will to force her body to relax.

Slowly Janet stands, looking as if she wears a living turtleneck sweater made of bees. Gently she shakes her head and arms so that most of the bees fly back to the hive. Pretending to feel calm—almost bored—Janet cleans the camera lens, checks the connections and battery pack, then rebolts the camera against the hive wall and flips the power switch.

Two cameras later, Janet walks back to the feeding station to find Charles staring in horrified awe. "How many stings?"

"Only one," Janet answers, rubbing the growing knot on her shoulder.

Carol Gibson, Janet's other assistant, holds out a tube. "Here's some ointment."

Janet waits fifteen minutes for the hive activity to return to normal and releases two marked bees right above the feeding station. One zooms out into the field. The other settles on the lip of the cup, dabbing at the sugar water. It rises into the air, makes two short zags to get its bearings, and drives straight to the hive along the land-marked path Janet has created.

"Roll cameras!" Janet orders.

Charles clicks remotes. Red and green lights blink on all three cameras.

Janet says, "The dance should take about thirty seconds. Carol, you wait forty-five seconds then begin a count of how many bees emerge from the hive. Charles, roam the field and search for other places the bees congregate. I'll count how many fly to this feeding station."

Thirty minutes later Janet calls out, "Stop the counts. Retrieve the cameras. That'll be good enough." By this time, 150 bees have emerged from the hive. 120 have flown straight to Janet's sugar water. She points west toward a billowing, dark cloudbank, "Besides, it's about to rain."

Back at Notre Dame, the trio reviews their videos in slow motion. Janet announces, "That proves it! This bee's dance lasted thirty percent longer and contained forty-five percent more turns than the bees I released yesterday from the same feeding station. It had to be the extra visual landmarks that slowed the dance."

"It proves nothing," Professor Esch counters. "This bee might be naturally slower in its dance. It could be providing more detailed directions or distance information of a non-visual nature. It might have embellished its tale like some human storytellers."

Janet interrupts. "But the number of turns and the duration of the dance seemed to increase proportionately with the number of new landmarks we set out along the path. I say this is solid evidence."

"Evidence, yes," answers Esch. "But proof? No. To *prove* our theory, we have to trick the bees."

"Trick the bees?" asks Charles.

"We must make the bees communicate visual information that will lead other bees somewhere other than the feeding station— somewhere the bees would only go if they were following this false visual information."

"How do you fool bees?" Charles asks.

Janet glances at Professor Esch. "You think we need to build a shadow tube?"

Esch shrugged and nodded. "It's the only way to *prove* it."

Professor Esch's lab work suggested that bees visually recorded the dark shadow of a landmark rather than the object, itself. A shadow tube was a large plastic tube with a pattern of black rectangles painted on the inside to simulate shadows. A bee flying through the tube would *think* it had passed many landmarks. If Harrington and Esch were right, a bee that later left the hive and *didn't* fly through the tube would have to fly much farther to pass the same number of landmarks.

Armed with a three-foot diameter, thirty-foot long plastic tube that looked like a painted black-and-white checkerboard on the inside, Janet, Carol, and Charles return to their test field the next afternoon.

Janet lays the shadow tube along the ground pointing toward the hive. She places a feeding station (cup of sugar water) just inside the far end of the tube. Finally ready, she releases a marked bee at the station and closes that end of tube behind it. The bee tastes sugar water, pauses at the lip of the cup, and then flies a zigzag course down the tube. Carol and Janet cheer as their bee emerges into daylight where it hesitates and then zooms straight to the hive.

Janet orders, "Roll cameras and collapse the tube. We'll use the same counting plan as yesterday. Charles, if we're right, bees should fly toward the far corner of the field. Start out there."

Over the next thirty minutes, 140 bees emerge from the hive. 109 fly straight to an area of the field 120 yards away. There they buzz back and forth as if confused and desperately searching for something. Only two fly to the feeding station for Janet to count.

Now Janet can ride in triumph back to the lab with her cameras and notes.

After Words

This small adventure in a summer bee field proved how bees communicate and just how smart bees really are. Dr. Janet Harrington's work has created a more accurate picture of the wondrous insect world around us and a better understanding of insect communications. It has led to a far better appreciation of the intelligence and intricacies of bees, in particular, and insects, in general.

* * *

Suggested Topics to Explore

This story deals with bee intelligence and behavioral research. Here are some starting questions that will help you discuss and research both.

1. Why study bees, a mere insect? Why study the lives and habits of any one species?

2. How does it help human scientists to know how intelligent bees are?

3. Do you think humans tend to underestimate the intelligence of many other species? Why? What species do you think are intelligent? Which do you think aren't? How can intelligence

be tested in other species? Can you design an experiment to find out? Research animal intelligence in the library and on the Internet.

For Further Reading About This Story

Brimner, G. *Bees.* Danbury, CT: Children's Press, 1999.

Fischer-Nagel, Heiderose. *Life of the Honey Bee.* Minneapolis, MN: Carolrhoda Books, 1990.

Frisch, Karl. *The Dancing Bees.* New York: Harcourt, Brace, Jovanovich, 1963.

Gibbins, Gail. *The Honey Makers.* New York: Morrow Junior Books, 1997.

Hartley, Karen. *Bee.* Portsmouth, NH: Heinemann Library, 1998.

Heilegman, Deborah. *Honey Bees.* Washington, DC: National Geographic Society, 2002.

Holmes, Kevin. *Bees.* Chicago: Bridgestone Books, 1998.

Hughes, Kevin. *A Closer Look at Bees and Wasps.* New York: Franklin Watts, 1989.

Ispen, D. *What Does a Bee See?* New York: Addison Wesley, 1991.

Patent, Dorothy. *How Smart Are Animals?* San Diego, CA: Harcourt Brace Jovanovich, 1990.

Dorothy Hodgkin

"Picture" Perfect: X-Ray
A Science Adventure   Crystallographer

Imagine trying to identify and locate every person in a room just by looking at their collective shadows cast on the walls. Imagine trying to do this with fifty people in the room. That's very close to what Dorothy Hodgkin had to do in order to save millions of lives by creating synthetic penicillin.

A Science Adventure in the X-Ray Lab

Dr. Ernst Chain slammed the museum doors as he rushed in out of the cold English rain. The echo rolled off cavernous walls. Colonel Jeffery Stanton marched beside Ernst, the heels of his stiff military boots clicking on the marble floor. Above their heads spectral skeletons of ancient whales and dinosaurs hung from the dimly lit ceiling. Collections of dead beetles, moths, and lizards covered the distant walls.

Dr. Chain led the colonel to a side door along one wall of this Oxford University museum. Opening it, and nodding toward the narrow stairway beyond, he said, "Dorothy Hodgkin's office is down here."

Dr. Hodgkin's office was a cramped alcove, hardly big enough for the three of them to sit without moving piles of reports and rearranging stacks of test equipment. After preliminary handshakes, Colonel Stanton rose. His thick red mustache quivered as he spoke in crisp, precise diction.

"It is now March of 1942, Dr. Hodgkin. The war drags on. Hundreds of good English lads are dying every day. More of them die from battlefield infections than German bullets. We need a steady supply of those. . . . " The colonel fumbled for the right word and then gestured to Dr. Chain.

"Antibiotics," responded the doctor.

"Precisely! Antibiotics," continued the Colonel. "And we need them now!"

Dorothy Hodgkin shrugged. "Why come to me? I'm a chemical researcher."

"Ah, precisely. It has everything to do with you and your . . . your X crystals . . . " Again he motioned for Dr. Chain to take over.

"X-ray diffraction crystallography," corrected Ernst.

Colonel Stanton appeared a trifle bewildered, so Dr. Hodgkin explained. "We shoot X-rays at molecules locked inside a crystal structure and watch how individual atoms bend or diffract the X-rays."

"Ahh, precisely!" Colonel Stanton rocked slowly on his polished heels, gestured to Ernst, and sat.

"The army needs massive quantities of penicillin," said Chain. "Dr. Fleming discovered penicillin mold in 1928. Following his original work, I have tried to grow it, but the penicillin mold grows too slowly. We need to *synthetically* create penicillin in a factory. But we can't, because we don't know what's in it. We don't know the arrangement of atoms in a penicillin molecule, or even which atoms are in there to be arranged."

Dorothy nodded. "And you're hoping I can find out using X-ray diffraction."

Col. Stanton fidgeted in his chair. "My wife collects crystals, you know."

Dorothy laughed and rocked back in her desk chair. "Crystals are all around us, Colonel. Table salt is a crystal. So is sugar. So are snowflakes. Aspirin forms crystals. Some single crystals are as large as two thousand tons. Some are microscopic.

"A crystal is any solid whose molecules are locked into a regular, repeating pattern and shape. It is that repeating regularity that lets us look inside the crystal's molecules. If I could get my hands on a penicillin crystal, I believe I could tell you the arrangement and identity of the atoms that are in it."

Dr. Chain smiled and opened his brief case. "Just what I hoped you'd say."

He lifted out a small padded case, much like a jewelry box, and slowly opened the lid. "Will these do?" Inside on fluffy cotton wadding sat three tiny crystals, each the size of the eraser on the end of a pencil. Each gleamed with the pale milky translucence of pearls. Very carefully Ernst lifted one out and set it in Dorothy's out-stretched hand.

"The first penicillin crystals ever made. This stuff doesn't crystallize easily. Took me two months to make this batch crystallize after I ground and boiled it."

Colonel Stanton leaned forward and grabbed Dorothy Hodgkin's wrist, his eyes filled with harsh urgency. "This is a national top priority, Dr. Hodgkin. The war depends on it. We need the formula for penicillin. And, if Britain is to survive, we need it now!"

Dr. Hodgkin's X-ray diffraction lab—hardly bigger than a closet—was down the hall from her office. One wall was covered by a stack of equipment required to generate the X-ray pulses she would aim at a thin slice of crystallized material. Opposite that stack, a curved housing that held the X-ray film was mounted on the far wall.

The day after Chain's and Stanton's visit, Dorothy used surgical saws to cut a slice of penicillin crystal far thinner than a sheet of paper. She hung it in front of the X-ray gun and shot one strip of film just to see what sort of challenge they would face.

"Gad!" she muttered, studying the blur of white smudges piled thickly on top of each other across the developed film. It was the first X-ray diffraction film ever shot at penicillin molecules. "It must be a massive molecule."

Dorothy's assistant, Barbara Lowe, said, "We've never attempted to decipher one so large. How much film will this take?"

Dorothy sighed and shook her head. "I have no idea if we even *can* decipher this beast."

A week later, Colonel Stanton's polished heels again clicked across the Oxford museum floor and down the narrow side stairway. As he marched into Dorothy's small office, he heard the whir of fan motors and the whine of test equipment from her lab. His mustached face poked through the doorway just in time to see Barbara Lowe climb a ladder.

"What are the new settings, Dr. Hodgkin?" she called over her shoulder as she reached the top.

Glancing at a mound of jumbled notes and scribbled pads of calculations balanced on her lap, Dorothy called back, "Rotate the crystal fifteen degrees clockwise and thirty degrees down, please, Barbara."

Stacks of black-boxed test equipment were bolted to the walls and hung from the ceiling. Trays of pungent chemicals climbed up one wall, stacked atop each other. Cables snaked across chairs and were tacked over the door. Two large adding machines perched on the one table with long tails of used paper trailing across the floor.

"Doctor Hodgkin. Hard at work I see. Do you have a penicillin formula for us yet?"

Dorothy looked up, smiled, and extended her hand. "Welcome, Colonel. You're just in time to watch us shoot the next piece of film."

"Ahh, good show, Doctor. Shall I turn off the lights?"

Dorothy laughed, as she so regularly did. "X-ray film, Colonel, is not sensitive to visible light, only to high frequency X-rays. We don't normally darken the room."

"Ahh, precisely, yes . . . " The Colonel looked confused. "And what, exactly, do your X-rays *do?*"

"X-rays are smaller than visible light waves. They can penetrate into things that visible light can't. X-rays can actually see and react to individual atoms."

Barbara Lowe fitted a ten-inch-high, thirty-inch-long strip of X-ray film onto a semicircular wooden bracket. Dr. Hodgkin had cut a new, paper-thin sliver of penicillin crystal with surgical saws. It hung in a glass mount right in the center of that circle. The cone-shaped black nozzle of an X-ray gun stood several inches away, aimed at the crystal sliver.

Dorothy stopped her calculations and looked up. "Imagine this, Colonel. Forty people are stuffed into the middle of a room. One light somewhere along a wall shines onto those people, casting their shadow across to the far wall. Just looking at a picture of their collective shadow could you correctly identify and place all forty people in the room?"

"Certainly not," replied Colonel Stanton with an indigent snort.

Dorothy shrugged. "But that is exactly what we're doing. By rotating that crystal sliver to get different views of the shadow of a penicillin molecule, and by knowing what the X-ray shadows of different atoms look like, we can slowly piece together a map of where the atoms must be in the natural structure of a penicillin molecule. I suppose it's like finding only a fingerprint on the wall, and trying to figure out the height, weight, and age of the person who made it."

"And you can *do* that?"

"We have to, if you're going to get your penicillin."

His face hardened. "We need penicillin, doctor. We need it desperately."

Dorothy reached back for a sketchy diagram on a piece of white paper. "Actually, we're making good headway. I've already identified and located five atoms, and think I have a good sense of the size and overall shape of the molecule."

Barbara climbed back down the ladder. "The crystal's repositioned. Film's in place. Ready to shoot."

Dorothy reached for a large red button mounted on the wall near her. "All clear?"

"All clear," answered her research assistant.

Dorothy hit the button. Motors whirred. There was a short series of loud "Ka-lunks!" Barbara climbed the ladder to retrieve this new piece of exposed film.

"That was it?" asked the Colonel. "I didn't see anything."

"Sorry to disappoint you, Colonel. But you can't see X-rays."

Barbara developed the film in the chemical trays stacked on one wall and laid the still wet X-ray negative onto a large light box.

As the two women hunched over the film, Colonel Stanton peered over their shoulders. Again, he was disappointed. He saw not pictures of atoms and molecules; rather, he saw a maze of fuzzy white splotches on a black background. Dorothy and Barbara busily measured the size of, and distance between, each white spec in this pattern of fuzzy white dots.

Numbers were hurriedly punched into adding machines. The paper tape rolled out across the floor. Each computation was entered on a foldout paper grid to compare it with previous calculations concerning each potential atom in the penicillin molecule.

It would take almost a day to complete these calculations and decide how to align the crystal structure of their next shot. It took over fifteen months of constant, high-pressure work and almost 1,000 pieces of X-ray film to identify and place each of the thirty three atoms in a basic penicillin molecule and the almost seventy in several of the salts of penicillin.

After Words

Dr. Hodgkin's hard-won discovery allowed penicillin to be produced by the ton instead of by the ounce, and has saved countless millions of lives. It also won the 1964 Nobel Prize for Dr. Dorothy Hodgkin. Her work has led to a much better understanding of how crystals function, and to the invention of that now common electronic crystal: the transistor. But that was a different adventure.

* * *

Suggested Topics to Explore

This story deals with X-ray diffraction, crystallography, and penicillin. Here are starting questions that will help you discuss and research all three.

1. What are crystals? What can be made into a crystal? Have you ever seen a crystal? Do you use crystals every day? Make a collection of commonly used crystals and research the properties of crystals

2. Why use crystals of a substance to study the molecular structure of the substance?

3. What are X-rays? Why are they better than light or sound waves for studying things as small as molecules and atoms? Why do we use X-rays to take pictures of bones?

4. What is penicillin? What does it do? Where does it come from? Who discovered it? How? When?

For Further Reading About This Story

Balibar, Francoise. *The Science of Crystals.* New York: McGraw-Hill, 1993.

Frank-Kamenetskii, M. *Unraveling DNA.* New York: Addison Wesley, 1997.

Haber, Louis. *Women Pioneers of Science.* New York: Harcourt, Brace, Jovanovich, 1989.

Hammond, C. *Introduction to Crystallography.* London: Oxford University Press, 1990.

Opfell, Olga. *The Lady Laureate.* Lanham, MD: Scarecrow Press, 1986.

Shiels, Barbara. *Winners: Women and the Nobel Prize.* Minneapolis, MN: Dillon Press, 1991.

Watson, James. *The Double Helix: A Personal Account of the Discovery.* New York: Atheneum, 1968.

Wilcox, Frank. *DNA, the Thread of Life.* New York: Lerner Publications, 1988.

Grace Hopper

Amazing Grace:
A Science Adventure

Mathematician/
Computer
Scientist

Grace Hopper stood face-to-face with the world's first computer, under an urgent order to complete top-priority wartime Navy calculations, only to find that this machine had no working computer language or operating code. The pressure was on. Grace had to figure out how she could make this machine really work—and she had to do it fast.

A Science Adventure in America's First Computer Lab

"You're late!" barked the man with close-cropped graying hair, and small, tight mouth as he glared from behind his desk. Grace Hopper fumbled with her briefcase and a stack of orders and directions.

The hum of distant machinery rumbled through this basement office, as did the buzz from banks of overhead florescent lights that created dazzling reflections off the polished linoleum floor. The stifling heat of this July 2, 1944, day had even wormed its way down here into this buried cellar world.

"Is this the right basement for the Navy Bureau of Ordinance Computation Project?" she asked, trying to gather her belongings into her left hand so she could salute with her right. Her trim, brown hair squeezed out from under her Navy officer's hat.

"You're in the Navy. It's a *deck,* not a basement. And you're late." The pencil clamped in his teeth wiggled up and down as he talked.

Her cheeks blushed bright red. "I'm Lieutenant JG Grace Hopper and I'm looking for Professor Howard Aiken."

"I'm *Commander* Aiken to you. We're *all* in the Navy here. Now why are you late?"

This was not how thirty-seven-year-old Grace had envisioned that her first meeting with her first commander on her first Navy assignment would go. Flustered, she tried to click her heels and salute. "Sir, I had to report to District Headquarters in Boston. It took *four* offices to tell me that the Bureau of Ordinance Computation Project was in Croft Hall at Harvard. It took two just to find out *what* it was. . . . "

"I don't mean *today.*"

Grace was taken aback. "I was with my parents this weekend, sir, after graduation on Friday."

Commander Aiken rose and pounded the desk. Grace Hopper stood barely five feet, so her commander now towered over her. "You're *two months* late, Lieutenant! I needed you *before* you went to Midshipman's School when this project was first being assembled."

A shock trembled through Lt. Hopper. This was not going well at all. "I . . . I didn't know. . . . My orders said . . . "

But Aiken was already marching toward double doors at one end of this office room. "I hope you're ready to work."

"Yes, sir!"

"Has anyone told you about Mark I?"

"Mark who?"

Aiken stopped at the doors and spun back to face Grace. "Not *who,* its a *what.* Mark I is the world's first computing engine."

He threw open the double doors and led Grace into a much larger room marked "Restricted. Authorized Access Only." Before her stood Mark I, the world's first computer. Over fifty feet long and eight feet high, Mark I was endless banks of black metal boxes in gray metal frames with columns of floor to ceiling lights. Each panel was enclosed in a glass case that could be opened for access and maintenance. Five hundred miles of wire and 800,000 moving mechanical parts were magically woven together to make calculations at the undreamed-of speed of three computations per second!

Behind the main console, a whining four-horsepower motor drove the fifty foot-long main shaft. Mark I was an electromechanical machine. That is, it used bulky mechanical switches to store and process data instead of vacuum tubes, transistors, or microchips.

Two Navy ensigns busily monitored the monster as it hummed, clicked, and whirred. An enlisted man prepared punch cards on what looked like an overgrown typewriter.

With 4,000 mechanical relays clicking open and closed, it sounded to Grace like an auditorium full of people quietly knitting.

Aiken nodded toward the ensigns. "As soon as they're through with this problem, you're on."

Grace stared at this wondrous sight straight out of science-fiction stories, a mathematician's dream, on the basement floor—or, deck—before her. "What can it do?" she asked, sounding like an anxious car buyer.

"That's what you're here to find out. You're first job will be to calculate the coefficients for the interpolation of the arc tangent."

"When do you need them?" asked Grace. As a mathematics professor with an engineering background, she knew what these coefficients were and what they were for.

Aiken pushed back through the double doors. Over his shoulder he said, "You're already late. They were due in to a Navy office last Wednesday."

Rooted where she stood next to the door, Grace Hopper's eyes widened as she stared in awe at the gleaming Mark I. At first sight, she fell in love with this whirling dervish, this knit-clicking marvel. Reverently she tiptoed forward as if in a cathedral, and reached out to touch it, cautiously, with only one finger at first, as if it were alive, as it rumbled, hummed, flashed, and clicked.

The hardware had been built over the past year as a joint project of Professor Aiken of Harvard, the IBM Corporation, and the Navy. But in their rush to create the computing machine, itself, no one had thought much about how they would communicate with this mechanical marvel, how they would command and control it. With her mathematics and science background, Grace Hopper had been assigned both to work *on* the Mark I, and to explore better ways to work *with* the machine.

The two ensigns stopped their work, jokingly elbowed each other and nodded toward Grace. "Here to meet our temperamental baby?" asked tall, slender Richard Bloch.

The shorter, chunkier man, Robert Campbell said, "It's quite a gadget." And then added, "*If* you like to spend most of your time coaxing it to work."

"I've been assigned to work on the Mark I," said Grace, extending her hand to formally meet her new co-workers.

"*Another* woman," groaned Bloch.

"There are other women here?" asked Grace.

"Some old Navy officer was assigned to us. But she's two months late."

"I heard she's a white-haired school teacher who'll wrap our knuckles with a ruler every time this contraption breaks down," nodded Campbell.

"That officer is me," laughed Grace. Then she tried to look stern. "And that's Lieutenant Hopper to you, Ensign!"

But even before the ensigns could snap back a "Yes, ma'am!" Grace broke out laughing again. "Actually, it's just Grace."

Bloch's head jerked toward the Mark I. His hands shot out like a traffic cop signaling "stop." "Shhhh!" He froze, head slightly cocked. "A click is out of sync. A relay must be jammed."

A computer warning light flashed on, a signal that the Mark I couldn't complete an ordered operation.

Campbell bellowed, "Lights!" and reached back to flip a switch and plunge the room into total darkness.

Panel by panel the two ensigns groped their way along the computer's length.

"What are you doing?" Grace asked.

"Searching for a telltale spark that will identify the culprit relay."

"Got it!" Bloch called. "Lights!"

Their enlisted aid felt his way along the wall from his punchcard terminal to the master light switch.

Campbell yanked a screwdriver from a slot in his belt and flipped the latches to release the glass cover plate and locking mechanism on the jammed relay.

"A moth," he sighed. "I might have known." He rubbed mashed moth out of the relay with rubbing alcohol and cotton swab.

"Does that happen often?" Grace asked.

"They fly into the machine and get pounded to death by the mechanical relays—which are then shorted out, gummed up, and jammed. We have to stop and clean them out five or six times a day."

"So, rather than work with this computer," Grace bristled, "I am going to spend my time debugging it?"

"Good name for it," laughed Bloch.

"That's the only way to keep the beast running," sighed Campbell.

Grace forced a deep breath and whispered to herself, "I can do this."

She had always been good with mechanical things. As a seven-year-old she had once taken apart all seven alarm clocks in the family's rambling summerhouse at the lake. She hadn't been able to put any of them back together, and she never quite figured out how they worked, but she was a pro at taking them apart!

Still running her hands over the banks of lights and switches, she added, "This machine is beautiful—more than beautiful, it's glamorous—even with the bugs."

"Wow. I think we have a convert." And both ensigns chuckled.

Grace asked, "How do you tell it what to do?"

"Write code."

"What's code?"

Bloch said, "We have to write every detail of each step of every computation in number codes. Those codes get transferred onto punched cards that Mark I can read."

Grace asked, "Who designed the system of codes?"

"That's the problem," admitted Campbell. "A few code commands were hardwired into the machine—like the command to add two numbers. (That's 07.) We're trying to create more as we go. But it's sort of hodge-podge."

An excited gleam flashed in Grace's eyes. Again she whispered to herself, "*This* I can do."

The codebook was embarrassingly short and simple. Still, it took Grace two hours to write the program to calculate her coefficients for the interpolation of the arc tangent.

Grace complained, "It's too slow having to write out every tiny step."

"You get used to it," Block answered.

Grace thought a second and laid down her pencil. "You know, this computer doesn't do very much. It should be smarter. My slide rule is a lot faster and easier to use."

"At figuring *one* of your coefficients, yes," Campbell replied. "But if you have to calculate a thousand, or a hundred-thousand, then this baby'll beat your slide rule by a mile!"

Thumbing through her sheets of paper, Grace said, "Just to calculate these simple coefficients my program has 227 lines of code."

"Your *what?*" Bloch asked.

"Program sounds more elegant and impressive than code. I write programs."

Both ensigns nodded, their eyebrows raised. "Program—I like it."

"We need a better control language. We talk to this machine as if it were a kindergarten child," Grace continued. "Starting next week, I'm gong to create a control language for this machine so our programs don't have to be so unwieldy."

"Do you know how to do that?" Campbell asked.

"Not yet. But apparently, no one else does either."

But Grace wasn't through. "And I want three fans brought in here tomorrow and set up behind the computer."

"To keep the motor cool?" Campbell asked.

"To blow wandering bugs away from our computer so we'll have to debug it less often."

Standing in the doorway, Commander Aiken smiled. "Welcome to the Mark I, Lieutenant. You'll fit in just fine."

After Words

Grace Hopper designed the root language and operating systems for the Mark I, Mark II, ENIAC, BINAC, and UNIVAC computers—the UNIVAC being the first mass-produced, commercially available computer in the world. Besides writing programs, Grace was a true pioneer in designing and developing whole languages for computers including COBAL, the most successful general purpose business and accounting program for over thirty years.

* * *

Suggested Topics to Explore

This story deals with computers and computer languages. Here are starting questions that will help you discuss and research both.

1. What is a computer? How is a computer different than a calculator or an abacus?

2. When and by whom was the first computer designed? When was the first computer actually built? Research the history and evolution of calculators and computers from ancient times to the present.

3. What is a computer language? How does a computer language work? How does it let us talk to machines? If you were going

to create a computer language, what would it look like? What would you want to be able to tell the computer to do?

For Further Reading About This Story

Billings, Charlene. *Grace Hopper, Navy Admiral and Computer Pioneer.* Hillside, NJ: Enslow Publishers, Inc., 1989.

Osen, Lynn. *Women in Mathematics.* Cambridge, MA: MIT Press, 1990.

Perl, Teri. *Math Equals: Biographies of Women Mathematicians.* Menlo Park, CA: Addison-Wesley, 1988.

Wade, Ira. "Women in Mathematics." *The Arithmetic Teacher* 18, no. 4 (1990): 26–39.

Yount, Lisa. *Contemporary Women Scientists.* New York: Facts on File, 1994.

Louise Hose

Cravin' Cavin':   Speleologist
A Science Adventure

Imagine exploring a cave with water and walls corrosive enough to blister skin, with air filled with deadly H_2S (hydrogen sulfide) and CO (carbon monoxide) gasses, a coffin-black cave filled with bizarre life that exists no where else on Earth. Louise Hose slithered through tiny crevices in just such a cave half a mile underground, when she got stuck, and her light began to fail.

A Science Adventure in a Mexican Cave

"Holly, can you hear me?" Thirty-two-year-old Louise Hose repeated the call, "Holly, anyone, come in." Louise wiggled her shoulders and arms to create enough room to push the tiny hand-held radio into the beam of her carbide headlight.

"Nuts!" Thick, rust-colored ooze bubbled from the battery housing. The flexible antenna had been replaced by a pool of warped plastic and smoking wires. It looked like the radio had been dropped into a vat of battery acid.

Louise muttered, "It must have scraped the wall."

Outside it was October 15, 2000. Inside the Villa Luz cave, located in the extreme southern end of Mexico in the dense jungles of the State of Tobasco, dates had no meaning. Neither did day or night in the cave's perpetual coffin-black.

Deep in the bowels of Villa Luz, Louise tried to push forward through this "squirmhole" no bigger around than a toilet bowl. She began to feel dizzy. Breathing came hard through the filters of her chemical respirator. She sucked for every breath as if there were no air left.

"It's just low O_2 (oxygen) and high H_2S (hydrogen sulfide). Stay calm," she panted. "Better get a sample of this air." Louise reached ahead of her with a sample jar and uncapped the lid. She let the poisonous air flowing from the next room fill the container and snapped the cap shut. Woozie and more disoriented with every breath, she felt as if she had swallowed a handful of fiberglass. "Time to back out of here."

Louise began the agonizingly slow process of squirming backward, trying to remember each bend, lip, and rock she had wiggled past. Her legs, arms, and body were soaked in the gruel-like acid mud that coated the passageway floor. It oozed through small tears and holes in her Tyvek chemical protection suit and began to blister her skin.

Near lethal concentrations of H_2S burned into her lungs with the vile stench of raw sewage. Louise felt pinned beneath two hundred feet of solid limestone. Even though she was a veteran of over a thousand spelunking descents into caves, she struggled to control the upwelling panic.

Louise realized that she was wiggling out too slowly. Her arms felt too heavy to move. She had trouble concentrating. She couldn't remember which way was up. Her mind began to drift. With dismay, she realized she might not make it out at all.

Suddenly a pair of hands grabbed her boots and gently pulled her back into the safety of a small chamber. Three minutes later, Louise collapsed to the floor in the spacious comfort of Sala Grande, the biggest room in the Villa Luz cave system. She panted in the cleaner air and open spaces of this large chamber.

Holly Shugardt said, "Your filters are caked yellow with sulfur. You better head back to town."

Louise nodded, her head still spinning from the toxic air of the passageway. Holly added, "Why didn't you call for a backup?"

Louise held up what was left of her radio.

Holly whistled low and shook her head. "That must be the most corrosive wall yet. Did you see any sign of life?"

"It's teaming in there," Louise answered. "Those walls are worse than battery acid. The mud is acidic enough to raise blisters. The air almost killed me even with the filters and chemical respirator. Yet I saw a bat—a mammal—in there, happy as a clam. Several lizards scurried past. It's got spiders, centipedes, and a thick coating of microbes on the walls. . . . "

After a pause for deep gulps of fresh air, Louise continued, "I could see a pool just beyond. It's *got* to have deadly concentrations of sulfur. Yet it was jammed with shrimp and translucent fish. Huge blue eyes and I could see their internal organs. That place should be a death trap. It's worse than the worst toxic nightmare humans could dream up. . . . And yet, the place has a thriving ecosystem. Somehow they've all adapted."

"Did you get any samples for the lab?" Holly asked.

"Microbes from the wall, mud, air, and water," Louise answered, tapping her mesh sample bag. Again, she thanked Holly for her rescue and rose, still disoriented and wobbly from her bout with deadly air, for her hike to the cave entrance. From there, a jeep waited to carry her back to the team's base camp in a nearby village.

Formed in solid limestone, laced with thick sulfur deposits, the action of water over the eons has produced the unique and deadly mix of toxic gasses and acidic water that characterize the five-mile-long cave system.

By all accounts, Villa Luz should be a barren wasteland. Its toxic water and air should kill every living thing that wandered inside. Yet its thriving food web is every bit as lush and vibrant as that of the jungle above. It shouldn't be. But it is.

Villa Luz has a unique and flourishing ecosystem. DNA analysis on sample species retrieved from the cave confirm that many of the life-forms in Villa Luz exist nowhere else on Earth. Studying this cave and its ecosystem could have great value to industry as well as to environmental scientists. In 2000, Louise Hose was in her second year as team leader for the cave's exploration and study.

A restored colonial village, Tapijulapa, poked through the jungle canopy a half mile from the cave entrance. One building had been taken over as office and in-town lab for the team to use during their survey missions. There, Louise handed her samples to the team's two chemists. "From a small chamber just beyond the Yellow Rose room. Be careful. I think they're *very* corrosive—and toxic."

One of the chemists who doubled as the team medic said, "I'm worried about the cavers' health. The breathing filter packs show not only deadly high concentrations of H_2S . . . "

"We've known that for two years," Louise interrupted, laughing.

" . . . But *also,*" he continued, scowling, "HF (hydrogen floride), SO_2 (sulfur dioxide), and CO. Any one of those could kill you on its own. But they're *all* in there and I'm afraid those over-the-counter respirators won't protect you."

Louise smiled and patted his shoulder. "You worry too much, Carl. Caving is dangerous. It's always dangerous. The cave floor could give way beneath me and I'd fall to my death. Cavers fall into pools and are trapped and drowned. Cavers become wedged and trapped and die slowly, all alone in the dark. There are more things to worry about down there than just toxic air."

"All I'm asking is that you don't take unnecessary risks."

Louise put her hands on her hips. "And I'm saying that we have an incredible opportunity to explore and study something unique and unknown here. This place is like no other cave in the world. It's incredible down there! Did you know the average room in that cave has ten-million-million microbes clinging to it? That's thousands of times more than you'd expect from the same area of a surface ecosystem. And it does it with no solar energy and no photosynthesis. Our funding only allows us to come down here three weeks a year. I plan to use every minute of every one of them. So don't tell me to hold back!"

The other chemist whistled shrilly. "Wow! I just measured pH on that wall slime you brought back, Louise. Two-point-one! This stuff should dissolve those critters, not help them thrive."

Louise smiled and shrugged at Carl. "See? We *gotta'* spend all the time we can observing and sampling this place."

Back at the cave entrance after a shower and food, Louise gathered her three-person team. "There is a tight passage beyond Battery [the name they had given to one room because the walls dripped acid as strong as battery acid]. I want to explore whatever is beyond that passage and collect samples and population counts. Wear all the protective gear you can."

Holly Shugardt said, "We can't wear or bring much gear or we'll never make it through any tight passages."

"I know. But wear as much as you can."

After donning neoprene bib overalls, Tyvek chem suits, miners helmets, and with gloves, knee and elbow pads, and multiple chemical exposure monitors clipped to their chests, the team crawled past the toxic sludge of Battery. They waded through a chest-deep acidic sulfur spring, and started into the squirm hole, hardly bigger around than a large tennis racquet.

It took almost twenty minutes for the team to worm their way sixty feet along that tiny passage and into a chamber beyond. Bats fluttered overhead. A swarm of midges crowded around their faces and exposed skin. All three cavers were sweating and panting from the exertion of their crawl. Air hissed through the filters of their respirators. Shadows leapt across the slime-coated walls as their miner's lights swung with each head turn.

"Let's hope nothing goes wrong back here," Holly said. "We'd never get out in time for a rescue."

"Watch your monitors," Louise cautioned.

Doug Soroko, a microbiologist, pointed at dripping stalactites. "Would you get a load of those!"

Thick mucuslike ooze drooled down delicate spikes to form bulbous globs at the bottom, only to finally splat to the floor below.

"Looks just like snot," Holly laughed with a shiver.

"This room is now Snot Heaven," Louise announced. "Mark that on your charts."

The team fanned out to collect samples: water, wall microbes, the mucus stalactites they named Snotties, and air. Holly probed under rocks searching for insects. "Watch out," she cautioned. "We've got tarantulas and black widow spiders in here."

Louise collected an air sample and water samples from a bubbling sulfur spring where she found an albino, shell-less turtle and a thick school of small fish. Doug collected a dozen samples of microscopic life.

"My chem monitor is flashing," Louise announced. "We better scram."

"I show nothing on mine," Doug protested.

"Wait. Mine's flashing, too," said Holly.

"Let's go. Everybody out!"

Holly squirmed into the passage tube first. Louise said to Doug, "This place could kill any of us in less than a minute. How can all this life thrive in here?"

By the time the trio reached Sala Grande and fresher air, Holly was beginning to moan and writhe under her chem suit. A large tear down one side showed where she had scraped along the passage wall. All of their gloves and kneepads were eaten through by the toxic sludge on the cave floor.

Holly began to shiver. She peeled off her chem suit to reveal bright red body welts all along the side of the rip. In spots the welts were beginning to blister. As Louise and Doug carried her toward the cave's entrance, Holly moaned, "It feels like I'm being wrapped in a red-hot blanket of fiberglass."

In the office twenty minutes later, Carl slathered an antihistamine salve across the welts. Louise said, "I think we just named that tunnel: 'Itchy Passage.' We'll have to get microbe and moisture samples off the wall."

"Now?" Doug groaned.

"No. Tomorrow will be fine. 'Till then, showers, food and rest."

Tomorrow would be another adventure in Villa Luz.

After Words

Study results from this cave, combined with those collected from a number of other extreme (and toxic) environments are rapidly altering science's view of life on earth and on ecosystem structure and flexibility. Additionally, industry and several universities are actively studying these ecosystems for clues to new medical cures and ways to strengthen human immune and other defensive systems. The careful and courageous science work of Louise Hose, her team, and others like them, make it all possible.

* * *

Suggested Topics to Explore

This story deals with unique, extreme ecosystems and spelunking. Here are starting questions that will help you discuss and research both.

1. Where did the word "spelunking" come from to describe descending into caves? Is spelunking a sport or a job?

2. Why would groups of animals make themselves adapt to the hostile and extreme conditions in a cave like Villa Luz? What is in it for those animals that do adapt?

3. What can people learn from studying life in such hostile and extreme environments?

4. Can you identify and research famous caves in the United States? Are there any caves in your area?

For Further Reading About This Story

Gibbons, Gail. *Caves and Caverns*. New York: Harcourt Brace, 1993.

Halliday, William. *American Caves and Caving*. New York: Harper and Row, 1986.

————. *Depths of the Earth.* New York: Harper Row, 1989.
Jackson, Donald. *Underground World.* New York: Time-Life Books, 1988.
Kerbo, Ronald. *Caves.* Danbury, CT: Children's Press, 1991.
Lyon, Ben. *Venturing Underground.* McLean, VA: EPM Publications, 1992.
Mohr, Charles. *The Life of the Cave.* New York: McGraw-Hill, 1993.

Rose Kellman

Big Bad Wolf: Biologist
A Science Adventure

Rose Kellman was the only human for sixty miles in any direction across the Arctic tundra. Her survey was going fine until the wolf pack she was studying turned on her one night.

A Science Adventure in the Arctic Tundra

Twenty-six-year-old Rose Kellman stood perfectly still on the crusty snow and concentrated on the receding thump-thump-thump sound of the helicopter's engine, suddenly feeling that she needed to hold onto at least that one connection with the civilized world. All too soon the aircraft had left—to go back to its base in Fairbanks, Alaska; and its comforting roar was replaced by the low and lonely moan of the endless Arctic wind on this afternoon of April 18, 1978.

As a graduate student, Rose Kellman had read the scholarly papers and their conclusions about the lives of arctic wolves—all based on observations made during fly overs and spot tagging runs. "How dare they," she scoffed, "claim to *know* the life of an arctic wolf without actually watching one—living with one—day after day?"

So Kellman had proposed to conduct a six-month, onsite study of one Arctic wolf family. It seemed glamorous and noble at the university in Montana. Now here she stood, painfully alone next to a rickety shed built six summers ago as part of another research project.

After the chopper left, Rose felt a close-to-panic weight of isolation, as if there was nothing other than ice and wind within a thousand square miles except Rose, her boxes of paper and pens, five-gallon cans of kerosene, one radio, binoculars, camera, a shovel, a pick, a hammer, clothes, three boxes of kitchen and cabin supplies, and a small mound of food. For six months there would be only Rose, the wolves, the wind, and her struggle for survival. The sun circled low above the horizon and wouldn't set until 8:00 P.M. In two months it would go over a week without ever touching the horizon.

Short, stocky, with red curls that tumbled across her forehead and usually hid her ice-blue eyes, Rose stood on a low ridge near a tributary of the Selawik River in western Alaska. Before her stretched miles of open tundra extending farther than eyes could see or legs could walk over flat plains, low rolling hills, and occasional jagged ridgelines. Above her stretched a sapphire sky with only a few traces of white cloud near the far-off horizon.

The Schwatka Mountains knifed into the sky to the north. The nearest town—Kobuk with its 300 people—sat eighty miles away. Eighty miles didn't seem like much in Montana. Here it felt like forever. According to her map, Rose was standing right on the Arctic Circle, surrounded by undulating, snow-covered emptiness. She had been dropped here because a wolf pack had been spotted nearby during university-sponsored flyovers. Now, Rose's job would be to find and study that family.

Almost a week disappeared while Rose stowed her gear and repaired cracks in the shed walls. There was no wood. There were no trees. Still, she was able to use rocks and to find pools of spongy peat and mud where the snow had melted in advance of the coming summer thaw. There was no bed for her sleeping bag. She had to build one out of stones with layers of peat for a mattress.

She also set up stations to begin her precipitation, evaporation, and biomass production studies. A study of one species—the wolf—had to include a study of the ecosystem that supported them.

Rose shivered through the bitter Arctic nights and the deep, unrelenting cold—cold that felt like it would never go away—amazed that any plant or animal could survive its entire life in this frozen desert. Each day she recorded the occasional precipitation and miniscule evaporation and scant plant production in her test squares, hoping to create a baseline for complete ecosystem studies.

By April 26, Rose began taking long hikes, systematically exploring her domain. The ground had turned soggy and spongelike as daytime temperatures edged above freezing. Thick peat with tiny pink and purple flowers covered the rolling tundra.

On May 3, Rose finally located the wolf pack. They had dug a den less than half a mile from her shed. Rose knew the family would stay in this territory all summer, helping the pups (born blind, deaf, and toothless in that den) to grow into strapping eighty-pound teenagers ready to survive their first Arctic winter.

Rose couldn't help but shudder when she first spotted two of the wolves loping along a ridgeline at sunset. In stories, wolves always represented the darkest and most evil corners of humanity—things like werewolves, and the Wolfman. Folktale characters—Little Red Riding Hood, the Three Little Pigs, and Peter—all met the embodiment of their greatest fears in a wolf. Wolves even looked scary—gray creatures of the twilight with yellow slant eyes and an eerie, bone-chilling howl that sounds strangely human.

She forced herself not to recoil in fear and run but to follow the wolves, cautiously, ever watching for another wolf to emerge from the growing shadows behind her. At dusk she lost their trail. The next morning she was able to pick it up and followed it to the den.

With her binoculars, Rose could comfortably watch from the cover of a rock outcropping 100 yards away. She focused on a lone female wolf sitting near the trampled den entrance.

The wolf hunched her back to the biting wind that gusted out of the northwest and yawned. Streaks of gray played through her snow-white winter coat. Soon shades of brown and dark gray would appear as she shed her heavy fur with the thaw.

The wolf's head turned to the den entrance as four gangly bundles of fur tumbled out. Rose guessed that this female was an aunt—a babysitter—watching the pups while their mother hunted to bring back food for her cubs.

The wolf dropped her head and nuzzled the pups as they pawed and nipped at her legs and muzzle. All adult wolves dote over pups, heaping lavish attention and care onto each. Wolves never outgrow their love of play. And there is no better excuse for a romping, rolling game of tag than a brood of five-week-old pups with sturdy bodies, long, gangly legs they are just beginning to control, and an insatiable appetite for fun.

The adult female allowed two of the twelve-pound balls of brown fuzz to chew on the thick fur of one leg until one nipped some skin. The babysitter growled and kicked with her leg. Both pups scampered toward the den in a rolling, yelping tumble of retreat. In less than a minute they were back, tails wagging so hard their whole back ends shook. One wagged so hard his wobbly back legs collapsed and he happily rolled onto his back, pawing at his sister to play with him.

The wolf bent down and licked the pups, nuzzling her nose against their faces. The other two romped nearby, pouncing and wrestling with a rock. At the moment, the rock seemed to be winning.

Rose bolted upright and spun around. The soft sound of breathing and padding feet through the squishy peat penetrated her fascination with the cubs. Two wolves jogged past her—less than thirty yards away—on their way to the den. Neither seemed to pay her any attention, as if in one glance they had already determined that Rose could not pose a threat.

Still Rose's heart hammered in her chest and she gasped for breath. Her hands and legs trembled as she slid out of the rocks and jogged back toward her shed.

By May 15, Rose realized that her food supply would not last through the summer. She thought of radioing for supplies to be brought in by helicopter. But a stubborn streak made her hesitate. The wolves would make it through the summer without relief airdrops. So would she. If they ate caribou, she'd eat caribou.

Rose had a rifle and she could hunt. She had tried moose, buffalo, and elk. How different could caribou be? She was low on kerosene and had no wood to cook with, but she'd think of something. Maybe she could dry and burn peat.

On her daily treks to the rock outcropping, Kellman decided to pay more attention to what the wolves ate instead of concentrating just on family structure and relationships. In her notebook, she kept separate pages for each of the seven adults (the dominate—alpha—male, the dominate female, two young females—including Rose's favorite aunt babysitter, and three young males) and for the four cubs.

This afternoon the cub's mother returned, loping leisurely across the rocks and tundra. Her shadow streaked across the bare ground from the sun perched low over the horizon. The babysitter turned to make her greeting. Keeping her head submissively low, she wagged her tail.

The mother barked and snarled as if sensing that the younger female harbored resentment and wasn't sincere in her greeting. The babysitter rolled onto her back, acknowledging the mother's dominant position, and whined, begging for forgiveness. The mother lapsed into friendly licking. Her tail wagged, too. Within the pack, the bonds between wolves were strong and affectionate, even while being ever-conscious of rank.

Most of the eating was done away from the den. Rather than carry meat back for the cubs, the mother ate at the kill site and then regurgitated much of her catch for her pups. It is a better way to feed pups still too young to travel. It keeps the meat warm, clean, and fresh until they can eat. Besides, meat is much easier to carry in an extended stomach than dragging a carcass by one's teeth through the rocks, dirt, and snow.

Late that afternoon Rose watched from the rocks as the small pack gathered: two young males, two young females, and the dominant pair. Everyone wagged their tails, heads submissively low for the powerful silver-gray male who led the pack. With neck hair bristling and teeth bared, he issued warning barks and growls at each pack member to remind them of his dominance.

Each wolf wagged and pawed the ground, excited to begin the hunt. There was much yelping and yapping, much leaping and rolling. Then one of the wolves started the howl. Everyone else stopped their play to join. All adult wolves howled in chorus, heads thrown back and mouths wide open, each adopting a different key. The seventh adult—the evening's babysitter—watched, but did not join the howl. If two wolves slid onto the same note, one quickly changed so that the different tones wove together into an eerie, humanlike, chorus that drifted in shimmering waves across the quiet, frozen landscape. From the far distance, a second pack of wolves answered with their own howl. The air filled with waves of the ghostly music and chilled the blood of every mammal on the tundra. With a deep shiver of dread, Rose scampered for her shed. She would follow the hunt some other night.

Toward the end of May, Rose began to wander at night—the wolves' primary hunting time—hoping to catch a glimpse of big game and of the wolves in action. What she saw shocked her. Food was now more abundant. Life seemed to spring from each crevice of the tundra. The wolves now ignored passing oxen and elk. Apparently they were too much of an effort to chase. Instead they loved to chase rabbits, ground squirrels, and mice.

Even from a hundred yards away, Rose could hear the crunch and snap as wolves ground up and ate even the bones of their prey. A wolf will eat every part of a rabbit—skin, fur, even the bones, which it grinds up with its hind teeth and steel-trap strong jaws.

Rose took to carrying her rifle on her afternoon hikes to hunt her share of the wolves' preferred food and stretch her meager food supplies. She found that mice and squirrels made a fine stew. She, however, ate only the meat. No bones or fur for Rose. By June, she craved pasta and broccoli but had to make do with her remaining food stock of peanut butter, dried potatoes, and dried peas.

June became Rose's least favorite month in the tundra. Mosquitoes hatched, by the thousands, by the millions. Buzzing mosquitoes penetrated every fiber, every nook, every inch of ground. Rose was chased by clouds of them. There was no way to escape—either day or night—from the whining hordes of hungry bloodsuckers.

Then great flocks of birds arrived to feast on the mosquitoes. Hundreds of species covered the sky in noisy rainbow profusion. The endless din of chirping and squawking reminded Rose of the constant honking clatter of big city traffic. Sleep became a rare luxury in June.

On the night of June 17, with the midnight sun hovering half below the horizon, Rose watched her wolf family surround an old and obviously sick ox with a lame foot.

One wolf leapt at the haunches of this exhausted ox, whose wheezing breath and white, terror-filled eyes said he was too tired to resist. The wolf nipped at the hamstring muscle and bounded back to avoid the ox's hooves that instinctively lashed out with the power to splinter rock.

A second wolf sprang at the ox's muzzle, locking onto its snout as a diversion for the real attack. The babysitter and the dominant male raced in on the same side and crashed into the ox's rump.

It stumbled and bucked sideways, struggling to keep its balance. A fourth wolf darted in to bite and tear an Achilles' tendon in the ox's lower leg. The last wolf jumped at the ox's face, slashing at its eyes to keep it from properly reacting to the real attack behind.

Hurt, confused, and disoriented, the ox slipped on its injured back leg and sprawled to the ground. All five wolves dove to attack the now defenseless prey.

Wolves have neither the size nor power to kill quickly, as a lion does. The wolves' fangs and canine teeth slashed at the ox's throat and tore at its great leg muscles. Death would come slowly as the ox's blood stained the tundra grass.

Rose watched in morbid fascination—until she heard a soft growl behind her. Rose turned to face the great silverback male, his muzzle bright red from his attack on the ox, front legs spread, teeth bared, hair bristling. Two other wolves circled behind Rose, making it impossible for her to keep them all in her field of vision.

Frantically, Rose glanced left and right. In the open of rolling tundra there was no place to hide, nowhere to run to. Until that moment, it had never occurred to her that the wolves might attack and eat her.

Her rifle was slung on her shoulder, safety on. Even if she did swing it down to fire, she'd only stop one wolf. Yet, even in that moment of danger, Rose realized she didn't want to hurt any of these magnificent creatures that she had grown to know as family.

In her hands, Rose held only a pencil with which to mount her defense. Slowly she backed away from the alpha male and away from their oxen kill. It occurred to her that she should act submissive. She began to whine and forced her eyes to gaze down at the ground in front of the snarling wolf. Step by step she inched back, bleating, whining, waiting every second for the terrible attack that she saw happen to the ox happen to her.

But attack never came. Once the wolves had forced her back a good eighty feet from their kill, they turned with a final howl and trotted back to enjoy their meal. They had merely wanted to drive her away from their food.

Rose trembled through the night huddled on her bed, sweating, shaking, and shivering, as she listened to the familiar drone of mosquitoes, the call of birds, and the distant howl of wolves.

After Words

Rose survived her time in the Arctic and wrote detailed study papers describing this one wolf family, their structure, their life, and their interactions. Her study, combined with dozens of other detailed, onsite studies have greatly enhanced science's understanding of this important top predator. These long-term, onsite studies have dispelled myths about wolf family life, hunting practices, and food sources. Recent policy shifts by both Canadian and U.S. governments reflect the wisdom learned from these onsite studies.

* * *

Suggested Topics to Explore

This story deals with arctic wolves and biological field studies. Here are starting questions that will help you discuss and research both.

1. What role does the wolf play in maintaining a healthy Arctic ecosystem? What would happen to the ecosystem if the wolves

were removed? Why do wolves stay in the harsh Arctic north? Why don't they all migrate farther south where it is warmer?

2. Can you find advantages to being a field mouse (or a rabbit) in Arctic tundra over living in southern U.S. meadow?

3. Wolves form strong, loving family units. Is this important for Arctic wolves' survival? Research wolf families and how they function to support the survival of wolves.

4. Who preys on wolves? What limits Arctic wolf populations? Why are there fewer wolves in the United States and Canada now than there use to be? What do wolves need in order to successfully survive?

For Further Reading About This Story

Ballard, W. B., and T. Sparker. *Unit 13 Wolf Studies.* Juneau, AK: Alaska Department of Fish and Game, 1989.

Brandenburg, Jim. *To the Top of the World.* New York: Walker and Company, 1993.

Clark, K. *Food Habits and Behavior of the Tundra Wolf on Central Baffin Island.* Toronto, Canada: University of Toronto Press, 1981.

Clarkson, Ewan. *Wolf Country.* New York: E. P. Dutton & Co., 1994.

Fiennes, Richard. *The Order of Wolves.* New York: Bobbs-Merrill, 1986.

Fox, M. *Behavior of Wolves, Dogs, and Related Canids.* New York: Harper Row, 1981.

Harrington, Fred, and Paul Paquet (eds.). *Wolves of the World.* Park Ridge, NJ: Noyes Publications, 1992.

Klinghammer, E. (ed.). *The Behavior and Ecology of Wolves.* New York: Garland STMP Press, 1993.

Lawrence, R. D. *Wolves.* San Francisco: Sierra Club Books, 1990.

Lopez, Barry. *Of Wolves and Men.* New York: Charles Scribner's Sons, 1978.

Patent, Dorothy. *Gray Wolf, Red Wolf.* New York: Clarion Books, 1993.

Zimen, E., and L. Boitani. *The Wolf: A Species in Danger.* New York: Delacourt, 1991.

Darlene Ketten

"Sound" Discoveries: Marine Biologist
A Science Adventure

Darlene Ketten waved thick swarms of flies away from a dead fifteen-ton whale, as she cut into the beast with chain saw and surgical scalpel. All the while, government officials and Navy brass peered over her shoulder, demanding to know why the whale had beached itself and died.

A Science Adventure in Marine Biology

On March 18, 1999, the National Marine Fisheries helicopter circled low over the transparent turquoise water of the Providence Channel between the northern Bahamas Islands. It banked steeply over a line of gentle surf and dazzling white sand, then sped over waving palm trees and a thick and matted undergrowth of dense green, before circling back. It would have been a postcard perfect tropical paradise—except for the six great black masses lined on the beach like rotting piers jutting into the water.

Forty-two-year-old Darlene Ketten leaned out the helicopter side door. The headband of her earphones clamped her short, chestnut hair against her head like a thick barrette and kept it from flailing in the wind.

"Were they all beaked whales [a common local variety of whale]?" Before she got her answer, she added, "Are any still alive?"

Local government biologist Jeffery Stallings answered, "There were sixteen. Ten have been pushed back out to sea. Two of the final six were still alive this morning. But I don't think they'll make it."

Darlene nodded and leaned in to tap the pilot's arm. "Land farther away from the whales."

The down wash of the rotor blade created a mini sandstorm that swirled down the beach as the helicopter landed. A cloud of flies buzzed into the air before settling back onto the decaying carcasses of the dead whales. Waves of noxious odor, so strong that they almost knocked Darlene down, overpowered the normally sweet scent of tropical flowers.

A hundred tons of dead whale was a startling and sobering sight, even for someone who had seen it all before. The six whales lay neatly parallel almost as if they had carefully driven into parking stalls. Five were dead. One still struggled to breathe. Two had been dead several days and were badly decomposed.

An assistant of Dr. Stallings ran over, nose and mouth covered with a bandana. "That last one will die any minute. There's nothing we can do."

Picturesque puffs of cloud drifted above swaying palms. Today this vacation paradise was the grizzly sight of the mass death of beautiful whales.

But was it suicide or murder? Darlene Ketten was here to find out.

A thick tourist crowd hung back, lining the road, held at bay by the stench. The constant click of cameras filled the air.

Darlene accepted a surgical mask to help curb the smell and marched the line of whales. Stallings and his assistant followed at her heels. She pointed at the three that were best preserved. "These three. The others are too decayed. I only need the heads."

She shook a can of white spray paint and sprayed cut lines on her three chosen specimens. "Chain saws and long-pole flensing knives."

"The long ones that old-time whalers used?" Stallings asked.

Darlene nodded and continued, spraying dotted lines well back from each whale's head. "Cut here. Get construction equipment to load them on flat beds and pack them in ice. I'll do my work in a warehouse." She paused and pointed at the one that still clung to life. "And give that poor whale a lethal injection to put it out of its misery."

A local deputy sheriff walked over, still talking into his walkie-talkie. "Dr. Ketten? Welcome. I have cranes and semi-trucks on the way to haul out the bodies. What else do you need?"

Darlene answered, "These three heads, packed in ice and hauled to a warehouse that stays cool. One hundred and fifty bags per head should be enough to preserve the tissue."

"One hundred and fifty bags of ice? . . . for *each* head?" the policeman stammered.

"Grocery stores, convenience stores, hotels, restaurants. Get as much as you can. I also want the organs of one of the bodies examined before disposal for signs of illness or parasites that might have caused the whales to beach."

"I can do that," Stallings volunteered.

Heavy construction equipment moved in. Winches and thick chains dragged twenty-ton bodies to hoists that hefted them onto flatbeds for the trip to a disposal sight. Long flensing knives lashed through jet-black skin and creamy-white layers of blubber. Chain saws whined and tore through bone and gristle.

As always, Darlene was amazed how lovely and dazzling the milk-white whale blubber was. As she watched the two-ton heads forklifted into a long-bed dump truck and packed with ice, she asked, "Is my operating team here yet?"

Stallings shook his head. "They'll fly in late tonight." Then he asked, "What are you going to do?"

"Two things," she answered. "First, see if high-powered sonar pulses from the Navy's sonar testing in the area killed them. Second, learn more about whale hearing."

Stallings snorted, "You academics always want to learn more. How much more can you learn about whales?"

Darlene bristled and counted off her points on her fingers. "Humans have thirty-eight optic nerves for every auditory nerve. In whales the ratio is one-to-one. Their central auditory nerve is the size of a TV cable. Some whales can hear ten times the frequency range of a human.

"*That's* how important hearing is to whales. But we don't know how it works. No one knows if a whale's external ears do anything. They might be blind pouches. We don't know if they detect sound through their ears or from a yellow fatty deposit along their jaw. We don't even know what they actually hear." She concluded, "We can't protect them if we don't understand them."

The next morning, Darlene's five-person surgery team assembled in a concrete warehouse often used for government vehicle storage. Two wore scuba wet suits. All wore surgical scrubs, gloves, and masks. Three wore heavy rubber aprons. All clomped into the warehouse wearing heavy rubber boots. They carried flensing knives, sets of long butcher knives, and trays of surgical scalpels and clamps. Two wore construction tool belts to carry measuring tapes, cameras, and cutting tools. The three whale heads lay on their sides in a neat row.

Darlene started with tape measure and calipers, measuring every dimension of the nearest head, jaw, and ear.

"Be particularly alert for any signs of internal bleeding, swelling, or tissue trauma," Darlene cautioned the team as they started in with their knives.

Flensing knives—wielded as by whalers of a century ago—peeled back thick layers of milk-white blubber. The team switched to butcher knives as they neared the whale's jaw and jaw muscles.

Darlene signaled a halt and moved in with surgical scalpels. Working now with the patience of an archeologist, she slowly peeled blubber away from a thin membrane housing a blob of creamy yellow, softer fat.

"What's that?" Jeffrey Stallings asked, peering over her shoulder.

"I believe it is how whales hear. These rabbit ear-shaped lobes of fat tucked along the jaw seem to amplify sound waves." She turned to an assistant cutting along the upper end of the lobe. "Careful Julie. I need to examine the nerve fibers at that end." Louder she called, "Ray, set up the microscope, please. Julie, pack this lobe for shipment to the lab."

Twenty minutes later Darlene sat back from her microscope with a satisfied nod. "Inflammation. Something irritated or overloaded these nerves."

"The Navy's sonar test?"

Darlene shrugged. "Too early to tell."

Julie poured a blue tracer dye into the whale's exposed outer ear, a small opening shaped like the sound well of a violin. In less than two inches, the dye hit a block. "It looks like a dead end. This ear canal goes nowhere—just like on the other whales," she called. "Maybe whales' outer ears *are* evolutionary relics that serve no purpose anymore."

"Maybe," Darlene agreed. "But we have to make sure. Use scalpels. Cut wide and deep around that canal. I want to examine those tissues in the lab to see if they somehow still channel sound."

"What are you looking for now?" Stallings asked as Darlene used butcher knives to slice through blubber and skin behind the jaw.

"The tympano-periotic bulla."

"The what?"

"The dense bone housing the middle and inner ear. Last night you established that the whales were not being attacked by any virus, bacteria, infection, or parasite. That means the whales beached because the balance center in the middle ear was damaged."

"There," she finally said, pointing at a thick band of ligaments. "Behind those."

Scalpels and surgical saws cut through the tough ligament bands. " Julie, can you clamp this tissue back? . . . There. . . . And that flap, too."

Darlene gently tugged a bony mass forward. "Look at the size of that auditory nerve!" It looked like a thick electrical cable running from the mass of the bulla back through the skull and into the whale's brain.

"Lift the bulla out while I cut the auditory nerve," Darlene said to Jeffery Stallings. Two assistants knowingly smiled. One giggled.

"Wow! This thing weighs a ton!" Jeffery stammered, almost stumbling under the dense weight of this grapefruit sized bone mass. "Cement doesn't weigh this much!" Everyone laughed.

"Heavy, aren't they? The most dense bone in the world," answered Darlene. "It protects the inner ear from the pressures of a deep dive."

Darlene turned to one of her assistants. "Box the bulla in ice and ship it back for CT scans."

"Why not just X-ray it?" Jeffery asked.

"Too dense. X-rays won't penetrate that bone."

One of Darlene's assistants climbed into a forklift parked nearby and revved the engine.

"Now what?" Stallings asked.

"We turn this head over and do the same to the other side. Then we move on to the other two heads. Then we fly back for about two weeks of lab work. After that, if we're lucky, we might—*just might*—know something definite."

After Words

Darlene Ketten's preliminary findings confirmed that Navy sonar and other high-frequency, high-energy emissions can and do severely damage the auditory systems of many whale species. Based on these findings, the Navy, Coast Guard, and several research universities have changed their policies on underwater sonar testing, setting much lower limits on the energy and volume allowed in any one sonar or acoustic pulse.

Ketten's work on almost twenty beached whales has greatly improved human understanding of whale hearing and sensitivity to sonar pulses and is being used by governments and scientists around the world in trying to protect whales from sound damage.

* * *

Suggested Topics to Explore

This story deals with whale hearing and anatomy and with sonar technology. Here are starting questions that will help you discuss and research both.

1. Are whales the only animals to use sonar for locating objects? Who else uses sonar?

2. What is sonar? How are sonar pulses made? What do they do? How does a whale "hear" them?

3. Research the uses of sonar by humans. What do we do with sonar? What is the difference between sonar and radar?

4. Once an animal is dead, how can a scientist hope to figure out how and what the animal heard while it was alive?

For Further Reading About This Story

Asimov, Isaac. *Why Are Whales Vanishing?* New York: Gareth Stevens Children's Books, 1991.
Cole, Melissa. *Whales.* Woodbridge, CT: Blackbirch Press, 2001.
Collard, Sneed. *A Whale Biologist at Work.* New York: Franklin Watts, 2000.
Faiella, Graham. *Whales.* New York: Grosset & Dunlap, 2002.
Gowell, Elizabeth. *Whales and Dolphins: What They Have in Common.* New York: Franklin Watts, 1999.
Moritz, Reiver. *Theme and Variation: Echolocation in Mammals.* London: British Broadcast Corporation, 1989.
Morton, Alexandra. *Listening to Whales.* New York: Ballantine Books, 2002.
Simon, Seymour. *Whale.* New York: Crowell, 1989.

Jane Kirkwalter

Star Light, Star Bright: Physicist
A Science Adventure

Do you think it's possible to create a fist-sized sun with all the churning, explosive power of a blazing star? Is it possible to turn this new sun into a steady source of power without allowing it to explode out of control and turn into a nuclear bomb? Jane Kirkwalter thinks so.

A Science Adventure in the Physics Lab

For one glorious half-second, the donut-shaped mass of gas blazed supernova bright, like a blinding sun burning at seventy million degrees Fahrenheit. Unimaginably bright and hot, the gas became a two-foot diameter seething, explosively powerful pool of hydrogen plasma. Then it faded to dull purple, and, two seconds after it first ignited, turned back to black.

For a flickering moment, Jane Kirkwalter's physics team had created a new star—almost. But no one outside that warehouse, or beyond the tucked-away cluster of plain, numbered buildings ever knew.

That small campus of anonymous buildings three miles north of Princeton University in New Jersey was protected only by a chain link fence and one guarded entrance. No sign announced that this was the Princeton Plasma Physics Laboratory, a $300 million dollar fusion reactor—the most advanced fusion research facility in the world. In late May 1985, with spring in full bloom, the lab and surrounding woods were a profusion of spring-green leaves, a rainbow of buds, and the fresh smell of rain-washed air.

Inside one of the gym-sized concrete warehouses, the smell was of sizzling electricity. The giant room was crammed with tangled merry-go-rounds of red copper coils, a maze of copper pipes looking like a wild and giant erector set. Scattered across the room were banks of power converters and laser generators, a profusion of dials, lights, and switches to match the spring blossoms outside, overhead conveyor belts carrying rivers of gray electrical wire and cables, scaffolding, cat walks, and shiny black control panels. Workers in the warehouse wore hardhats, not science lab coats.

In the middle of it all, with an American flag rising from the top of a ten-foot pole, sat a squat structure that looked like an alien space ship with all its wiring and piping on the outside. Twelve red semicircular magnets stood on end around the outside of the structure like giant spider legs—each of them twelve feet tall. Banks of gray electrical boxes were stuffed between the magnets. Buried deep in the heart of this structure, controlled by the tremendous force of the magnetic field, surrounded by 27,000 heat-absorbing graphite tiles, sat the donut shaped fusion reactor (called a tokamak reactor), itself no bigger than many desk-top computers.

Thirty-two-year-old Princeton physicist Jane Kirkwalter sat in a side office of the warehouse with Richard Endmoor, University Assistant Director of Research, following this latest in her series of plasma tests. She slammed her palm on the metal desk. "You can't put these kinds of restrictions on my work. The country can't survive on *fission* power. We need to push forward with *fusion* research."

Nuclear *fission* is the act of splitting an atom in two smaller atoms. Nuclear power plants and atomic bombs use this process to create energy. Nuclear *fusion* is the act of fusing two smaller atoms together to form one, larger atom. Usually hydrogen atoms are fused to form helium atoms. Fusion releases many times more energy than does fission. If fusion power plants could be made to work, they would represent an inexhaustible supply of cheap electricity—*if* they could be made to work.

Endmoor paced the small room as he replied. "And if anything goes wrong with your work, this building turns into a three-hundred-million-dollar nuclear bomb that wipes out a quarter of New Jersey!"

"You greatly overexaggerate the risks."

"And I don't want some fusion plasma accident to spray radioactivity over this building and turn it into a radioactive grave."

Jane insisted, "I need to test the fusion reactor at near full power if I am to learn anything about hydrogen plasma fusion. This last test reached less than sixty million degrees. I learn nothing new that way. I need to heat the plasma to at least one hundred and eighty million degrees."

Endmoor shook his head. "That's a grave risk just to create a more efficient way to boil water." (The heat created by a fusion reaction would be used in power plants to superheat steam as a way of producing electricity.)

She pleaded, "The fusion reactor *is* safe—even at those temperatures. I'll show you my calculations and a dozen computer simulations."

Endmoor countered, "And I'll show you a stack of computer models that turned out to be wrong once something was actually tested." He stopped his pacing and pointed first at Jane and then through the glass door toward the reactor.

"Continue with low power tests and show me you can control that . . . beast. Prove to me it's safe. *Then* we'll talk about trying to produce energy."

Jane Kirkwalter sat seething with frustration for ten minutes after Endmoor left.

Inside a working hydrogen fusion reactor, microwave beams drove the temperature of hydrogen gas—trapped in the reactor by a powerful magnetic field—up to 180 million degrees (or more). At those extreme temperatures, hydrogen gas changed into hydrogen plasma. Superheated atoms smashed into each other so hard, that they often fused into helium atoms, releasing amazing amounts of energy in the process. But raising anything to the temperature of the sun—a temperature high enough to vaporize virtually any material on earth—is dangerous. Raising a potentially explosive gas, such as hydrogen, to those temperatures is especially so.

Back out on the test floor, Jane met with her chief engineer. "Did we get good visuals on the last test?"

A tall, thin man, the engineer shrugged. "Sure. The video probe held up very well. But there's not much to see since we only reached fifty-five million degrees."

Jane stomped her foot. "We're wasting time . . . and my research budget with these low power tests." She thought for a moment. "Could we go again?"

The engineer nodded, "Control panel's all green. The test crew is still here."

"Get the temperature up to one hundred and eighty million this time."

He frowned. "This facility isn't cleared for over seventy-five million yet."

Jane countered, "It was designed to withstand up to two hundred and twenty million degrees."

The engineer said, "That's all just theory. We're not sure we can really go that high. And we're not entirely sure what would happen at that kind of temperature—or if the graphite tiles could stand it."

"I'll settle for one hundred and forty to one hundred and fifty million," answered Jane.

"Five hundred milliseconds enough time for you?"

Jane nodded, "I can live with a half-second long experiment."

The engineer thoughtfully rubbed his lip. "The atoms in plasma do a whole lot of living in five hundred milliseconds." Then he added, "You know, it will only take that plasma a couple of milliseconds to go out of control, if it's going to."

Jane snapped, "Fusion reactors are *safe*. I'll prove it to the whole world if I need to." She called a test alert over the building loudspeaker system and hit the alarm buzzer to warn everyone to stand well clear of the reactor.

"All stations and systems ready and clear," the engineer announced from his rolling chair at the master control panel.

He began the system count down. "Magnetic field on. . . . Hydrogen gas injected. . . . Microwave generator ready . . . "

"Start the test," directed Jane.

He nervously rubbed his upper lip. "Computer says one hundred and thirty-five seconds of microwave at full power to reach one hundred and fifty million degrees."

"Do it!" she commanded.

"Microwave on. . . . All monitoring systems on and functioning."

Fan motors howled. The magnets' hum grew to a high-pitched whine. Jane could feel the magnetic field and the surging electrical power around her tug on the hairs on her arms until they stood straight up. The faint smell of sizzling plasma reminded Jane of the burnt ozone smell when lightning strikes.

Inside the reactor the donut-shaped mass of hydrogen plasma flashed unimaginably bright. It was like standing next to a new sun, a star. In less than the time it took for one quick breath, the light ignited, lived, and was completely gone.

The engineer called, "All clear." Workers moved in to inspect the reactor and to retrieve data from the monitors and sensors.

Jane still stared at the now-blank monitor connected to the video probe mounted inside the reactor. "For just a moment while that fusion reaction was going, we held more power in our hands than thirty power plants can create."

The engineer smiled. "Good thing your hands were protected by three feet of graphite tiles. One hundred and sixty-six-million-degree plasma is a bit too hot to hold."

Jane continued, "It felt like I held creation, like I held the future—for a moment." She turned to her engineer. "One hundred and sixty-six million? That's better than I had hoped. What was our power output?"

He checked his computer screen and shook his head. "Only ten percent."

Jane exclaimed, "Ten percent?! For a half-second we created a glowing, working star, and you tell me that that star only produced ten percent as much energy as we used to create and hold it?"

The engineer shrugged, "The tokamak fusion reactor design may never create more energy than it uses." He ruffled through a stack of papers on the work station desk. "Professor Martin Peng is proposing . . ."

Jane interrupted, "Yes. Yes, I know Martin. We teach in the same department."

The engineer continued, "Well, he is proposing to use a torus fusion reactor." A torus reactor forced plasma into the shape of a cored apple instead of into a donut shape as in the tokamak. Torus reactors required smaller (and cheaper) magnets.

Jane nodded. "I've read his paper. Maybe he's right. Maybe smaller is the way to go."

The engineer asked, "So what will you do with this monster?"

"Run a thousand more tests," Jane answered. "We still don't know very much about plasma flow and interactions at over one hundred and seventy million degrees. Even if it won't produce more energy than it uses, this reactor will teach us a lot of what we need to know before fusion can replace fission as the source for electric power."

Jane smiled and added, "And I still have to convince Richard Endmoor that it's safe for us to test at those temperatures where we can really learn something." She glanced at the wall clock. "But first I have to teach a class."

After Words

Research on both torus and tokamak type nuclear fusion reactors continues in both the United States and Europe. No one has yet been able to make a fusion reactor produce more energy than it consumes. But researchers are getting very close, and they believe that, within the next ten years, a working fusion power plant will be online in America.

* * *

Suggested Topics to Explore

This story deals with nuclear fusion. Here are starting questions that will help you discuss and research that topic.

1. What is fusion? What's the difference between fusion and fission? Why is fusion so much harder to create than is fission?

2. What is plasma? Look it up in the dictionary and on the Internet. Research how scientists create hydrogen plasma. Can they create plasma from other elements?

For Further Reading About This Story

Fowler, T. *The Fusion Quest.* New York: Johns Hopkins University Press, 1997.
Heiman, Robin. *Fusion: The Search for Endless Energy.* London: Cambridge University Press, 1990.
Peat, F. *Cold Fusion.* New York: Contemporary Books, 1989.
Richardson, Hazel. *How to Split the Atom.* New York: Franklin Watts, 2001.

Mary Leakey

Diggin' It:
A Science Adventure

Paleontologist/
Archeologist

Mary Leakey and her team spent months scraping through the baked African dirt and rock of this particular site with small picks and brushes searching for a fossil bone or two that she hoped would prove to be several hundreds of thousands of years old. Imagine her surprise when she stumbled on a fossilized footprint that proved humanoids walked upright 3.5 *million* years ago.

A Science Adventure in Africa

Late on the morning of December 14, 1975, lanky Bill MacAfee opened his front door to find an angular, stately woman. So this is who had knocked loudly enough to rattle him from his newspaper reading. Her eyes blazed and almost seemed to glare at him.

"Is something wrong, Mary?"

Wearing a floppy, sweat-stained hat to protect her from the relentless African sun, Mary Leakey answered, "Constance wrote that you found fossils?"

"Yes. We did. In a load of sand."

"Sand?"

"It was delivered for a construction project. We're building a new barn."

Bill and Constance MacAfee owned a sprawling cattle ranch in Northern Tanzania, twenty miles east of Lake Victoria and thirty miles northwest of the Leakeys' famous archeological dig at Olduvai Gorge. The MacAfees had known Louis and Mary Leakey since they first moved to Africa with their archeological work in the early 1950s.

Mary asked, "Do you still have the fossils?"

"Constance has them round back." Then he added, "Do come in."

Mary managed a smile and then marched past, wearing the khaki pants and faded shirt she typically wore at digs. "Oh, and Merry Christmas, Bill." Sixty-three-year-old Mary Leakey's skin was deeply tanned and wrinkled from years of sun exposure at her archeological digs. Her eyebrows naturally dipped into a scowl. Combined with her large brown eyes that stared without blinking, they created a fierce and angry look that was frightening at first meeting.

Mary followed Bill to the screened veranda that overlooked miles of rolling African grassland. There, petite Constance MacAfee hunched over a magnifying glass and table of artifacts. A ceiling fan softly spun a breeze across her as she worked. After greetings, Constance pointed to a pile of bleached bones at the end of her table. "Those are the fossils I wrote about."

Mary reverently held each bone fragment in her hands, as if weighing, measuring, memorizing it. She gazed intently at each surface against the incoming light as she turned it over and over and paused when she lifted a nearly complete jawbone.

She spoke more to herself than to the MacAfees. "Definitely humanoid. . . . Rather old, I should say. . . . Very well preserved . . . "

She finally set the jaw down and tapped her fingers gently on it as she spoke. "Where did this come from?"

"The sand," answered Constance.

"I know. But where'd the sand come from?"

"From the sand company."

Mary's eyes flared with impatience. "Yes. But where did *they* get it?"

Constance shrugged and turned to Bill. "Ah, yes. I believe from the Laetolil Beds."

"Are you sure?"

"Sure? Well, I suppose. I mean it *is* the sand company. And I *did* ask."

Mary frowned and shook her head. "I have explored the Laetolil Beds before and found nothing."

Bill swallowed hard. "Well, it *is* a large area . . . "

"I have dug there three times with no success." The intensity of her gaze almost made Bill want to apologize, although he wasn't sure for what.

Mary asked, "Do you have a telephone?"

"No. Not yet." Most of rural Africa still lacked telephone service.

Constance asked, "Will you stay for tea, Mary?"

"No. I must find out where this sand came from as soon as possible."

"Merry Christmas, then," Constance called as Mary swept toward the front door.

At the door Bill nodded his head toward the back veranda and asked, "Do you think these fossils are really important?"

"I won't know for sure until I have explored the site. And if the sand company destroys it before I arrive, I can learn nothing." She started away, then stopped, "And thanks to both of you for alerting me to this find."

Later, from her own home, built near the Leakeys' Olduvai Gorge dig, Mary phoned the sand company manager.

"Yes, ma'am. Good sand. . . . The MacAfees? From our site at the Laetolil Beds, ma'am. Very good sand. . . . Yes, I'm sure. I supervised the digging myself . . ."

Thirty miles south of Olduvai Gorge, the Laetolil Beds were rolling tuffs of volcanic ash laid down by the Sadiman volcano twenty miles to the east. It was a desolate and forbidding site—hard-packed dirt and rock, scrub bushes, a few dwarf trees—all of which seemed to suffer terribly from the shimmering African heat. The month made no difference here. It was always fearfully hot and dusty.

Constance drove to the site with Mary and the five diggers she brought from her Olduvai works.

Squinting into the parched desolation, Constance asked, "Do you think you'll really find something of interest?"

Mary thoughtfully shrugged. "I think those bones were old—possibly hundreds of thousands of years old. If we can find the spot they came from . . ."

"I mean, do you think you'll succeed without Louis."

Louis Leakey, Mary's husband and founder of their African digs, had died in 1974 from a heart attack. This would be Mary's first completely solo expedition.

Mary glared at her friend. "*I* have been in charge of our digs for over a decade."

"Well, yes. But, Mary, you're also over sixty . . . "

Mary snorted, "These old knees can still handle a five-hour shift on a kneeboard while I scrape away with a dental pick."

Constance stared over the expanse of rolling tuffs. "How will you know where to look?"

Mary smiled, thinking back over her many years of archeological digs. "It's like that famous jawbone we found at Olduvai. We had searched that gully wall for months. Then one day I happened to be at exactly the right spot with the right light and looked in just the right direction. And there it was, actually sticking partway out of the ground. It had been there all the time, just waiting to be discovered."

The blank look on Constance's face said that she couldn't make the connection. "It's the same here. We'll mark out a grid on the ground and work systematically through that grid. But discovery may come anywhere, at anytime—or nowhere."

Mary shaded her eyes and pointed off to the left. "We'll start over there, near the sand company's excavation."

Mary's diggers staked out markers to form a wide grid over the general area. First they inspected each grid square—slowly, painstakingly. They brushed aside loose dirt and carefully examined each exposed rock face. Progress was measured in inches. After ten days of careful searching they had found nothing.

Mary chose one grid section near the sand company's operation to being the digging. Their first job was to dig away dirt. Ancient fossils would be imbedded in rock. But even dirt had to be scooped away slowly. The dirt here was baked adobe—hard as bricks and bleached as pale as many of the sedimentary rocks. It was slow, hard work to scrape and brush away the packed dirt, no digger ever free from the worry that any pick or shovel blow might break a fragile fossil bone embedded in the rock hidden below. Often a digger didn't see a treasure until it was too late—if they saw it at all.

Trowels, hand picks, and brushes were used more commonly than shovels and pick axes. Day by day trenches slowly sank deeper into the hardscrabble ground. Day after day passed by, but nothing but dirt, heat, and rock were found. Each night sitting by the campfire outside her tent, Mary studied the fossils from the MacAfee's sand—more for encouragement than for scientific study. Once a week, someone drove Mary's Land Rover into town for food and supplies.

"Luck and hard work," Mary told her team. "Patient hard work will give the luck more opportunity to appear."

Open pit digs are all about patience, perseverance, and faith. A site seems to give up its secrets only when it is good and ready. Yet every day the team dug, scraped, chipped, and swept their way farther into the past as they descended inch by inch, deeper and deeper.

No trench was dug deeper than four feet. At that depth, Mary believed that they had dug too deep to find any human remains and the spot was abandoned. Another spot would be picked and another trench begun.

Late in the second month of the dig, one of Mary's assistants made a find. He almost missed it as he picked, scraped, and brushed dirt away from a solid rock layer below. It looked like a meaningless depression in the rock. He almost turned to dig in another area. But the general shape of the slight depression caught his eye. He had been looking for bones—for things—and had almost missed the significance of a hole in the rock. But it caught his eye when he realized it was in the shape of a human foot.

Even then he shrugged it off at first. They were looking for prehistoric bones, not footprints left in the mud by a passing human. He actually began work in another area, and only mentioned the footprint during casual dinnertime conversation.

Mary spent an entire day hunched over a kneeboard with dental picks and whiskbroom cleaning that print. She then made a plaster cast of the print and chipped out a small chunk of rock next to it to send off for potassium-argon dating (more accurate than traditional carbon dating).

"How old do you think it is?" Constance asked.

"Several hundred thousand years most likely," Mary answered. "Interesting, but not terribly important."

Two weeks later the report came back. Mary was dumbstruck. She stared in reverent awe at the simple footprint, a seemingly insignificant marker from the past.

That footprint was between 3.5 and 3.8 *million* years old! It had been made by the oldest erect walkers ever discovered. By hundreds of thousands of years, it was the earliest evidence of erect humanoid presence on Earth. Mary's footprint became one of the most significant archeological finds of the century.

After Words

By late 1977, Mary's team had excavated over eighty feet of this ancient trail and had found prints from three early humanoids who walked along a muddy path one day 3.5 million years ago. Within the next year they found the remains of twenty-five humanoids and a wide array of early animals including fifteen new species (a record for one site).

Mary Leakey's work at sites throughout Africa (but mainly at Olduvai and Laetolil) provided much of the hard evidence to support our modern theories of the origins of humans on this planet.

* * *

Suggested Topics to Explore

This story deals with archeology and archeological digging. Here are starting questions that will help you discuss and research both.

1. What do archeologists do? How do they decide where to dig? What do they look for and dig up? Research the field and practice of archeology.

2. Research Mary Leakey and her husband, Louis, both famous archeologists. What did they discover? Where? How?

3. How can scientists tell how old something is? What techniques do they use? Research the process of dating old objects. Would you use the same techniques to decide that an object is 100 years old that you would use if it were 100,000 years old? What is the difference in the two techniques? Why are they different?

For Further Reading About This Story

Avi-Yonah, Michael. *Dig This!* Denver, CO: Runestone Press, 1993.
Heiligman, Deborah. *Mary Leakey: In Search of Human Beginnings.* New York: Franklin Watts, 1998.
Leakey, Mary. *Discovering the Past.* New York: Doubleday, 1984.
Leroi-Gourhan, Andre. *The Hunters of Prehistory.* New York: Atheneum, 1990.
McIntosh, Jane. *The Practical Archaeologist.* New York: Facts on File, 1999.
Morell, Virginia. *Ancestral Passions: The Leakey Family.* New York: Simon & Schuster, 1995.
Scheller, William. *Amazing Archaeologists and Their Finds.* New York: Atheneum, 1994.

Holly Lisanby

Magnetic Personalities:
A Science Adventure

Neurological
Researcher

Testing a new medical procedure on lab animals is usually easy and safe. But, at some point, a researcher has to find out if it works on humans. Holly Lisanby was the first to test an experimental treatment on the brains of live human patients. Until she tried it, she'd never know if it would really help or harm her human volunteers.

A Science Adventure in the Medical Lab

Pink and white spring blooms painted the trees leading to the five-story brick laboratory building of the Columbia University College of Physicians and Surgeons in New York on this glorious afternoon of April 24, 1990.

In a large, third-floor consultation and lab room, a man reclined on a comfortable dentist-style chair—trying to joke with the lab tech, but still tense and apprehensive. The tech busily jotted notes at a side counter, preparing the chart on this new patient. Clusters of blossoms swayed like pom-poms past the windows in the gusty breeze.

"Should I take my glasses off?"

"No need. Just sit back and relax. Dr. Lisanby has successfully done this procedure on lots of patients."

"How many?" The man's voice sounded urgent, pleading for reassurance.

"Just relax. She'll be here in a minute."

The man nervously rubbed the back of one hand with the opposing thumb. "Will I be . . . put under?"

The lab tech had shifted to testing the electronic equipment stacked on a rolling cart. "No. We won't use any anesthetic. You'll hardly feel a thing."

"What's *that?* You're not going to shave my head, are you?" The man had pushed back against his chair, shrinking away from the lab tech.

The tech shrugged and laughed. "It's just a white skullcap. It helps focus the magnetic field." The tech carried a skullcap of wire mesh covered with white nylon gauze. "You'll need to put this on before Dr. Lisanby arrives."

Fifty-two-year-old Dr. Holly Lisanby entered through a side door, followed by a younger colleague who wanted to watch this new procedure. Both wore green hospital pants and smocks. Dr. Lisanby's hair was held back in a barrette.

She marched in front of the chair and extended her hand. "Hello, I'm Holly Lisanby. This is Dr. Olstein. He's just here to observe."

The patient nodded and glanced nervously around the room.

She continued, "You have volunteered to be part of an experimental treatment program. Has anyone explained the TMS procedure to you?"

The man shook his head and appeared noticeably worried. Beads of perspiration formed along his upper lip.

Holly explained, "You've heard of shock therapy . . . "

The man gasped, "You're going to *zap* me!?" His eyes widened.

"Certainly not." Dr. Lisanby smiled confidently and continued. "Shock therapy is a brutal and generally invasive treatment that affects the whole brain, not just the one specific spot we want to adjust. Electrotherapy must use large voltages and currents because the bones of the skull are such a poor electrical conductors. Electrotherapy can cause memory loss, seizures, and headaches. But the skull does *not* resist a magnetic field. That's what we do here— Transcranial Magnetic Stimulation or TMS. A weak magnetic field can induce the localized electrical responses in the brain that electroshock theory *hoped* to achieve. But we do it in a controlled way. There are more benefits and *no* side effects." She paused and smiled. "Do you have any questions?"

The man stammered, "Wi . . . will it hurt?"

"Because of TMS's low power levels, we need no anesthesia. You'll suffer no memory loss, no seizures, and you can return to work immediately after. Most feel only a light tapping on the head."

The man nodded tensely and closed his eyes. Holly radiated as much confidence as she could. "Good. Let's proceed."

She turned to Dr. Olstein. "William is a forty-one-year-old man suffering from chronic severe depression and anxiety that have not responded well to medication. Otherwise his health is good. This is our first session of ten I have ordered over the next two weeks."

The lab tech rolled the cart to just behind the patient's chair and clicked on the power amplifier and control units.

Dr. Lisanby lifted the magnetic field generating paddle that looked like an oversized windup key for a toy car. Holly Lisanby described it as an eight-inch-long figure eight with thick electrical cable running to the middle of it. She called it the wand. Engineers called it a donut magnet.

Standing behind the patient's chair, she leaned down and touched his shoulder. "Are you comfortable? Good. Relax, breathe normally, and close your eyes. That's your job for the next thirty minutes. Here are ear plugs to wear."

"Why ear plugs?" he asked.

"The magnet sounds loud when it's right next to your ear."

She turned to the lab tech, now perched on a stool in front of the equipment controls. "Set for ten cycles per second in eight second bursts at a power level of two-point-five. Set the clock for one burst every ninety seconds."

Dr. Olstein asked, "Why those settings?"

Holly motioned with her head toward the next room and reached down to pat the patient's shoulder. "I have to step out for just a moment. Get comfy. I'll be right back."

With the office door closed behind them, Holly said, "I don't like to mention any uncertainty in front of the patients. It makes them tense and may adversely affect the treatment."

When Olstein nodded his understanding, Holly continued. "TMS is brand new. We only have data on two dozen patients. So we're still experimenting to see the effect of different doses on different patients and on different parts of the brain. I still have to guess at what levels will be appropriate and effective without risking damage to brain tissues."

Olstein chuckled. "I can see why you didn't want to say that in front of the patient. He'd probably bolt from the chair."

Holly bristled. "Even in its experimental stage, TMS is far safer than electroshock. The pattern of voltage and current I ordered in there has worked in the past. I think it's a good place to start with a new patient until I see how he responds."

Back in treatment room Dr. Lisanby flashed a confident smile at her patient. "All ready? Good." With her fingers, Holly measured a spot several inches above and in front of the man's left ear. "I'll hold the paddle over the prefrontal cortex since this site is linked to chronic depression."

Holly nodded. The lab tech flipped a switch. Fan motors purred. The paddle emitted a high-pitched hum—almost a whine—that seemed to pulse for a few seconds and stop.

"There's the first burst." She leaned forward. "Still comfortable?"

The patient whispered, "I felt the tapping . . . "

Thirty minutes later, with the equipment turned off, Holly removed the skullcap. The patient rose to leave. "My scalp's a little sore."

"That's normal," reassured Holly. "We'll see you tomorrow. Same time."

After the patient left, Olstein said, "Congratulations. That seemed to go smoothly."

Lisanby answered, "Smoothly, yes. But I won't know for days if that treatment level was appropriate for his problem. Three hundred patients from now, I won't have to cautiously tiptoe up from these low settings, hoping to do some good. I'll know *exactly* what power and pattern to start with. *Then* congratulations will be in order."

In the staff room Holly sighed with relief and collapsed onto a couch. The session had gone well. But every experimental treatment has unforeseen risks and dangers—especially when dealing with something as complex and mysterious as the human brain. TMS seemed to work. But on every patient? Could it have disastrous side effects that Holly would never anticipate? Were there some patients for whom it would do more harm than good? But how would she ever learn enough to be sure if she didn't experiment?

Holly grabbed a cup of coffee and sank back into the couch when Dr. James Harrison, School Medical Director, stormed in to confront her. "I am uncomfortable with you experimenting on live humans."

She snapped, "You would rather have me prescribe electroshock therapy?"

"I would rather have you stick to approved treatments."

Holly rose to her fullest 5'10" height. "But TMS *works,* and the only way to ever get it approved is to complete an experimental treatment program with it."

They were standing only inches apart, glaring at each other.

"But at what risk to the patients?"

Others in the staff room froze and watched. Holly answered, "No seizures. No memory loss. No headache. No impact on parts of the brain we don't specifically target. Besides, they have all knowingly volunteered."

Harrison insisted, "At least none you *know* about. And you know nothing about the long-term effects."

"And I won't until I've used TMS for a long time. Stick around for my next patient. A schizophrenic. Just one session relieved her auditory hallucinations for weeks!"

Harrison countered, "And in two years we might learn that you've given him cancer or turned him into an uncontrollable deviant."

"*Her*," said Holly. "My next patient is a woman."

Harrison snorted and continued, "If anything goes wrong with one of these experiments, you'll be sued. So will the hospital. And you'll be ruined. Finished!"

"I believe in TMS. I'll stake my career on it. I've completed all of the necessary lab tests. It's time for human trial studies."

Harrison sighed and rubbed his face. "Look, Holly. Early mammograms seemed like a good idea, too. But the X-ray dose was so high that they created more problems than they solved. I'm just asking you to go slow. Use minimum voltage and current."

"I use three percent of the current and voltage that electroshock therapy would use to do the same thing."

"Can't you do animal studies?" he asked.

"I have. In studies on rats and dogs, TMS has increased long-term activity in nerve-cell receptors and neurotransmitters. We've actually altered the structure of rat nerve cells. We've used MRI's to chart changes in blood flow in the brain. In lab animals, TMS does exactly what it is supposed to—and with no adverse side effects that we can detect."

Fifteen minutes later, Dr. Harrison stood, arms folded across his chest, watching Holly begin treatment of the schizophrenic woman. Her eyes darted around the room as if following unseen voices. "The voices are starting to tell me things again, doctor."

"We can quiet them, Dorothy. And maybe for longer this time."

Holly motioned to her lab tech. "Set power level to four-point-five. Same burst pattern, duration, and frequency as before."

Then she turned to Harrison. "Watch. If I hold the wand just above and behind the left ear, the right thumb twitches. See? If I move it up . . . here, I affect her color perception. TMS is teaching us about the nerve pathways in the brain as well as helping patients."

After Dorothy left—relieved to again be without her nagging voices—Dr. Harrison nervously shook his head, "It's just so unknown, so experimental."

"True," answered Holly. "We're still feeling our way. But it seems to be working."

Harrison raised a cautionary finger. "Not all the time. I've seen your records. Some patients show very little improvement."

Holly admitted, "There might well be more variation in brain circuitry between individuals than we thought—another reason we need to experiment more."

Harrison frowned, "It's just so dangerous to experiment on humans when there are still so many unknowns."

Holly smiled, "That's the adventure of medial research. Sure, we still have a lot of work to do. But remember, we don't really understand many of our treatments. But we use them anyway because they save lives."

After Words

Thanks to a decade of data compiled by Dr. Holly Lisanby and others on the effects of TMS, it is becoming the therapy of choice for a wide range of mental and emotional illnesses including obsessive-compulsive disorder, mania, schizophrenia, and severe depression. One patient was even cured of writer's block by a series of TMS treatments.

* * *

Suggested Topics to Explore

This story deals with electrical stimulation of the brain and with medical experiments. Here are starting questions that will help you discuss and research both.

1. Do you think it is all right to test a new therapy on humans? Are there some kinds of therapy that shouldn't be tested on humans? Which kinds? Why are some all right and others not? How should dangerous therapies be tested?

2. Research the different parts of the brain and the function of each. How does the brain work? How much does science know and not know about how the brain works?

3. In this story a magnetic field is used to stimulate electrical activity in the brain. What is the relationship between electrical current and magnetic fields? Research these two aspects of electrical energy.

For Further Reading About This Story

August, Paul. *Brain Function.* New York: Chelsea House, 1990.

Bailey, Donna. *All About Your Brain.* New York: Steck-Vaughn Library, 1991.

Barmeiser, Jim. *The Brain.* San Diego, CA: Lucent Books, 1996.

Behrman, Andy. *Electroboy.* New York: Random House, 2001.

Bennett, Paul. *My Brain and Senses.* New York: Silver Press, 1998.

Hobson, J. *The Chemistry of Conscious States: How the Brain Changes Its Mind.* Boston: Little, Brown & Company, 1997.

Pouledge, Tabitha. *Your Brain: How You Got It and How It Works.* New York: Scribners, 1994.

Shannon Lucid

The "Gravity" of the Situation:
A Science Adventure   Chemical/
Biological Engineer

Shannon Lucid was stuck on a science station for six months, conducting a long and tedious series of engineering and biological experiments, never once able to set foot outside the cramped station. Of course, she never really minded—especially since her station drifted 17,000 miles above the Earth in space.

A Science Adventure in Space

There was just a moment each morning as she first awoke when Shannon Lucid couldn't remember why her hair and body seemed to float without pressing down into her sleeping bag. But that moment always quickly passed. Why shouldn't hair float when you're sleeping in space?

This morning in late April 1996, Shannon stretched, pushed out of her sleeping bag—velcroed to a pole to keep her from drifting during her sleep shift—and floated to the window of the Russian space station, MIR, to watch spring march north across Earth's northern hemisphere. It amazed Shannon that she could see differences from one day to the next. Ice sheets darkened as they thinned. Thick, black cracks snaked across lake ice. Drab brown countrysides shifted to soft greens.

Shannon Lucid had ridden on the space shuttle Atlantis for four days to reach MIR, where she served on a six-month scientific assignment with two Russian cosmonauts, Yuri Usachev and Yuri Onufriyenko. Now, six weeks into her stay, Shannon was tiring of the constant meals of dehydrated borscht and watching the two Yuris smear American mayonnaise on everything they ate.

As on most mornings, Shannon slipped into her red-white-and-blue "American Flag" socks. She wouldn't be walking on the flag, because the only time she stood or walked was when she was strapped into the station treadmill for exercise. Otherwise, it was easier to float using your arms for guidance.

The two Yuris greeted Shannon. She answered in Russian, as neither of the cosmonauts spoke English. They offered her tea and cookies. Shannon accepted a Russian ginger cookie, took a bite, and instinctively plopped the cookie down on top of a handy console while she chewed and slurped hot tea through a straw. Shannon missed drinking out of a cup. But there was no way to tip a cup and pour tea into her mouth when there was no gravity to make it flow.

The cookie hit the console and ricocheted straight for the ceiling. Shannon had to stretch like a baseball outfielder to catch it on the rebound.

The two Yuris laughed. She still hadn't gotten use to the first law of space living: you can't do anything as you would on Earth. There's no gravity to hold it there. Gently let it go wherever it is and it will float there patiently until you grab it again.

Yuri Usachev made a joke in Russian about Shannon's cookie. Yuri Onufriyenko howled with laughter. Shannon frowned, concentrating. She understood the words, but not the joke. With her limited Russian, jokes were the hardest thing for Shannon to understand or to tell.

MIR consisted of three connected cylindrical modules. To Shannon it felt like being crammed into a camper shell on the back of a pickup truck that is overcrowded with equipment. . . . and its raining and you're stuck in there with your yelling, screaming kids, and you can't get out—not ever.

Half of the back module was reserved for science experiments. This was where Shannon spent most of her time. Gliding through the connector hatch, she scanned her experiment log and the long-term schedule she had prepared. Most of her experiments related to effects caused by the absence of gravity (zero-G).

Three petite Japanese quail eggs and embryos hovered in a see-through self-zipping plastic bag. That bag lay inside a second self-sealing plastic bag with two gloves built into it. Using the gloves, Shannon could open the inner bag without opening the outer bag. With the inner bag closed, she could open the outer bag to bring in, or take out, any equipment or chemicals she needed for the experiment. The idea was never have both bags open at the same time. It prevented contamination of the experiment, and prevented any dangerous elements of the experiment from escaping.

During her second week, Shannon had slipped and pulled open the outer bag while applying a chemical agent to her first set of quail eggs. Several drops of the chemical—capable of burning skin or destroying an eye—escaped and split into a thousand tiny droplets that scattered across the module.

Shannon hit the emergency warning button. The hatchway slid shut. She had to grab a facemask and breathing tank while pressurized cleaning gas hissed from spray nozzles as it was pumped through the compartment. Still all three cosmonauts suffered burns on their hands and arms when they later touched droplets that hadn't been washed away. One of the droplets fell onto Yuri Onufriyenko's cheek two days later. It hit just below his eye and sizzled his skin, leaving a large blister and a permanent scar.

Shannon was using the quail eggs to document the effects of zero-G on egg and embryonic growth and development. Would they develop faster? Slower? Bigger? Differently in any way than when anchored by Earth's gravity? Daily, she measured the size and mass of each egg. (She couldn't measure weight because weight depends on gravity.) She used onboard equipment to measure shell thickness and shape as well as embryo density.

In zero-Gs, this batch of shells had grown too thin and fragile. That would never do on a permanent space station that had to grow much of its own food. Today Shannon planned to paint a chemical growth stimulator on one of the shells to see if she could encourage the egg to grow a tougher shell.

Shannon opened the outer bag and placed the bottle of growth agent and a brush inside. She zipped that bag closed and shoved her hands into the built-in gloves. Visually she checked to make sure the outer bag was sealed before she opened the inner bag with her gloved hands.

Each step took so much longer in space because there was no gravity to hold things down. She carefully dipped her brush in the liquid chemical and eased it back out of the plastic jar. She gently stroked her brush across the egg labeled A-12 making sure none of the liquid escaped to drift over to the other eggs and affect their development.

Finally, she resealed everything and wrote in the experiment's log hooked to the wall behind it.

Next Shannon turned to her plant growth experiments. Would plants and trees grow faster and taller in space? Did a lack of gravity affect the development of roots, or the thickness and toughness of stalk or trunk? How did zero-Gs affect a plant's ability to draw water into and through itself?

Shannon had carried the seedlings of fifty species of plants into space. During her second week in space, she transferred them into MIR soil beds. Every day she measured growth, examined root structure, and compared the growth of these dirt-bound plants with that for her hydroponic plants (those grown in nutrient-enriched water). She also searched for abnormalities or unexpected affects of zero-G life on her plants, the first plants ever planted and raised in zero-G. Plants had never experienced life without gravity and no one knew what the removal of that constant, ever-present force would do to their development. She used a microscope to examine leaf thickness and structure. She measured oxygen production and water consumption.

For Shannon, the hardest part was watering her plants with no gravity to hold the water down. It was hard to get the water to go where the roots were. As part of her plant growth experiments, she was testing three watering systems proposed by NASA (National Aeronautics and Space Administration) engineers.

Shannon spent four hours tending and testing her "garden," and then an hour of exercise split between the treadmill and the weight-bearing exercises she called "Russian torture." A big problem during exercise was sweat. It tended to drift off and coat the module with a watery film. It also upped the humidity to sauna levels. The cosmonauts were testing a newly designed exercise vacuum pump to collect sweat as it was produced and eject it into space. A fine spray of tiny ice crystals drifted away from MIR during each exercise period.

Then more borscht—this time with dehydrated meat and vegetables, cookies, and tea—before turning to Shannon's engineering experiments. In order to design the International Space Station, NASA engineers needed more data on how fluids flowed and acted in space.

Shannon's expertise was in chemistry and plant physiology. These engineering studies made her nervous. Her job today was to study the affect of zero-G on the formation of turbulence in liquid flows. When mountain streams tumble, swirl, and fill with air bubbles, that's turbulence. Turbulence is bad. It reduces flow efficiency and requires much more energy to pump the same amount of liquid.

Shannon's job this day was to test five different thicknesses (viscosities) of liquid. She had to pump each one through a series of clear tubes to see how changes in pressure, velocity, and the roughness of the pipe's inner surface would affect the formation of turbulence.

Using a nozzle, she poured the first liquid into the test reserve chamber. She clicked on the pump and set speed and pressure. Fluid gurgled out of the reserve chamber and surged through clear plastic tubes. Shannon recorded the pressure and flow-rate gage in each tube and watched for signs of turbulence. In small increments, she increased pump speed and pressure until chaotic turbulence occurred in each pipe.

Shannon shut down the pump, carefully drained that liquid back into its plastic storage container, and poured a second liquid into the reserve chamber. After one deep breath and a quick stretch, Shannon began the experiment all over again with this second liquid.

Two hours later, she was ready for her last experiment of the day—and her least favorite. Fire was deadly dangerous on board a space station—far worse than on a ship or in an airplane—because flames seemed to jump and move in unpredictable ways in the absence of gravity. MIR was filled with breathable air, oxygen canisters, and countless opportunities for an electrical fire to begin. The same would be true on any space station. It was important for planners to learn more about fire in zero-G.

Shannon called Yuri Usachev into the science module. During any open-flame experiment, a second cosmonaut had to be standing by with a fire extinguisher. Shannon prepared thin lines (about a foot long each) of burnable material on a steel counter—pastes, gels, wood fibers, wires, etc. Next to each line she placed a metal ruler so they could record the exact rate at which the flame moved.

She signaled to Yuri. He shut down the module's automatic fire suppression system, clutched the extinguisher, and nodded that he was ready. Shannon started a video recorder and timer.

She lit the end of the first line—a flammable gel. The flame wavered, then stretched high and thin, as if riding on unseen air currents. It shifted and jumped several inches down the line, flared, and soared over a foot into the air—thin and orange-blue. Just as suddenly, it squatted low and spread to the side igniting two adjacent lines of material.

These new lines both flared into burning life. Their flames swirled like interlocking snakes and joined into a bright orange campfire.

Searing flames spread out in all directions. Shannon heard a deep whooshing sound as the growing fire sucked air like a powerful pump.

Yuri blasted the fire extinguisher. The module filled with cool, white specks. The fire withered and died to ash and smoke. Ventilation fans kicked on, sucking out the smoke and floating particles and forcing in clean, filtered air.

Shannon spent half an hour reviewing the video and documenting the moment-by-moment progression of the fire. Ground engineers would review her data and then suggest changes for her to use when she continued this experiment another day.

After a light evening meal, Shannon had less than an hour for her chosen hobby—reading—before she zipped back into her sleeping bag. Another day on MIR had ended.

After Words

The data from Shannon Lucid's many experiments helped NASA engineers to design vastly improved onboard systems for the International Space Station orbiting Earth at the beginning of the twenty-first century. Her results also provided essential data for long-range planners designing star ships and space stations the size of cities.

Shannon Lucid has spent more time in space than any other American astronaut, and more than any woman in the world. She continues to work in NASA's space program.

* * *

Suggested Topics to Explore

This story deals with zero gravity and the process of science experiments. Here are starting questions that will help you discuss and research both.

1. How does gravity affect your life? In what ways do you depend on gravity every day? Keep a one-day log of every time you use and depend on gravity to make your life easy and safe. Did you do anything that didn't depend on gravity? Can you imagine what your same day would be like without gravity?

2. Shannon Lucid was the second American woman in space. Who was the first? Research American and Russian women astronauts. How many have there been? What were their jobs?

Were their entry requirements or training any different from those for male astronauts?

For Further Reading About This Story

Briggs, Carole. *Women in Space.* Minneapolis, MN: Carolrhoda Books, 1988.

Burdett, Gerald, ed. *The Human Quest in Space.* San Diego, CA: Univelt, Inc., 1987.

Hansen, Rosanna. *Astronauts.* New York: Random House, 1997.

NASA Web site: <http://www.jsc.nasa.gov>.

O'Connor, Karen. *Sally Ride and the New Astronauts: Scientists in Space.* New York: Franklin Watts, 1983.

Yenne, Bill. *Astronauts.* New York: Simon & Schuster, 1991.

Barbara McClintock

"Sowing" Lesson: A Science Adventure

Geneticist

Barbara McClintock worked alone in a small, windswept cornfield for a decade, shoved aside and ignored by mainstream science. She worked there because it was the only job in her specialty she could get, even though she had written a dozen acclaimed articles and two widely used textbooks. Imagine the world's surprise when she made a Nobel prize–winning discovery in that cornfield.

A Science Adventure in Genetics

The moon poured soft light into Barbara McClintock's apartment as she paced through the night of April 20, 1950. A chilling wind rattled the windows. But the steady, biting cold wind off Long Island Sound was why they named the place Cold Spring Harbor.

Barbara lived in a trim two-room apartment over the bright green painted garage of the Carnegie Institute Cold Spring Harbor Research Facility. It only took eight steps for her to pace from wall to wall.

As she paced her small home, Barbara argued both sides of an internal debate. "I *am* right! We look at genetic control all wrong. Genes aren't fixed. They move; they jump."

She reached the windows and spun on her heel for another lap across the well-worn rug. "But if I can't even convince Marcus Rhodes that I'm *serious,* let alone that I'm right, how can I hope to convince anyone else?"

A small, slight woman, Barbara stood barely five feet tall and weighed under ninety pounds. Her face and hands were worn and wrinkled from long exposure to wind and sun.

A self-confident, frustratingly independent scientist, Barbara McClintock was a former professor of Marcus Rhoades'. The locals in Cold Spring Harbor called her "odd" and a "loner." Scientific contemporaries of the forty-eight-year-old genetic researcher called her a "past-by relic of the old ways." Marcus Rhoades, who had spent the day visiting her corn patch and reviewing her research, called her a friend. He was one of the very few who still did.

Reaching the wall next to the file cabinets, Barbara turned back for her next lap. "If I write it compellingly, forcefully, if I make it vivid and impassioned, if I carefully present my data, then I'll make them see." Turn. New lap. "But am I absolutely sure? Could I be wrong? Marcus thinks I am." Turn. "I've got six drawers of data. I've watched six generations of corn. How much surer can I be?" Turn.

This day had started so well when she learned that Marcus Rhoades was on his way out for a visit, and ended so poorly when he left with a chuckle, thinking her research was somehow a grand joke.

Cold Spring Harbor was an isolated spot on northern Long Island, filled with wind, rolling sand dunes, and waving shore grass. Marcus didn't find her until almost noon.

He located his old professor stooping in a small half-acre corn-field tucked between the facility's cluster of buildings and the choppy waters of the sound. She was planting corn seeds in carefully laid out rows by hand. She paused to consult a notebook diagram before shoving each seed into the cold dirt with her thumb.

"Barbara!" he called, waving his hands. "What are you doing in a cornfield? You said you were doing important research"

This was 1950, and research into the structure, function, and genetic coding of a cell was a bustling world of new technologies: electron microscopes, X-ray crystallography, and radioisotopes. There was no room for an old fashioned fool who divided her time between a cornfield and an ordinary microscope.

Barbara wiped off her hands, knee socks, skirt, and thin sweater—seemingly immune to the wind's icy spell—and bounded across to greet her old student.

Barbara's bright eyes twinkled and she laughed a loud, horsey laugh. "Marcus, being here in this field is a tremendous joy—the careful process of finding an answer where none existed before—just pure joy . . . " Then her face clouded. "Besides, you know perfectly well there are no university professorships for a woman."

"But, what do you *do* way out here, day after day, year after year?"

1950 was Barbara's sixth year of planting, growing, and studying the genes of these corn plants as they passed from generation to generation. She now felt more like a farmer than a genetics researcher.

How Barbara spent her days depended on the season. In summer, most of her time was spent in the cornfield, nurturing the plants that would produce her data for the year, weeding, checking for pests and disease that could ruin her experiments. In the fall she harvested each ear by hand, carefully labeled it, and began her lab analysis of each gene's location and structure on the chromosomes of each ear. Her lab consisted of one powerful microscope, chemical lab trays, and stacks of journals to record her findings. This work would consume the long hours through winter.

In spring, she split her time between numerical analysis of the previous year's data and field planning and preparation for the next generation of corn plants.

Marcus looked puzzled. "Twenty-five years ago you identified and decoded the corn chromosomes. What's still out here to learn?"

McClintock harrumphed and pointed at her rows of wild Indian corn with the bright blue, brown, and red kernels. "We don't know how heredity *really* works, not at all. Why do some corn kernels turn out blue while others are red? Why do dark mutation spots appear in some generations, and not in others? What really *controls* how genetic information is passed from generation to generation?"

Now Marcus sounded surprised. "We *do* know. First Mendel said it, and then Dr. Morgan at Cornell. Everybody knows that *genes* carry heredity information, that they are fixed like tiny strings of pearls onto *chromosomes,* and that they pass—in the same fixed order—from generation to generation. Every one knows *that,* Barbara. That's how heredity works"

Barbara snorted and pointed to her cornfield. "For six years I've studied each and every plant in this field. I've tracked color mutations, patterns, and changes. Here's what I've found. Genes are *not* fixed along chromosomes as everyone thinks. They can move. They *do* move. Some genes seem able to direct other genes, telling them where to go and when to act. These genetic directors control the movement and action of other genes that jump positions on command and then turn-on—or turn-off—the genes next to them in their new location."

Barbara McClintock was known for her humor and mischievous pranks. Marcus began to feel that his leg was being severely pulled. He laughed and shook his head. "Good one, Barbara. You had me going there. That's quite a joke . . . "

"But I'm serious. And I'm right. Everyone else is wrong. Sooner or later, they'll see."

"But . . . but that's scientific heresy. With just a microscope how can you defy the best minds and research equipment of the twentieth century?"

Barbara had led Marcus up to her apartment, and she now pointed at two bulging, five-drawer file cabinets. "Six years; six drawers filled with careful notes, data, and observations. My corn plants don't lie. Genes *do* move along a chromosome. They jump—seemingly almost at random—from spot to spot, generation to generation. But it's not random. It's controlled. Understand what controls that jumping, and you *really* understand genetics. That's why everyone else's research is stalling and falling apart. Look at all the trouble other researchers are running into. They aren't accounting for gene movement."

Marcus Rhoades left just after sunset, still shaking his head, still suspecting this must be a grand Barbara McClintock prank. How could one woman working all alone in a remote cornfield be right, and the greatest minds at the greatest universities in the country all be wrong?

So now the night passed, as Barbara paced, worried, and debated. "Should I wait another year—or two—to be more sure? How much surer can I be?" Turn. "Maybe one more year of study. Then I'll write and present my findings at the 1951 symposium." Turn. "Why can no one else see what is so clear to me?" Turn. "Will anyone ever listen to me?" Turn. Turn. Turn.

Barbara submitted a proposal to present at the 1951 national symposium on genetic research. The conference was scheduled for September—harvesting time. But Barbara could start that process a week late. She felt it was more important that she share her findings.

Barbara McClintock's seminar was one of fifteen concurrent sessions scheduled for 10:00 A.M. on Friday, September 22, the first full day of the conference. Her room had seats for 200. Thirty attended. A few more straggled in during her talk.

For forty minutes, she nervously described her painstaking fieldwork, her research methods, her carefully documented research findings. She hoped for excited questions and looks of sudden understanding. Secretly, she expected attack, heated debate, and argument. That, at least, would give her a chance to defend her data and her ideas.

She concluded early, with fifteen minutes left for discussion, and braced for an onslaught of criticism as she called for questions. The attack never came.

She was not asked a single question. Those few left in the room simply stood and left, hoping to find a session of greater interest in the next hour.

As so often happens with radically new ideas, Barbara McClintock was simply dismissed by the audience with a bored and indifferent shrug. She was ignored. They couldn't understand the implications of what she said.

Feeling both helpless and frustrated, Barbara returned to harvest her cornfield and start her analysis of this seventh year's crop. She never received even one comment, question, query, or criticism of her presentation.

After Words

Twenty-five years after she first announced her discoveries, the world caught up to Barbara McClintock and realized *what* she had discovered. The 1983 Nobel Prize Committee called Barbara McClintock's pioneering work "one of the two great discoveries of our time in genetics." They called her the greatest genetics field researcher of the century and awarded her the Nobel Prize.

Barbara McClintock's work in the Cold Harbor cornfield became the base building block for a dozen major medical and disease fighting breakthroughs. She continued to tend her corn plants and to gather annual genetics data until she retired from the station in 1987 at the age of eighty-five.

* * *

Suggested Topics to Explore

This story deals with genetics and the role of women in science. Here are starting questions that will help you discuss and research both.

1. Why study genetics? What can scientist learn by figuring out how traits are passed form generation to generation?

2. Why do genetic researchers use pea plants, corn plants, and fruit flies to study heredity instead of looking at people?

3. Why do you think some researchers get shoved aside and ignored by other scientists? How would you feel if you were Barbara McClintock and had been pushed out of universities and forced to work all alone in a small cornfield? Research the life and work of this scientist.

For Further Reading About This Story

Dash, Joan. *The Triumph of Discovery.* New York: Simon and Schuster, 1991.

Keller, Evelyn. *A Feeling for the Organism: The Life and Work of Barbara McClintock.* San Francisco: W. H. Freeman, 1983.

Maranto, Gina. "At Long Last—A Nobel for a Loner." *Discover* (December 1983): 26.

McClintock, Barbara. "Induction of Instability of Selected Loci in Maize." *Genetics* 38 (1953): 579–99.

Opfell, Olga. *The Lady Laureates: Women Who Have Won the Nobel Prize.* Metuchen, NJ: Scarecrow Press, 1993.

Shiels, Barbara. *Winners: Women and the Nobel Prize.* Minneapolis: Dillon Press, 1992.

Karen McComb

"Call" of the Wild: Field Biologist
A Science Adventure

A rampaging bull elephant charged straight at Karen McComb. Sure, it was a deadly dangerous situation. But it was one Karen had intentionally created. After all, driving elephants into such a defensive frenzy was her job.

A Science Adventure in the African Wild

The radio on twenty-eight-year-old Karen McComb's belt squawked, "Can you tell the age of the matriarch? Over."

Karen wore thick khaki shorts, hiking boots, a heavy denim shirt, and a wide-brimmed hat to ward off the fierce sun here in Kenya, Africa, on this late afternoon of May 18, 2001. A water canteen and her intercom radio were strapped to her belt. Binoculars dangled around her neck. Next to her, she lugged a battery powered loud speaker/CD player. She had pushed through a thick line of stiff, bristly bushes, edging closer to an elephant family grazing on the far side.

She lowered the binoculars, squinted towards the sun hanging low in the west, wiped the sweat from her forehead, slapped at two pesky flies, and grabbed the handset of her intercom. "The matriarch is young. No more than forty, I'd say."

"How large is the family? Over."

Karen chuckled. She had taught eighteen-year-old Nijob how to use the radio when she hired him as a guide for the summer from a nearby village. Even though they were the only two people for miles (Nijob at the truck and Karen hiking nearby), he still insisted on using formal radio procedure.

"You don't have to say 'over' every time, Nijob."

"Roger. Over."

Karen smiled and shook her head, then peered back through the binoculars. "Looks like eight adults (five female and three male) and three—no, four—calves."

One of Nijob's tasks was to keep thorough logs on the elephant families they encountered. "Are there two notches on the matriarch's left ear? Over."

"Yes. Have we seen this family before?"

"Yes. Two weeks ago. Over."

Karen thought for a moment. "I want to test them with a familiar call. Which calls are we sure they should recognize?"

Nijob's reply was almost instant. "Calls numbers three and eighteen on your CD tape. Over."

Karen, a biologist at Sussex University in England, was testing a theory she had developed about elephant family behavior. Large elephant herds travel in small, spread out family groups.

Elephants approaching a family unit announced their presence by rumbling loudly, a practice known as contact calling. A family should recognize the call of elephants from their own herd. On hearing an unfamiliar call, a family stopped all activity, grouped tightly, and raised their trunks to sniff for the scent of an intruder. It wasted time, agitated the family, and pulled important time and energy away from feeding and survival.

Responding to Nijob's information, Karen punched in track eighteen on her CD and cranked up the volume. The recorded contact call rumbled across African grass, bush, tree, and plain.

This *should* have been a familiar call, taped from a bull elephant in this family's herd. The matriarch *should* have paused for a moment, listening, and then returned to grazing, thus reassuring her family that she recognized the call and all was safe.

The matriarch paused, turning her head, shifting nervously from foot to foot. Then she trumpeted harshly. Instantly her family stopped grazing and lumbered into a tight knot. Adults faced outward, trunks raised, sniffing the air for the scent of an intruder. Calves were hurriedly scooted safely into the center.

Karen turned off the tape and backed deeper into the bushes. This was a dangerous time. Nervous elephants might charge if they believed a threat existed or even if they simply didn't like her scent as detected by their sensitive noses.

"That was all wrong. Over. They should have recognized that call. Over. Why are they in defensive mode? Over."

Karen smiled. Nijob ran his sentences and his "over's" together every time he was excited.

She settled onto a soft clump of grass to wait. It often took twenty minutes or more for the elephants to fully relax and return to feeding after a false alarm. She would wait and try one more call on this family—another call that should be familiar.

She knew she didn't have to remind Nijob to record exactly what had happened. He had proved to be excellent at documenting everything they did.

Karen theorized that the family matriarch (the oldest female) decided if a contact call was familiar or not and ordered the family into defense action. She had traveled to Africa to test her theory.

Renowned elephant biologist Cynthia Moss had noted that the average age of African elephant family matriarchs was declining because older elephants' longer tusks were more highly prized by poachers. Instead of having matriarchs who were seventy or older, many families had matriarchs still in their twenties or thirties. Families with old matriarchs fared much better. They grew healthier. They bore more new calves each year.

Karen McComb postulated that young matriarchs lacked the necessary experience and training to consistently identify contact calls as familiar or stranger, and so disrupted feeding and threw the family into a defensive tizzy far too often.

It was as if female elephants needed years of study to learn their duties and techniques under a wise and older mistress. Young matriarchs arrived on the job unprepared. As a result, the entire elephant population was suffering.

Nijob's voice screeched over the intercom, sounding frantic. "Two female lions nearing your position. Over. I don't know how I missed them until now. Over."

Karen sighed. Sticking around to test this family with another call wasn't worth facing a pair of hungry lions. "Roger. I'm on my way back. Will I have any trouble getting there?"

"Stay north of the tree line and come now. Over."

Dr. McComb lugged the loud speaker at a jog, angling along the tree line toward the truck. Reaching an open space she'd have to cross, Karen ducked between two bushes and froze, listening, trying to still her own heavy breathing. "Can you see the lions, Nijob? I think I hear them close by."

"They are on the other side of the trees. Over. Don't stop. Over."

Karen could hear the lions snarling behind her during her final fifty-yard dash to the truck. If she had hesitated with the elephants a minute longer, it could have turned into a disastrous moment.

The next morning, Karen and Nijob headed out early, tracking a new family group. By 9:00, they had crept as close as they dared in the truck. Karen hoofed the last one-third mile on foot, keeping behind the cover of a thick line of acacia trees. "I'm in position. The matriarch looks very young. Is this a new family for us?"

"We have never followed this family before. Over."

"I'll try track one, and see how they respond."

Karen played the track. The matriarch paused for a moment, trumpeted softly to her family, and continued to munch the ripe grass. It had been recognized as a familiar contact call.

Karen waited ten minutes and played track twelve.

The matriarch roared. Returning trumpets from two unseen elephants told Karen she had made a big mistake. She had let two roving family males get behind her as they grazed. Now she was trapped between two rampaging bull elephants and the main family pack of five additional adults.

One of the rogue males charged.

Karen punched the CD to play the next track, hoping it would sooth (or at least confuse and divert) the elephants, and dashed away from the recorder. She hoped the charger would head for the sound instead of for her.

The new call seemed to set the elephants into a frenzy—trumpeting, pawing the dry ground, kicking boiling clouds of dust into the air.

As Karen frantically wiggled into a thicket, hoping to avoid being trampled by an enraged rogue, she bumped straight into a baby elephant. No wonder the family was upset! They were missing one calf. The calf raised its trunk and called in a weak, pleading trumpet.

Instantly the matriarch and two other females bellowed a reply and thundered straight at Karen's hiding spot.

She was now in the worst of all possible predicaments. She was trapped between a baby elephant and its angry mother on one side, and if she fled the opposite way, she'd come face-to-face with two raging males.

Karen had only seconds to do something before she'd be discovered and literally trampled to death.

She dove through a line of bushes and scurried in an ape-like sprint toward a small gully she hoped would offer some protection. She dove in and hugged the ground, afraid to look over the lip.

She waited for several minutes that felt like hours, hoping an elephant wouldn't detect her and charge. Then she crawled down the gully and scurried past thick bushes and back to her loud speaker.

Her CD player and speaker were smashed, splintered into a thousand pieces by an enraged elephant's foot. The pieces were scattered over the trampled grass.

Karen's hands still shook twenty minutes later when she reached Nijob and the truck. "I called and called," he scolded. "Why didn't you answer?"

Karen simply shook her head. "There wasn't exactly time for me to talk."

Karen quietly rode back to the Center to wait for new equipment and another day when she would use her backup CD to continue her research. But, with every test, she became more and more convinced of her theory.

After Words

By the end of the summer, Karen McComb had demonstrated that matriarchs fifty and older made mistakes in identifying familiar from unfamiliar calls only once in 2,000 attempts. Matriarchs in their thirties made mistakes one in three times. The difference in family lifestyle and success was staggering. Karen's work will help African countries improve their national polices and laws regarding elephant matriarchs, and elephant herds in general.

✳ ✳ ✳

Suggested Topics to Explore

This story deals with elephant communication, elephant behavior, and large game poaching. Here are some starting questions that will help you discuss and research each.

1. Elephants live in matriarchal societies. What does that mean? Have humans ever created matriarchal societies? Can you identity and research any of them? What are the advantages and disadvantages of the matriarchal model?

168 / Women at the Edge of Discovery

2. Why is it important for elephant families to identify intruders? Do humans do the same thing? If a stranger walked into your classroom, how would you decide if that person should or shouldn't be there? Is there one person to whom you would look to show you how you should react to that stranger? Is a classroom like a matriarchal society?

For Further Reading About This Story

Dorros, Auther. *Elephant Families*. New York: Harper Collins, 1994.

Groning, Karl. *Elephants: A Cultural History*. New York: Konemann, 1999.

Jackson, Peter. *Elephant*. Miami, FL: Chartwell Books, 1990.

Patent, Dorothy. *African Elephants*. New York: Holiday House, 1991.

Payne, Katherine. *Elephant Society*. New York: Crown Publications, 1992.

Petty, Kate. *Elephant*. Boston, MA: Gloucester Press, 1990.

Tibbitts, Alison. *African Elephants*. Philadelphia: Capstone Press, 1992.

Margaret Mead

Ta-lo-fa to You: Anthropologist
A Science Adventure

What would it be like to be dumped all alone on a small island where you don't speak the natives' language, where you have no way to contact the outside world, and where you'll live for nine months to complete an important study about those same natives? Margaret Mead found out.

A Science Adventure in the South Pacific

"There's Ta'u, that island up ahead," beamed Navy Ensign Charles O'Rourke, white teeth flashing under a bushy mustache. "Just off to port. That's 'left' to you city folk."

Wearily, twenty-four-year-old fledgling anthropologist Margaret Mead gazed at the distant speck barely eleven miles long by eight miles wide shimmering on the horizon, one in the long chain of South Pacific islands called American Samoa. Ta'u looked tiny. The thought made Margaret smile. At 5'1" and under 100 pounds, Margaret Mead usually thought everything else looked big.

"Seas are calm. Light, regular swells. The U.S. Navy'll have you at the dock in two hours." O'Rourke bounded back through the hatchway.

Left alone in the small cabin Margaret groaned as the boat slammed through a slightly larger wave. It was late June 1924, and stuffy hot. She had been seasick for days. But, as this tiny boat shouldered its way through the waves toward Ta'u, what made her truly miserable was the feeling that she was totally unprepared for this adventure.

The boat's engine slowed. Margaret rose to find Ta'u, lush, green, thick, and steamy. The boat glided through a small bay, drifting toward a rickety wooden pier. Palms criss-crossed the thin strip of sandy beach. Dense forest hid the rest of the island behind a solid green blanket sprinkled with brilliantly colored flower blotches. The air hung as wet and thick as in a sauna.

With a heavy heart, Margaret Mead stepped onto the wobbling pier carrying one bag of clothes, a typewriter, and two boxes of paper, ribbon, drawing paper, and notebooks. With the boat engine off, the sounds of life in a tropical forest flooded into her ears. Staring back at her from the shade of wide mango trees at the end of the pier were eighty pairs of solemn, inquisitive eyes set in handsome brown Samoan faces. No one spoke. No one stepped forward to greet this white-skinned woman. They just stood and stared.

Margaret gulped and tried to smile. "Ta-lo-fa," she called. It was the standard Samoan greeting and literally means, "Love to you."

Some giggled at her strange accent and mispronunciation. Many smiled and nodded. An elderly man said something in a singsong voice that rolled like the ocean. Many nodded. Then all eighty Somoans looked back at Margaret.

Margaret realized they were waiting for something—expecting her to do something. But what? She nervously smiled while sweat rolled down her back and dripped from her chin. Not knowing what else to do, she repeated, "Ta-lo-fa."

More giggles. Then a general discussion with much nodding and pointing. Two burly men marched forward and scooped her bag and boxes onto beefy shoulders. They marched off the pier and turned down the beach. The crowd followed.

Margaret called after them, "Wait! Where are you taking that? Be careful with my typewriter!" Were they confiscating her belongings? Stealing them? Did they think they were gifts? She lifted her long skirt and jogged after her luggage as the Navy boat revved its motor and backed away from the pier.

Margaret turned back toward the boat. "No, wait!" she called.

O'Rourke smiled and waved. "Looks like you're pretty well settled in." Crystal blue water swirled around the bow as his boat backed into the bay.

Margaret Mead had arrived at Ta'u.

She followed her greeting party through a meandering village nestled in trees along the bay. Samoan houses had no walls, just a thatched roof held up by poles. Margaret decided the only reason they needed roofs was to protect from the rain that showered, drizzled, fell, sprinkled, or poured four or five times each day.

The luggage haulers stopped in front of the one western style building on the island. A sign read "U.S. Navy." Below that was a faded plaque that said the supply depot was run by Pharmacist's Mate Edward Holt. Behind the supply shack stood a bungalow with wooden walls and broad, screened windows.

They piled her boxes on the doorstep and silently backed away. For a long moment, they lingered in a wide circle watching this new arrival. Margaret again felt the need to do *something.* She bowed and said, "Thank you." Then realized that she had spoken English, but was too frazzled to remember the word in Samoan.

Margaret set up cot and typewriter on the back porch of Edward Holt's bungalow. Holt spent one week a month on Ta'u to run the Navy's one-man supply depot and was the island's only English speaker. The walls of his depot gave Margaret privacy when she typed up her notes and observations each evening.

Margaret arrived as the first anthropologist and first outsider to study the South Pacific cultures. Particularly, Margaret wanted to study Samoan teenage girls to see if they experienced the same rebellious anxiety and turmoil so characteristic of teenagers in America. It had seemed so interesting a study while sitting in her New York apartment. Now she wondered why in the world she had wanted to do it—or *how* she was ever going to do it.

All through the spring semester at Columbia University Margaret had laughed when teachers, friends, and family said she shouldn't go. She had no field experience. She had been an English major as an undergraduate. She lacked a science background. She'd be over 1,000 miles from help. There would be no telephones, no radio, no way to communicate with the outside world. Besides, the area was infested with snakes, wild animals, disease carrying insects, and fierce natives.

Then she had scoffed at their concerns. Now, however . . . "Just calm down," she hissed at herself. "You can do this." The sinking feeling deep in her stomach told her she was no longer convinced.

Margaret had formed only a vague plan to live as one of the native teenagers and observe them as closely as she could. Was it the correct plan? Would her presence change local girls' behavior so much that her observations would lose all validity? Margaret had no idea. Anthropology was still so new; it had no recognized methods of field research.

Margaret stepped out of the bungalow at sunset, hungry and nervous. What should she do for food? A bowl of food already sat waiting for her on one of the outdoor tables. She ate, not knowing what it was, smiling and nodding as all around her solemn brown faces watched her and nodded back. She sat there long into the steamy, buggy night, nibbling on baked fish and letting the musical, rhythmic sound of the Ta'u language wash over her. By the time a quarter moon rose, glistening silver, over the ocean, she decided that she might somehow survive her time here.

Next morning Margaret found a sarong draped over the bungalow doorknob. She wore it instead of her "western safari dress" and found a circle of teenage girls in the shade of a towering tree. She asked if she could join them. They giggled behind their hands.

Margaret gestured that she wanted to sit. Again they giggled but made space for her in the circle before they returned to their sewing and talk. Margaret kicked off her shoes to go barefoot as they did. Again they giggled and continued to sew, but studied her closely out of the corners of their eyes.

Margaret fidgeted, not sure of what to do. She picked up a spare needle and gestured that she'll like to sew. A young girl next to her handed her material and spoke instructions Margaret couldn't understand. Then she backed up the words with precise, flowing gestures.

As Margaret began to sew, the girl nodded. The conversation and giggles continued. Margaret Mead's study had begun.

Margaret dressed in a sarong—just as the Samoans dressed. She walked barefoot with the local teenaged girls. She adopted a Samoan name, Makelita. During the day, she ate with the girls, wove baskets with them, swam with them, bathed with them, carried torches for night fishing with them, danced, wove mats, worked in the sugar cane fields, and joked and giggled with them.

All the while she listened, watched, and wrote in her notebooks. Each night she tried to assess what she had seen that day. What did these girls think? How did they relate to each other, to boys, to their parents? What were their concerns and fears? What were their hopes and dreams? Why did they feel the way they did? What cultural teachings lay behind their thoughts, beliefs, and attitudes? Then late at night, before she drifted off to sleep, Makelita studied the local dialect.

Margaret mapped every house and inhabitant on the island as well as each family's wealth and status. She described the role each girl played within the family and what chores were hers.

She interviewed each girl and adult, asking about the girls and their lives. The girls loved to talk. The adults expected to be paid for information. Within the first month Margaret's interviews cost her 100 envelopes, 200 sheets of paper, dozens of cigarettes, and countless matches, onions, and sewing needles.

Margaret found that these Samoan girls showed no sign of the turmoil, rebellion, and family conflict so common in America. However, they also lacked the drive, ambition, and longing to expand and improve themselves and their lives that characterized American teens. Samoan girls were generally happy and content and had completely accepted their life and their place in the community. But their whole life was laid out for them in this village and would never change.

Margaret watched two of the older girls get married, girls she had come to know. Neither showed the nervous jitters and anxiety of American brides. Neither did they show the joy and exuberance of their American counterparts. Was the Samoan way better? Good? Bad? No. It just was. Margaret's job was to observe and record, not to judge.

Nine months after she arrived, Margaret stood waiting to leave Ta'u as a Navy Inter-Island Shuttle idled up to the same rickety pier. She carried one bag of clothes, one typewriter, and seven boxes of notes, drawings, and observations. Staring back at her from the shade of wide mango trees at the end of the pier were eighty pairs of solemn, inquisitive eyes set in handsome brown Samoan faces. No one spoke.

As a Navy ensign lugged Margaret's boxes onto the tiny launch, Margaret felt flooded with emotion. She was leaving home and going home. She was leaving family and going to family. She was ending her study, and yet just beginning the study. Joy and sorrow surged within her in equal measures.

She raised one hand and waved. "Ta-lo-fa." Eighty faces smiled and waved back. The adventure was over. The work was just beginning.

After Words

Margaret Mead returned to New York and compiled her volumes of notes into a book, *Coming of Age in Samoa*. It was a best-seller then (1926) and is still the most widely read anthropology book in the world. Margaret's studies helped refine and create accepted field research techniques for anthropology. She also did more than any other researcher to document and preserve cultures of South Pacific islands.

* * *

Suggested Topics to Explore

This story deals with the field of anthropology, the islands of Samoa, and Margaret Mead. Here are some starting questions that will help you discuss and research each.

1. What is anthropology? Look the word up in the dictionary, in an encyclopedia, and on the Internet. Unheard of even in the

late 1800s, anthropology is a true twentieth-century science. Early anthropologists had a double burden. They had to *conduct* their studies of other cultures at the same time they groped and struggled to discover *how* to conduct their studies. Research the beginnings of this scientific field in the early twentieth century. How have the field and its methods changed over the years?

2. Where is Samoa? What is it called now? What peoples live there? What is the history of the islands?

3. Research Margaret Mead. Where was she born and raised? How did she become interested in anthropology? Where else did she conduct studies? In what ways did she invent and create the field of anthropology?

For Further Reading About This Story

Cassidy, Robert. *Margaret Mead: A Voice for the Century.* New York: Universe Books, 1993.

Freeman, Derek. *Margaret Mead and Samoa: The Making and Unmaking of an Anthropological Myth.* Cambridge, MA: Harvard University Press, 1983.

Howard, Jane. *Margaret Mead: A Life.* New York: Simon & Schuster, 1994.

Kostmen, Samuel. *Twentieth Century Women of Achievement,* Chapter 7, Margaret Mead. New York: Richard Rosen Press, 1986.

Mead, Margaret. *An Anthropologist at Work.* New York: Avon Books, 1973.

———. *Blackberry Winter: My Earlier Years.* New York: Morrow, 1972. (Autobiography)

———. *Coming of Age in Samoa: A Psychological Study of Primitive Youth for Western Civilization.* New York: American Museum of Natural History, 1928.

Peavy, Linda, and Ursula Smith. *Dreams into Deeds: Nine Women Who Dared.* New York: Charles Scribner's Sons, 1985.

Rice, Edward. *Margaret Mead: A Portrait.* New York: Harper & Row, 1989.

Saunders, Susan. *Margaret Mead: The World was her Family.* New York: Viking Kestrel, 1987.

Stoddard, Hope. *Famous American Women.* New York: Thomas Crowell, 1990.

Ziesk, Erda. *Margaret Mead.* New York: Chelsea House, 1990.

Lise Meitner

A "Splitting" Headache: Physicist
A Science Adventure

For twenty years, Lise Meitner struggled to create new artificial, radioactive elements. Only then did she realize that, while failing, she had discovered the key to the most important energy source the world had yet known—nuclear fission.

A Science Adventure

Forty-four-year-old Lise Meitner peered across the dingy basement laboratory from her workbench. "Is the sample ready, Dr. Hahn?"

Frizzy-haired Otto Hahn nodded. "Close. I have dissolved the granules with a strong acid. Now, if I add the right base, I should be able to precipitate a salt of thorium plus any new transuranic element we have created. . . . Only a few more minutes."

Lise returned to her calculations and, as she as often did, drifted into the singing of a German folk song, this one by Brahms.

Hahn continued, "There. Now to dry and compress the sample and you can start your radioactivity counts."

Five minutes later, Hahn turned off the blower motor and poured the dried grains of radioactive thorium from his drying dish into Lise's hands. "Quickly now!" she ordered. "I need decay rates and beta particle emission rates. We must reach the counter before the sample decays."

"You carry," he answered. "I'll get the door and clear the way."

Lise Meitner and Otto Hahn dashed up the stone steps to ground level on this gray, wintry afternoon in 1932 and sprinted across the Kaiser Wilhelm campus in Berlin, Germany, toward the Physics Institute over half a mile away. Both were in their forties and formally dressed—he in tall, stiff collar and tie, she in floor-length dress with high, lace neck. In her bare hands Lise Meitner cradled a precious sample of their laboratory work—a few grains of a radioactive metal they hoped included a substance heavier than uranium (transuranic). Otto Hahn ran interference, shouting for everyone to get out of their way.

They would have preferred lab space in the Institute building. But Lise was a woman. A musty, poorly equipped basement lab at the edge of campus was the only place a woman was allowed. Besides, there were no bathrooms for women on campus. Lise had to use the facilities in a restaurant down the block.

After the Institute radiation detection equipment completed its work, one of the physics professors sadly shook his head. "I see characteristic emissions of thorium and of a radioactive isotope of barium plus the same kind of intense array of subatomic particles you have brought in your samples before. But I see no evidence of a transuranic element."

The hopeful expressions on Lise's and Otto's faces drooped in an all-too-familiar disappointment. "Are you sure?"

"The profiles exactly match known emission patterns—except for this excessive scatter of subatomic particles." The professor added, "How are your hands?"

"No worse than usual," Lise answered, gently kneading lotion into her reddened and blistered palms. It usually took several hours after each run to the Physics Institute for Lise's hands to be covered with blisters, burns, and open sores that would take weeks to heal. She had found that rubbing lotion into her hands early on minimized the pain. Lise knew that radioactivity somehow caused the burns, but it was not yet known that radiation was anything more than a bothersome irritant.

As part of their study of radioactive elements and radioactivity, Lise and Otto had struggled for years to create atoms heavier than uranium (transuranic elements). Using the crude lab equipment they could afford, they bombarded uranium atoms with free protons. Some would surely hit the nucleus and stick, creating an element heavier than uranium (one with more protons than uranium's ninety-two protons in its nucleus). It never worked.

They had tested their methods with thorium, barium, and other heavy metals. Each performed exactly as expected. *Everything* worked as Lise's physics equations said it should—until they reached uranium, the heaviest known element. When they tried to create a nucleus bigger than uranium (with more than ninety-two protons) it always failed. No one could figure out why.

"Maybe you should give up," the physics professor suggested. "You've tried a hundred times. Maybe it is simply impossible to produce elements heavier than uranium. Maybe there just aren't any."

"There *must* be," Lise snapped. "There is no physical reason why heavier atoms cannot exist. I still intend to create them." Then she went back to rubbing lotion into her blistering and scarred hands.

Late into the evening Meitner and Hahn sat glumly in their basement lab, a dim electric bulb glowing from the ceiling, and analyzed the results of this latest test at the Physics Institute.

"Look here, Dr. Meitner," said Hahn, tapping a pencil on one set of numbers. "These numbers indicate the presence of radium with an atomic number of eighty-eight. But there was no radium in the sample when we left this lab."

"I agree, Dr. Hahn," Lise answered. "But where did the radium come from?"

Lise and Otto had collaborated for almost twenty years in this shabby basement lab but still kept their working relationship very formal and proper. For all these years, they had not called one another by their first names and never socialized outside the laboratory, not even to eat lunch together.

"I see only one possibility," Hahn answered. "When we added protons to uranium, it decayed into radium and must have given off the four extra protons and neutrons as alpha and beta particles."

"And look at these numbers" added Lise tapping her finger at another column of numbers on their table of results. "Higher than expected alpha and beta particles in the emissions counts. That would support your theory, Dr. Hahn."

A long silence followed while each scientist tried to absorb this new idea and decide what it meant.

Finally Lise sighed. "But *why* would uranium decay that way? And what does this mean for our effort to create transuranic elements?"

Otto Hahn was a chemist by training, and he discovered, studied, and chemically purified radioactive elements. Physicist Lise Meitner studied and measured the radiation they gave off. Their equipment was crude and dangerous. The work inched forward at a snail's pace—slow and tedious. They commonly worked with their bare hands in order to complete their assessments before their radioactive materials disintegrated, getting burns that took weeks to heal.

"We must devise a new—and clever—test to find out, Dr. Meitner. A very clever test."

For four months the two scientists struggled to create a way to prove exactly what happened to uranium when it was bombarded with free protons. Finally Otto conceived a plan using nonradioactive barium as a marker to continuously detect and measure the presence of radioactive radium. If uranium decayed into radium, the barium would detect it.

Three more months were consumed with preliminary tests to establish how barium reacted to radioactive radium in the presence of uranium and to remeasure the exact decay rates and decay patterns of radium.

Before they could finish and conduct their actual experiment, Lise had to leave the country to escape the rise of Hitler's Nazi party. In 1938 she fled to Sweden to live with a nephew. There, however, as a single woman, she was unable to obtain any lab space or funding.

Otto Hahn had to conduct their grand experiment alone.

Two weeks after he had completed this test, Lise received a lengthy report describing his failure. He bombarded uranium with a concentrated stream of protons. But he didn't even get radium. He detected only more barium—far more barium than he started with. Bewildered, he begged Lise to help him figure out what had happened. Lise felt bitterly frustrated that she was stuck in Sweden with no facilities and could do nothing to help her colleague.

One week later, Lise and her nephew, Otto Frisch, took a long snowshoe walk through the early winter snows. As they sat on a fallen log gazing at the pastoral snow-covered serenity of the Swedish countryside, a flash image appeared in Lise's mind of atoms tearing themselves apart. The picture was so vivid, so startling, and so strong that she could almost feel the pulsing atomic nuclei and smell the sizzle of each atom as it ripped itself apart in her imagination.

Instantly, she knew that she had just been given their answer. Adding extra protons must have made the uranium nuclei unstable. They had split apart. But into what? Surely, barium—that's what Dr. Hahn had found. But why hadn't he found something else? The uranium had to tear apart into at least two somethings—barium and . . . what? And why didn't Otto detect that other something?

It only took two days of staring at the periodic chart for Lise to come up with a plausible answer. Still, she would need experimental results to be sure. Lise sent a letter to Otto directing him to repeat the experiment but to watch for the presence of a gas—probably krypton, because it had about the right atomic mass. A gas would have dissipated before Otto had a chance to test the sample and detect it. Besides, you only detected a gas if you were looking for one.

Otto's letter returned. Yes, he had found krypton. How could she have possibly known?

As Lise Meitner read Otto's words, a quiet satisfaction washed over her. Finally she understood. No, they had not created transuranic elements. That effort had failed. But they had discovered something that would soon be far more important. They had discovered that when radioactive uranium is bombarded with free protons, its natural decay is both sped up and altered so that each uranium atom splits in two. They created barium and krypton. In the process, immense amounts of energy were released.

After Words

Lise Meitner and Otto Hahn had accidentally discovered nuclear fission—the process of splitting an unstable atom into two, smaller, stable elements. The doorway to nuclear power and the atomic and nuclear bombs was opened. Otto Hahn (because he was a man) was awarded the Nobel Prize for their discovery. In his acceptance speech, Otto gave full credit to his longtime partner, Lise Meitner, the one who really solved the puzzle.

* * *

Suggested Topics to Explore

This story deals with uranium and nuclear fission. Here are starting questions that will help you discuss and research both.

1. What happens in nuclear fission? Does fission happen naturally? How does it create energy? How do we use nuclear fission today?

2. Is uranium the only naturally radioactive element? What are the others? In what ways are they all similar?

3. What is the difference between natural radioactivity and fission?

For Further Reading About This Story

Barron, Rachel. *Lise Meitner: Discoverer of Nuclear Fission.* New York: Franklin Watts, 2000.

Boorse, Henry, and Lloyd Motz. *The Atomic Scientist, A Biographical History.* New York: John Wiley & Sons, 1989.

Grinstein, Louise S., Rose K. Rose, and Miriam H. Rafailovich. *Women in Chemistry and Physics: A Biobibliographic Sourcebook.* Westport, CT: Greenwood Press, 1993.

Kass-Simon, G., and Patricia Farnes (eds.). *Women of Science: Righting the Record.* Bloomington: Indiana University Press, 1990.

McGrayne, Sharon Bertsch. *Nobel Prize Women in Science: Their Lives, Struggles, and Momentous Discoveries.* New York: Carol Publishing Group, A Birch Lane Press Book, 1993.

Sime, Ruth Lewis. *Lise Meitner: A Life in Physics.* Berkeley: University of California Press, 1996.

Stille, Darlene R. *Extraordinary Women Scientists.* Chicago, IL: Children's Press, 1995.

Yount, Lisa. *Twentieth-Century Women Scientists.* New York: Facts on File, 1996.

Cynthia Moss

African Call: Field Biologist
A Science Adventure

Cynthia Moss's whole life—even her idea of who she was—changed in one unexpected moment, a moment that made it impossible to go back to the life she had always known. After that one moment, Cynthia traded her comfortable New York apartment for a hut in the wilds of Africa.

A Science Adventure in Africa

A full moon glowed like a miniature sun as twenty-six-year-old Cynthia Moss—unable to sleep—gazed out the plane's window. Shadows fell across her arms and tray table, hard and crisp as noontime. Cynthia was in the third hour of her seven-hour overnight flight from New York to Cairo on this April 12, 1967, when nagging doubts buzzed across her mind and kept her from peaceful sleep.

She had given up her prime New York City apartment and quit her job . . . for what? For a one-month trip to Africa? How could one trip be worth it?

With one finger Cynthia twirled ringlets of her permed golden hair, the color of new straw in bright sunshine, as she argued with herself. No, this was far more than just a trip. She *had* to come. She had to . . . find something. But what?

Her practical side seemed to scold her. She was a reporter for *Newsweek* with three years' experience. How could she give that up? Sure, the magazine had set up a couple of interviews for her in Africa. But would there be anything to come home to? She had sunk her savings, her career, her *life* into this trip. She loved living in the city. She loved to ride horses on groomed bridal paths and stop for high tea. Why go to Africa?

It didn't matter. She *had* to go. Cynthia sighed and muttered, "It started with these letters." She fished a thin ribbon-wrapped packet of letters out of her carry-on backpack and tapped them on her tray table. A college friend had toured Africa the previous summer and had written graphic descriptions of tribal villages, of waving Savannah grass stretching as far as the eye could see as a shimmering, blood-red sun crept over the horizon, and of noisy marketplaces teaming with tantalizing rich and pungent smells and tastes.

The letters had kindled a deep longing in Moss—a *need* to make this trip. Logic and reason hadn't mattered. Carol Merchant, her best friend, had spent an entire evening showing Cynthia that every disease in her worst nightmares hung out in Africa. The food was lousy—and most likely rancid and worm infested. She wouldn't be able to communicate or read signs. It was hot, sticky and she'd be forever swatting flies and mosquitoes. Carol had arched her eyebrows and pointed a finger at Cynthia. "Wilderness, my friend, is overrated."

Cynthia agonized for the last two hours of her flight. Had she made a whopper of a mistake? What if there wasn't anything here for her to find?

Cynthia flew first to Cairo, Egypt. She was fascinated by the unfamiliar sounds of the music, the calls to prayer from towering minarets, the jingling bells of street water sellers, the pyramids and other ancient works. But still she felt an overpowering tug pulling her south, as if a string were attached to her heart reminding her that Cairo was not what she came here to find.

Cynthia completed her first interview with a husband and wife team of archeologists from a university in North Carolina, who were excavating a new site along the lower Nile. The couple slowly inched their way down through 4,000 years of history, hoping to stumble on some major revelation.

It took Cynthia only three days to write the article and wire it off to New York. Already she itched to head south from Cairo.

Moss hopped a plane to Nairobi, Kenya, the nearest city to her second interview. It felt good—correct—to have shifted south. Excitement and anticipation built in Cynthia as if every corner, every step held the promise of grand discovery.

On first walking the streets of this ancient city, Cynthia was surprised—no, actually alarmed—at the feeling of familiarity that washed over her. She almost seemed to know where to turn and what she'd find around each new corner. It was as if she had grown up in this African city—even though she had never set foot within 5,000 miles of it before.

She wrote to family and friends that "within a week of getting there, I had this overwhelming sense that I had come home . . . that this was where I belonged."

Foods she had never touched and could not identify tasted familiar. Pungent smells of unknown spices from shops along the market squares reminded her of her fondest childhood memories—a childhood spent in suburban Connecticut where baking apples were the strongest kitchen smell.

The flat-roofed and whitewashed architecture seemed more familiar than the peaked-roof New England clapboard houses in which she had grown up. Winding, narrow alleyways felt more familiar than Fifth Avenue in New York.

But still the unsettling tug on her heart pulled her on, as if even this brand new place that felt like home wasn't what she came to find.

From Nairobi, Cynthia took a bus to a small city where *Newsweek* had arranged for her to interview British zoologist Iain Douglas-Hamilton, who was conducting a pioneering ecology study of the region. She arrived a day and a half early and decided to explore. She hired a driver who promised to guide her to the sights of the region. "What would ma'am like to see?"

Gazing vaguely out the window, Cynthia answered, "I'm not sure . . ."

"Want to see animals, ma'am?"

"Animals?"

"*Big* game. I know where to look. This is not the best season. Better during or just after the rains. But I know a spot."

Cynthia offered a shrug and a slight nod.

Two hours later the guide parked just inside Kenya's Lake Manyara National Park. "We walk from here, ma'am. There is a watering hole . . ."

Flies buzzed in the afternoon heat as Cynthia squatted uncomfortably in the sloping grass near a small pool of brown mud, the last remnants of a rainy season watering hole. She felt the bite of one of the flies and swatted it away, wondering, as she squinted through the shimmering waves of heat, what she was doing here. This Africa was uncomfortably close to the picture Carol had painted back in New York. What could be here worth finding?

Then Cynthia heard a snort from across the watering hole that sounded like a long, weary sigh. She heard the rustling of dry grass being brushed aside. She felt the vibrations of heavy footsteps. Something tightened inside of her. Her heart raced and breathing came in shallow, expectant gasps.

Two towering female elephants shuffled leisurely out of the tall brush toward her. Their lumbering bodies swayed rhythmically with each step. A layer of dirt and dust had painted much of their gray skin a light brown. Their trunks lolled left and right as if groping for some relief. Their ears were held out, like radar antennas, scanning for the first blip of trouble.

All that separated these majestic mammoths from Cynthia Moss was fifteen feet of grass and brush and twenty feet of mud and brown puddles. The guide whispered, "Ma'am should crawl back now, very slowly. We are too close."

Instead, Cynthia stood. There was no thinking, no analysis. She simply did what her feelings told her to do.

"Duck back down, ma'am! Very dangerous. If they decide to charge. . . . "

Cynthia didn't respond to her guide. Instead, she walked forward, toward these largest of land mammals.

"I will not be responsible," hissed her guide as he scurried back through the brush.

As if transfixed, she held out her empty hand and sloshed forward through the muddy water. Both elephants paused to assess and watch this intruder.

One of the elephants snorted and extended its dust-covered trunk toward Cynthia. Fingers touched the bristly hairs at the tip of a trunk. The trunk tip curled around her hand, exploring this new smell and feel.

The contact lasted only a moment. The elephant returned to her work of searching the stagnant pools for drinkable water. But the feel of that elephant's gentle touch lingered in Cynthia's mind and fingers for hours.

Cynthia stood, ankle deep in muddy water, for twenty minutes after the elephants had shuffled away out of sight through the tall brush and trees. She alternately gazed after the elephants and then down at her hand.

What did that elephant think when they touched? It had seemed to nod—or was it just her imagination? Had it reached out specifically to her, or would it have done that with anyone?

Before she turned and waded back into the grass, Cynthia knew that this was the moment, the one event, she had come to Africa to find. It felt as if elephants had always been the central focus of her life. She had simply never noticed it before.

This brief but electric encounter with a wild elephant instantly rewrote who Cynthia thought she was and what she wanted to be. At a very deep level, Moss "became completely hooked on elephants." She had found what she came searching for.

In her resignation letter to *Newsweek,* Cynthia wrote that she "had never felt that kind of passionate attachment and commitment before in my life." She added that "elephants are such impressive, remarkable, and complex creatures that I instantly wanted to devote my life to studying them."

The next day, Cynthia turned her planned interview with British zoologist Iain Douglas-Hamilton into a job interview. When he offered her a research assistant position at his camp, she jumped at the opportunity without considering what effect this decision would have on her life or writing career.

After Words

Cynthia Moss never returned to the United States. She has studied elephants in the wild for over thirty years. Documenting the life, behavior, and social structure of any species requires years of dedicated, in-depth, onsite, careful, and systematic observation. She was the first to document elephant social structure, relationships, and interactions. She catalogued elephant emotional responses and personality traits. She was the first to build a concrete picture of elephant life and society. Cynthia Moss not only performed this daunting task with exceptional skill, she also helped redefine the standard methodology for conducting long-term field studies.

Moss has also acted as an advocate for the African elephants. She successfully lobbied for national and international laws protecting elephants and for a moratorium in the commercial trade of ivory. Her work has been described as an "irreplaceable" and "invaluable" contribution to our understanding of elephants and elephant society.

* * *

Suggested Topics to Explore

This story deals with elephants and field biology. Here are starting questions that will help you discuss and research both.

1. Research elephants. How many are there still in the wild? How many are in captivity? Where are they? Research elephant social structure and organization. Do elephant societies and organization resemble human social structure? Do they resemble the social structure of any of the great ape species?

2. Research Cynthia Moss. How did she get started in her work? What is she doing now? How has she changed scientific thinking about elephants and other large game species?

3. Besides Cynthia Moss, how many other women scientists are working in the field on long-term biological and ecological studies? See how many you can find. Why do you think so many women are working in this particular aspect of science?

For Further Reading About This Story

Dear, Pamela (ed.) *Contemporary Authors,* vol 12. Detroit: Gale Research, 1995.

DiSilvestro, Roger. *The African Elephant: Twilight of Eden.* New York: John Wiley & Sons, 1991.

Moritz, Charles (ed.) *Current Biography Yearbook,* 1993. New York: H. W. Wilson, 1994.

Moss, Cynthia. *Elephant Memories.* New York: Houghton, 1988.

———. *Portraits in the Wild: Behavioral Studies of East African Elephants.* New York: Houghton, 1975.

Pringle, Lawrence. *Elephant Woman.* New York: Atheneum Books for Young Readers, 1997.

Sukumar, Rama. *Elephant Days and Nights.* New York: Oxford University Press, 1994.

Ruth Patrick

River Rescue: River Ecologist
A Science Adventure (Limnologist)

Sometimes being a scientist means standing up for your beliefs—no matter what. When a corporate lawyer brought the police to arrest Ruth Patrick, she had to do some fast thinking—and some fast talking.

A Science Adventure on a New York River

Adjusting her slouched, wide-brimmed hat, fifty-eight-year-old Ruth Patrick slid down the embankment to a small gravel bar at the edge of the sluggish Canisteo River in upstate New York, just below the town of Hornell. She wore rubber hip boots over green pedal pushers with cruddy unlaced tennies underneath. Behind her, five other scientists piled out of the two vans that the team had driven along the dirt road that lined this west shore of the winding river. The men stretched and began to unload nets, rakes, wooden stakes, sample jars, an inflatable rubber boat, and other equipment they would need for this day's work.

This was the third day of the team's onsite survey. Small red flags they had planted along the bank on their first day marked the end of their quarter-mile-long survey section.

The date was May 10, 1950. The site Mrs. Patrick had chosen for this study lay half a mile below the Mohegan paper mill and the William Smith and Company clothes factory that made linen shirts and dresses. Both plants dumped their manufacturing waste directly into the river.

Ruth's five-man team assembled around her on the tiny sand and gravel spit with their array of equipment. Ruth said, "We've finished the physical survey and bottom profile. We've measured river flow and water velocity. Today I want water samples for algae and plankton studies. We'll take them at depths of one, five, and ten feet along center channel and near both banks every fifty yards. I'll also use a fine mesh net to collect plankton. Ben, you and Phil collect whatever samples you need for water chemistry analysis."

George Sanders, team ichthyologist, asked, "Do you think the paper plant will try to stop us again today?" The plant's lawyer had threatened legal action if the scientists did or said anything to defame the paper plant.

Ruth clenched her jaw. "Our work could *help* them. They should *support* us, not fight us."

In their rubber hip waders and stained and faded shirts, Ruth's team looked more like a group of fishermen playing hooky from work than a dedicated team of expert scientists on the hunt for whatever ailed this New York river.

George Sanders, by far the tallest member of the team, waded his way upstream carrying what looked like a posthole digger. Every few yards he stopped and pounded it down into the muddy bottom to collect a bottom core sample. Each he emptied into its own small glass jar. These he labeled with a grease pencil stored in a net bag slung over his shoulder.

Later he would sift, sort, and count the contents, looking for worms, snails, clams, and other bottom dwellers to see if this river had a healthy and normal population of critters living along and under its bed. He adjusted his wide-brimmed straw hat and called back over his shoulder. "Gonna get hot this afternoon."

Ben Hackman, short, muscular lead chemist, chuckled and called back, "If that lawyer comes back, it'll heat up real fast." Then he nodded toward Ruth. "You want the standard chemistry package today?"

"This river is in trouble. I want everything: oxygen, nutrient, pH, ammonia, metals, petroleum, and other pollutants. And I want chemical tags for every pollutant so we can track it back to a source."

Ben nodded again and clambered back up the bank to retrieve an extra case of chemicals he'd need for the additional on-site analysis. "I'll do what I can here. But some of that analysis will have to wait for the lab tonight." His bright yellow Hawaiian shirt stood out in gaudy contrast to the more traditional New England garb of the rest of the team.

Recently plowed farm fields spread out from this western side of the river beyond the dirt road and a narrow strip of bushes and trees that overhung the river. The river water, itself, flowed by more green than blue with considerable litter of floating leaves and puffballs of yellow foam. A thin band of woods, with a housing development just beyond, crowded the far bank of the river. Upstream from the survey sight a highway bridge and its rumbling traffic crossed the river and marked the edge of Hornell.

The sound of chirping birds and crickets blended with the steady rumble of traffic. Ruth clapped her hands, "Let's get to work! We have a busy day ahead of us."

Ruth led the rest of the team in laying out a grid pattern on the river. Ruth and one man started on the near shore. The other two rode the team's skiff across to the other side. Each pair carried a ten-yard chain and would work their way along the bank marking out a grid by tying colored ribbons or pounded brightly numbered metal stakes into the riverbank every ten yards. Corresponding red dots and numbers were already marked on their river maps. Every sample would be tagged according to these grid markers.

Glancing up form the folding table he was using to set up his chem lab, Ben Hackman groaned, "Uh-oh." Ruth peered up through the thick overgrowth and muttered, "Drat!"

A caravan of two police cars bounced along the dirt road, lights flashing, dust cloud billowing behind. Both cars stopped behind Ruth's vans. As soon as the swirling dust drifted away, a trim, middle-aged police lieutenant stepped from the lead car and leaned against his door as he watched Ruth's team fan out along the river below. He looked amused by the sight of the scientists slogging through the mud and river shallows.

A young deputy and a short, scowling man in a double-breasted suit and carrying a brief case emerged from the second car.

"This is the group, lieutenant. I want them evicted from this site," called the suited man. "And arrest them if they resist."

The lieutenant sighed and shouted, "Is one of you Ruth Patrick?"

Ruth waded back onto the gravel shoal and folded her arms over her chest. "That's me." Her team stopped their work to silently watch. The two in the skiff steered back toward the near shore. George Sanders sloshed his way back against the current to listen. Ben Hackman slammed his chemistry cases shut and rested his fists on his hips, as if daring anyone to touch his equipment.

"I have a complaint and order for you to cease your activity and vacate this river."

"What complaint?" demanded Ruth.

"Trespassing. The action was filed by the Mohegan Paper Company."

Ruth laughed and shook her head.

"This is no laughing matter, ma'am," said the cop.

The lawyer pursed his lips and smugly tapped his briefcase. "I have the papers right here."

Ruth explained, "When I was a teenager, my mother threatened to disown me if any of her friends saw me in hip boots. She thought it unladylike. Imagine her dismay if she knew I was being arrested wearing them."

To the deep chug-chug of his aging tractor, a farmer edged out of the field to see what the commotion was. He leaned over the tractor's steering wheel. "Morning Earl. Trouble?"

"Morning, Stewart," answered the lieutenant. "Nothing worth watching here."

The farmer pointed at Ruth's team. "I've been watchin' this bunch, Earl, and I say they're up to somethin' fishy. Yesterday they were chasin' May flies. Chasin' *after* 'em, for goodness sakes! I said if they wanted some sketters, they should just wait, and they said 'Thanks' like I'd been serious. One of 'em was scoopin' mud and sayin', 'Oh, boy! Good stuff.'"

Ruth smiled and shrugged. "Insects are an important part of a river's ecology—even those that fly above it."

The farmer pointed a finger at the lieutenant. "You gotta' find out what they're *really* doin' here, Earl. It's your duty."

The lieutenant sighed. "Thank you, Stewart. You get the rest of your beans in, and let me do my job."

The farmer shrugged as if to say, "I warned you."

The lawyer pointed a finger at Ruth. "I am Edward Coleman, attorney for the Mohegan Paper Company. Explain your presence here. You are trespassing."

"I'm director of the Limnology Department of the Academy of Natural Sciences in Philadelphia. The State of New York has contracted with us to study the ecological health of a number of their rivers—including the Canisteo."

The lieutenant rubbed his cheek. "The state, eh? No one told me anything about it." He scratched his cheek again. "Why study a river? Whatever happens in the water here today will wash down stream tomorrow."

"Not so," answered Ruth. "Water quality and aquatic life are surprisingly steady. We study and sample the river so that it will tell us what's wrong."

Both the lieutenant and his young deputy took a step toward the bank and stared at the flowing water with greater interest. "You saying something's *wrong* with the river?" The head cop frowned and turned toward the farmer. "You noticed anything, Stewart?"

"Don't you point any fingers at me, Earl Copeland. I'm just a farmer."

"Agricultural fertilizers are one of the top sources of river pollution," Ruth answered.

"Fertilizer is *good,*" insisted the farmer. "It makes my crops grow."

Ruth explained, "In a river, the nutrients in fertilizer makes harmful plankton—algae—grow in vast blooms. They choke out other plants, suck out the river's oxygen, and strangle fish." She turned to one of her team members, "George, grab my microscope." She turned back to the lieutenant. "I'll show you a diatom—one of the kind that blooms from agricultural waste."

George set up Ruth's 100-power microscope on the hood of their lead van. She scooped a jar of river water and held it up to the sunlight. "Should be plenty in here."

She used an eyedropper to squeeze a single drop on a glass slide and pushed it into the metal clamps of the microscope. Squinting through the eyepiece, she shifted the slide and adjusted the focus. Then she stepped back. "There, a diatom in the center left."

First the lieutenant and then the lawyer gazed at Ruth's diatom. "Looks like Wheat Chex® made out of glass."

"That's silica. Fertilizers help those diatoms grow."

"And these pollutants are caused by agriculture?" asked the lieutenant.

Ruth answered, "When enough nitrogen and phosphorous nutrients reach the river, diatoms bloom by the billions. That severely stresses the river chemistry and ecosystem."

Coleman smugly folded his arms. "So you agree that the harm to the river has nothing to do with the Mohegan Paper Company, Mrs. Patrick?"

Ruth scoffed, "Certainly not. Your industrial waste adds further stress on the river. Municipalities add yet more. The combination is deadly to river life."

The lieutenant rested one hand on his gun holster. "'Deadly' is a very strong word, Dr. Patrick."

Ben Hackman said, "Ohio's Cuyahoga River was so polluted it caught fire a couple years back."

"A river caught fire?" repeated the lieutenant.

George Sanders added, "River pilots have a saying to describe many Midwestern rivers: 'Too thin to cultivate; too thick to navigate.'"

Ruth concluded, "There are already some American rivers with no fish and water humans can't drink. Is that what you want for the Canisteo?"

Coleman insisted, "You can't prove any harm has been caused by my paper company. The pollutants could have come from anywhere."

Ruth smiled, "Tell him, Ben."

Chemist Ben Hackman counted off his points on his fingers, "We can tell how long pollutants have been in the water. We can sample water above and below your plant. We can look for unique chemical compounds and combinations of compounds that trace back to your specific plant. Oh, we can nail a good share of the problems here and probably for twenty miles downstream on your doorstep, Mr. Coleman."

Mr. Coleman said, "We can't shut the plant down. Society needs paper."

Ruth shrugged. "We wouldn't ask you to. You just need to reduce the flow to a level the river can safely handle. Science and technology created farmers' fertilizers and your industrial waste as well as virtually all other problems in this river. Why not use that same science and technology to repair the damage?"

Coleman fidgeted, shifting his briefcase from hand to hand. "We get first look at your results?"

The science team visibly relaxed. Ruth had won another argument. Their work would continue. Ruth simply nodded. "Yes, and you'll receive our suggestions on how to most economically minimize your contribution to the stresses on this river. Attack the problem now and you'll save bad publicity as well as money."

Ruth turned to her team. "I think we can continue our work, now." Then she glanced back at Mr. Coleman and the lieutenant and raised her eyebrows to see if they would object. "Would you like to stay and watch?"

The cop shook his head. "No thanks, Mrs. Patrick. I'm due back in town."

Mr. Coleman settled onto the bank. "I *will* stay. I plan to watch very carefully, so I can fully understand your results and be sure they are reliable." Then he asked, "Why do you need so many people?"

"Each is a specialist in a discipline we need to address," answered Ruth. "Chemists to study the water itself. An engineer to address river hydrology and river contour. Bacteriologists to study microscopic organisms. I study plankton and algae. Zoologists to study invertebrates (clams, snails, etc.). An ichthyologist to study fish." Ruth shrugged and smiled. "A river is really a very complicated environment."

The lieutenant turned off his engine and stepped out of his car. "Did you say you were going to catch some fish?"

Ruth nodded. "Fish are at the top of the river food chain. Many pollutants concentrate there. We will have to study the fish in this section of river."

"Do you have a fishing license?"

"But we won't kill or keep the fish."

The lieutenant smiled. He had finally found a violation. "You need a valid state fishing license to *catch* the fish. It doesn't matter what you do with them."

Ruth sighed and rolled her eyes. "Yes, officer. We will get a fishing license."

"Today."

"Yes, officer, today."

The two police cars spun around and started back to town. The farmer shook his head and ground his tractor's gears as he turned back for his field. Ruth Patrick and her team settled back into their adventure of building a picture of the health of the Canisteo River.

After Words

Ruth Patrick examined over examined 900 river sections worldwide during her thirty-year career and became an international leader in the effort to use modern technology to protect rivers and minimize waste dumping. She was a founding pioneer in the struggle to preserve and protest America's freshwater resources.

* * *

Suggested Topics to Explore

This story deals with river ecology and river pollution. Here are some starting questions that will help you discuss and research both.

1. What are the major elements in a healthy river ecosystem? Should those major parts (or niches) be in every river and stream? Research river ecology and see how much variation you can find in the structure of healthy river ecosystems.

2. What are the major sources of river pollution? What is the difference between "point" and "non-point" sources of pollution? Research a river near you and try to identify the major sources of pollution that enter that river.

3. What do pollutants do when they enter a river? How do they harm the ecosystem? Try to identify the major pollutants that enter U.S. rivers and research the effects they have once they are in a river ecosystem.

For Further Reading About This Story

Cole, Gerald. *Textbook of Limnology.* Los Angeles, CA: Waveland Press, 1994.

Doland, Edward. *Our Poisonous Water.* Sarasota, FL: Cobblehill Books, 1997.

Emberlin, Diane. *Contributions of Women Science.* Minneapolis, MN: Dillon Press, 1992.

Gay, Kathlyn. *Water Pollution.* New York: Franklin Watts, 1990.

Goldman, Linda. *Cleaning Up Our Waters.* Danbury, CT: Children's Press, 1994.

Hoff, Mary. *Rivers and Lakes.* New York: Lerner, 1991.

McKeever, Susan. *Fresh Water Life.* San Diego, CA: Thunder Bay Press, 1995.

Pringle, Lawrence. *Rivers and Lakes.* New York: Time-Life Books, 1989.

Usinger, Robert. *The Life in Rivers and Streams.* New York: McGraw-Hill, 1990.

Candace Pert

Brain Pain:
A Science Adventure

Brain Chemist

It might not appeal to you—scooping out and grinding up mouse brains as a normal part of your everyday job. But that's what Candace Pert did—for almost a year—to discover important breakthroughs about human brains and pain relief.

A Science Adventure in the Chemistry Lab

Candace Pert, a twenty-five-year-old graduate student, stood, arms angrily folded, in her Johns Hopkins University chemistry lab and glared at the page of calculations that showed the results of her experiment. Outside, dull gray clouds poured a fresh round of sleet over the dirty slush that lined Baltimore streets in this February of 1972.

Why didn't the experiment work? What had she done wrong? Inklings of self-doubt crept into her mind. Maybe it *was* true that she was hopelessly sloppy with her lab work. Maybe she wasn't fit for science. In her undergraduate days she had wanted to be a fashion magazine editor. After graduation she had become a cocktail waitress, and then a mother. Only recently had her interests turned to science, and that partly because her husband (who now served in the army) had received a science degree.

But science had come to excite Candace, especially the study of chemical compounds (peptides) that let the brain and body communicate. She had pulled every string she could find in order to land an assignment to this lab and to be allowed to take courses at Johns Hopkins toward a Ph.D. in chemistry.

However, if she failed at her first significant lab assignment, what science future could she possibly have? The pressure was on. It was time to prove herself or slide quietly out of science.

But so far, everything she had tried had failed. Ten hours a day in the lab didn't seem to be enough to find success.

Everyone knew that terrible pain anywhere in the body was almost instantly replaced by a rush of euphoric bliss when a person was given an opium based (opiate) drug—morphine, codeine, Demerol, and so on. But how did that happen? The injury still existed. The pain still existed. But the drug made the brain record a different sensation. These drugs somehow penetrated into the brain with amazing speed and effectiveness.

Candace and Dr. Snyder, the chemistry lab director at Johns Hopkins, suspected that brain cells had specific receptor molecules designed to catch and hold opiates. Opiates fit into these receptor molecules like a hand fits into a glove, or like a key fits into a lock.

Most scientists disagreed. Why should the body create a special receptor for an outside drug? Nature certainly couldn't have *planned* for people to use opium and heroin. In 1972, it was still a grand and important mystery.

Dr. Snyder had given Candace the job of proving that specific opiate receptors *did* exist in brain cells.

Candace's experiment plan was simple enough. (Candace Pert and Dr. Snyder both liked simple experiments that were "quick and dirty." You do it and—bam!—you get results.) Candace killed a lab mouse, removed its brain, and "homogenized" the brain tissue in a fancy, medical food mixer into a gray, sludgy "milk shake."

Candace mixed this sludge with an opiate drug that had been made radioactive. The radioactive tracer would make it possible to detect any opiate that stuck to individual brain cells. The process was slow and awkward because the mixing dish had to be locked behind a barrier wall to protect Candace from exposure to radioactivity. Candace used remote pincers to stir, rinse, and maneuver her glass dishes and delicate tissues.

Candace then washed the "mouse brain soup" with water to rinse off all unattached opiates. The remaining sludge was poured onto a photographic plate and exposed to an eight by ten inch photo negative. The resulting print showed Candace how many opiates stuck to mouse brain cells.

There was one problem. Opiates stuck in two ways. Some attached to receptor molecules. (This was called specific binding, what Candace was assigned to find.) Some opiates, however, just stuck randomly to brain cells as they would with any cells or tissue (nonspecific binding). Candace had to separate the two in order to prove that receptor cells exist.

Luckily, Candace found an article describing the mirror form of opiates—a molecule that looks identical to the opiate but is flip-flopped like a mirror image, like right-hand and left-hand gloves. Only left-handed opiates relieved pain. Only left-handed opiates entered and affected the brain. If Candace was correct, left-handed opiates worked because only they fit into brain receptor cells.

Having conducted the experiment with normal, left-handed, opiates, Candace repeated the experiment with a right-handed opiate. The same amount of right-handed opiate should randomly stick (nonspecific binding) to mouse brain cells that stuck in the left-handed experiment. But *no* right-handed opiate should bind with brain receptor cells. Thus, more radioactive opiates should show up in photos of her left-handed experiment than in her right-handed experiment. The difference would measure how much left-handed opiate specifically bound with receptor cells.

Simple. Except it didn't work.

Candace measured virtually no difference between left- and right-handed experiments. Something was wrong. Snyder, her husband, and her friends all pressured her to find an answer fast or give up.

Candace struggled to find ways to improve the experiment. She slowed her work down and took extra care—especially since she worked with such tiny quantities of material. Each experiment was run with less than a teaspoon of "mouse brains."

She decided that washing created too big a mess and introduced errors. So she reduced the wash water to one tablespoon. Results became more consistent.

Then she switched tracers to a more strongly radioactive drug called dihydromorphine. Results were now easier to count with a scintillation meter. However, to her dismay, Candace found that virtually no dihydromorphine remained in the soup after each experiment. It took four weeks of research to find out that the room lights in the lab broke down dihydromorphine and made it useless. She had to start all over again.

Finally, she learned to let the mixture stand for fifteen minutes at normal "mouse" temperature and to then chill it almost to freezing before washing. She learned to rinse the soup in a partial vacuum. Each change helped, but Candace still couldn't prove that opiates locked into special brain cell receptors.

After nine months of frustrated struggle, Candace happened to read a paper someone had left on a table in the university library. It described opiate "antagonists"—drugs that quickly reversed the effects of opiates—and how they could bring heroine overdose cases back from near death. The paper also described research with monkeys showing that these antagonists always counteracted and overrode the effects of an opiate.

To Candace this meant that opiate antagonists latched onto the same receptor keyholes, but did it better. Maybe she'd have more luck finding the receptors using antagonists than actual opiates.

After scrounging some naloxone (the antagonist used in the monkey research) from an army lab, Candace sent it off to be irradiated (made radioactive).

On September 22, 1972, Candace Pert added a small amount of this drug to a fresh batch of mouse brains. As she prepared to make her scintillation meter counts, she thought, "Either an experiment works or it doesn't. If this one flops, I quit."

But this one worked. The scintillation meter pegged off the charts. Massive amounts of her left-handed opiate antagonist had locked onto brain cells. Candace had finally succeeded.

After Words

After a raucous and jubilant celebration, both Candace and Dr. Snyder knew that their work was just beginning. They would have to test and retest. They would have to test rat, monkey, and guinea pig brains. They would have to isolate different parts of the brain for testing. They would have to test different kinds of tissues.

For Candace Pert, the initial hunt was successfully over. But the adventure was just beginning. Her research led to a better understanding of the human brain and a new generation of improved synthetic pain drug.

* * *

Suggested Topics to Explore

This story deals with brain chemistry and endorphins. Here are starting questions that will help you discuss and research both.

1. Do you think it's acceptable to use (and kill) lab animals as part of doing essential research to save human lives? What would it be all right for scientists to kill as part of their research? A bacteria? a worm? an ant? an elephant? a human?

When and why would it be acceptable to kill some species but not others?

2. Why do you think Candace Pert used mouse brains for her research—rather than brain tissue form some other type of animal?

3. How can researchers learn about the human brain—about the function of different parts of the brain, about how each part works?

For Further Reading About This Story

Arnold, Caroline. *Pain: What Is It?* New York: Morrow Junior Books, 1991.

Franklin, Jon. *Molecules of the Mind.* New York: Atheneum Books for Young Readers, 1987.

Kingdon, Ruth. *Handbook for Pain Management.* New York: Saunders, 1998.

Olilive, Marilyn. *Women in Science.* Cambridge, MA: MIT Press, 1986.

Pert, Candace. *Molecules of Emotion.* New York: Scribners, 1997.

Posner, Michael. *Images of the Mind.* New York: Scientific American Library, 1997.

Yount, Lisa. *Contemporary Women Scientists.* New York: Facts on File, 1994.

Anna Roosevelt

"Point" of Fact: Archeologist
A Science Adventure

Imagine hacking through the Amazon rain forest to make your first dive in a muddy, piranha-infested river—just to authenticate the age of a spear point. That's what archeologist Anna Roosevelt did. Why? Because she knew that if she were right, that one spear point would disprove the most basic scientific theory of how humans migrated into and through the Americas.

A Science Adventure in the Amazon Jungle

A ceiling fan squeaked as the blades sluggishly stirred thick equatorial air. Sweat trickled down the faces and necks of Anna Roosevelt and C. Vance Haynes as they argued in this third floor university office in the Brazilian port city of Belem. Outside the window this muggy July afternoon in 1999 a giant mango tree stood in full and fragrant bloom.

Trim, fifty-five-year-old Anna Roosevelt scowled as she held a seven and one-half inch stone spear point. "This Pedra Pintada point is completely different from Clovis points. See here? It's broader at the base—more triangular—and it has a barbed base. Suitable for fishing large river manatees, dolphins, and fish, but not for hunting."

Anna, whose cropped black hair had turned prematurely silver-gray, was considered a renegade archeologist because she consistently bucked the popular views of human migration into and through the Western hemisphere.

Dr. C. Vance Haynes of the University of Arizona dabbed his neck with a handkerchief and squinted as he took his turn holding the Pedra Pintada spear point against the window light. "Hmm. I'd say this spear point is nothing more than an adaptation from the Clovis points and not at all an indicator of a separate culture."

Famed Clovis spear points (first found in Clovis, New Mexico) had been dated as old as 11,500 years and were used as evidence to support the prevailing theory that humans migrated into North America from Asia around 13,000 years ago, and then migrated south through North, Central, and South America. Clovis points were used to "prove" the speed and direction of that migration from north to south. Now Anna was challenging that theory.

Anna snatched back her spear point. "This spear point dates from *13,000* years ago! It's *older* than any Clovis points. It can't be a migratory adaptation. The South American culture was here *first.*" She chortled and added, "It's more likely that this culture migrated *north* to Clovis."

"Preposterous!" snorted Dr. Haynes. He tapped out his straight pipe and lit a fresh bowl. Tobacco smoke curled toward the fan. "Look at your data. You only have one spear point found by a gold miner while exploring an undisclosed, uncharted underwater site. You'll look like a fool if you try to publish this. You don't have enough data to prove anything."

"Then I'll get it."

Dr. Haynes gave a short laugh. "Fly off into your jungle, Anna. But I doubt you'll find anything. Everybody *knows* migration occurred from North to South in the Americas."

One week later, Anna, two junior archeologists from the Belem museum (one a linguist trained in many of the Amazon native dialects), and Carlos Zajalla, a scuba instructor, flew due west five hundred miles to the river town of Santarem. There they chartered a smaller, twin-engine propeller plane. With her team, their equipment, and a pilot stuffed inside, Anna guided this plane three hundred miles south to the dirt runways of Novo Progresso, a mining and logging town not even listed on most maps. A bush pilot shuttled the team and equipment the last hundred miles from there to the village of Castelo dos Sonhos ("Castle of Dreams").

The trip to this remote village—no more than a collection of shacks—that was buried back in the thick undergrowth of the jungle, had taken two full days of slow, bumpy flying. During the flight Carlos asked, "Do you have diving charts on the lake we will explore?"

Anna laughed, "I don't even know where the lake is. All I have is the name of the miner who does."

"What are we diving for? Treasure? Artifacts?"

"Just for data," Anna answered. Carlos looked puzzled by her answer, so she explained. "I need to find the spot where a spear point was found, so I can prove how old it is."

In Castelo dos Sonhos Anna's interpreter found directions to the house of seventy-five-year-old miner Waldemar Caitano, retired because of a heart condition, who had found the spear point fifteen years before and sold it to a museum. It took three hours (and twice the cash Anna had planned to spend) to persuade Waldemar to reveal his secret spot.

When Anna unfolded a map, Waldemar laughed. "No, he couldn't locate the spot on a map because there weren't any accurate maps of this part of the jungle." Besides he hadn't had a map when he found the place. But—even though it had been more than a decade since he had explored that region—he believed that he could find it if he went with them.

For three days, the team drifted down a tributary of the Xingu River in two rented boats as Waldemar struggled to find familiar landmarks. The current was sluggish. Progress was frustratingly slow. Anna was constantly tempted to fire up the boat's engines. But she knew she needed to save every drop of fuel they had to run the dive air compressor and to power the boats back upstream on the return.

The jungle canopy stretched in layers 150 feet over their heads. Unseen roars, chatters, and howls crowded close along the river-bank. The pungent smell of the forest lay like a rich and fragrant blanket over the twisting waterway.

The small team spent their days steering—and often using long poles to push—the boat away from and off of shoals, rocks, and the thick undergrowth draping over the riverbank. They worked to the steady rhythm of hand slaps as these visiting humans struggled to defend themselves from the clouds of biting flies and mosquitoes that hovered over the river.

The first night, the team saw two points of orange light gliding along the river—the glowing eyes of a small Brazilian crocodile. Two guards kept a nervous watch all night.

For the next two days the river ran shallow, strewn with jagged rocks jumping at every splash and gurgle in the river. Progress was agonizingly slow and difficult. Twice the team had to hop into the river and drag one of the boats off a sand bar.

"Are there piranhas?" asked the interpreter, hesitating before he slipped a foot over the side.

Waldemar just shrugged and chuckled.

The second time a boat snagged on a sandbar, it took almost two hours to free it. They made less than twenty miles progress that whole day.

Anna had brought no radio or cell phone. They were far too remote to get a signal out. Anna figured that they were so far out into uncharted jungle that no one would ever find or rescue them even if they could call. Besides, they had had to save their precious cargo room at the beginning of the trip for scuba gear and the portable air compressor.

The team carried only what food they had been able to scrounge in Castelo dos Sonhos. They carried only one extra set of clothes per person. For drinking and cooking they boiled muddy river water. For firewood they hacked branches from the canopy with machetes. Dinner each night they had to catch from the river. They found that dragging a mosquito net behind the boat for twenty minutes usually produced a fine assortment of fish. Each night they slept, slathered in mosquito repellant and lying in hammocks encased in heavy nets, because local mosquitoes carried a nasty strain of malaria.

Anna's team was stopped by armed Brazilian soldiers when they floated past a small settlement at a district checkpoint. The soldiers forced Anna's entire group to wait under guard in a small hut while her boats were searched. Anna hadn't radioed ahead to announce their arrival, as Brazilian regulations said that they should. They might be smugglers, pirates, or drug dealers. All three frequented this part of the Amazon.

Anna tried to explain that they didn't have a radio. She showed her archeological permits. Still, the team sweltered for four hours in the windowless shack while soldiers poked and prodded into every nook and cranny of the boats. All that was missing when they were allowed to continue their journey was an envelope of cash with the equivalent of $200 in Brazilian currency.

Anna shrugged. Army patrols often expected bigger bribes than that before allowing passage.

On the fourth day, they reached a spot where the river flared into a small lake. Waldemar stared at a series of deep caves gouged into forty-foot cliffs on the northwest shore. "This is the place," he announced.

"Where did you find the spear point?" Anna insisted.

"Well . . . I was diving." He waved toward the middle of the lake. "More or less . . . out there."

It took three hours for Waldemar to find three trees he had marked along the lakeshore and to then use a compass to triangulate back to the position of his boat when he had made the dive and found the point.

Carlos Zajalla maneuvered the boat that housed the air compressor over this spot and dropped anchor. The other boat was run ashore. Hammocks and mosquito nets were off-loaded to set up a camp at the entrance of one of the larger caves.

The team fanned out for a quick survey of the area but saw no evidence of humans. Waldemar wheezed and chuckled, "Find one speck of gold, though, and they'll pour out from behind every tree trunk."

Carlos fired up the air compressor. Its steady chug-chug slowly pumped high-pressure air into a row of dive tanks.

Waldemar waded into the water for the short swim to the dive boat. "This part of the river is stuffed with piranha. But don't worry."

Anna recoiled, staring at the murky water. "Piranha?"

"This is still too close to the wet season for them to go after something as big as a human." Again he chuckled. "Wait three months 'till the river slows to a trickle and they're good and hungry. . . . Now *that's* a different story!"

Anna groaned, "I'm going to make my first-ever dive in a piranha-infested lake?"

The dive instructor explained the idea of using a systematic underwater search grid that would be marked by poles he would plant on the shallow lake bottom. He flopped overboard for the first dive and planted a five-foot white pole as a base marker. All dives would fan out from that spot.

Waldemar and Anna suited up for their first dive. The instructor cautioned, "It's so murky down there, you can't see your hand in front of your face. If you get disoriented, feel around your regulator to find your exhale bubbles. That'll tell you which way is up. I tied a fifty-foot white rope to the marker pole. Hold onto that to keep from drifting out of the grid area."

Waldemar said, "Look for a steep sloping drop off. Part way down that slope I found a layer of *lagresa* [a volcanic layer in which miners often found gold veins]. That's where I found the arrowhead."

"Spear point," corrected Anna.

Waldemar shrugged. "I'd rather find a speck or two of gold."

Carlos asked, "How will you know the exact spot where he found the spear point?"

"We don't have to find the *spot*," Anna answered. "We just need to find the rock layer it came from. That will establish how long ago the spear point was used before it was discarded and settled on the bottom of the lake."

"Wouldn't it be easier to carbon date the spear point, itself?"

Anna shook her head. "That would tell us how old the rock is, but not how long ago it was fashioned into a spear point."

Because of Waldemar's age and health, each dive lasted only ten minutes. Waldemar had spent his whole life hiking through the Brazilian jungle. Still, the passing years and a bad heart had left him frail.

Anna sucked hard on her scuba mouthpiece as she slipped overboard. Green water closed over her head. The sound of her breathing was magnified into a roar. Her heart pounded in the eerie gloom. She struggled to control her breathing and the sense of panic at being in an alien environment where she couldn't see.

Waldemar took Anna's hand so they wouldn't drift apart as they sank to the bottom and groped about in near-total darkness to find the marker pole and rope. Waldemar measured out six feet along the rope, and held it there as a guide while they swam a slow circle around the marker pole. Having completed a full lap, they measured out six more feet along the rope and made their next loop.

Anna quickly learned to swim several feet above the bottom so her fins wouldn't kick up clouds of silt to obscure what little visibility they had. Anna and Waldemar swam eight slowly increasing laps around the marker pole before they reached the end of the rope and kicked for the surface

They had found no sign of the drop-off.

"He thinks farther out," Anna reported after their dive. Waldemar slumped onto the deck, panting from his effort.

Carlos flopped back into the water and placed a second pole fifty feet from the first and tied a second rope between them. On the next dive they'd base their search from this new pole.

Meanwhile, the junior archeologists began a detailed ground search of the area surrounding the caves. Within hours they found evidence of an early settlement. Based on bone fragments, they decided that, besides fish and river porpoises, the dwellers ate turtles, frogs, and lizards.

In the gray, filtered light of late afternoon, Anna and Waldemar made a second dive. This time they found the sharp drop-off, thirty feet beyond the second marker pole.

Carlos moved their boat over this position and adjusted the marker poles. In the morning, Anna began a series of longer solo dives along that steep slope. She wore a battery-powered headlamp to improve her visibility and carried picks, hammers, and a nylon mesh bag to carry her finds.

Drifting to the lake's bottom forty feet below the dive boat, Anna was surprised to find how quickly she had become comfortable diving into this dark and murky world. Even the gnawing terror that something evil lurked just out of sight and over her shoulder was easing—a feeling that had her constantly jerking her head from side to side only a day before.

Foot-by-foot she drifted down the slope, brushing away the thick layer of silt. At a depth of fifty-five feet, she exposed a sparkly green-colored layer of volcanic matter (*lagresa*) that seemed to stretch like a horizontal ribbon across the lake.

She used a hammer to chip out hunks of rock and dropped them into her net sample bag. During over four hours of bottom time, she searched along that four-inch high horizontal layer, picking occasionally with the claws of her hammer. Silt and debris swirled in her face, making it hard to see more than a few inches. She had to press her facemask to the rock to see if it hid any treasures. By dusk she had found a few bone fragments but no additional spear points.

"That's it," she announced. "Tomorrow morning we break camp and head home."

"But we didn't find anything," one of the archeologists complained.

"If these rock samples date at 13,500 years old, we'll have proven the date when the original spear point was made. That's all we came to do."

"But don't you want to stay and excavate?"

Anna gestured around their meager camp. "We're not set up for it, or funded for it. If these rocks date correctly, we'll be back."

After Words

Carbon dating of Anna's rock samples confirmed that the spear point was made at least 13,000 years ago. Anna Roosevelt's work at this and at other deep jungle sites shattered the model of initial human migration into South America from North America and also established that human impact on the Amazon rain forest is both older and more pervasive than originally thought. She and other researchers continue to work to build more accurate pictures of the American human past.

* * *

Suggested Topics to Explore

This story deals with archeology and the Amazon Rain Forest. Here are starting questions that will help you discuss and research both.

1. How do archeologists "know" that human life began in Africa and spread from there to Europe and Asia, and finally from Asia across the Bering Straight to Alaska, and only then down the American hemisphere? What evidence do they use to back this theory?

2. How big is the Amazon rain forest? Compare it to the size of your own state and to the United States.

3. Why do small objects—like an arrow or spear point—become so important to archeologists? Don't they already have more artifacts than they could ever need?

4. What lives in the Amazon rain forest and nowhere else on Earth? Make a list of as many unique animal and plant species as you can. Why are so many unique species there?

For Further Reading About This Story

Ayer, Eleanor. *The Anasazi.* New York: Walker, 1994.

Bendick, Jeanne. *Tombs of the Ancient Americans.* New York: Franklin Watts, 1993.

Brody, J. *The Anasazi: Ancient Indian Peoples of America.* New York: Rizzoli, 1990.

Castern, James. *Rainforest Researchers.* New York: Benchmark Press, 2000.

Childrens, Diana. *Prehistoric People of North America.* New York: Chelsea Junior, 1997.

Dorst, Jean. *The Amazon.* New York: Steck-Vaughn Library. 1992.

Lauber, Pat. *Who Discovered America?* New York: HarperCollins, 1994.

Lewington, Anne. *Rainforest.* New York: Raintree, Steck-Vaughn, 1999.

McIntosh, Jane. *The Practical Archaeologist.* New York: Facts on File, 1999.

Scheller, William. *Amazing Archaeologists and Their Finds.* New York: Atheneum, 1994.

Untley, Beth. *Amazon Adventure.* New York: Garth Stevens, 1990.

Teri Roth

Family Matters: Biologist
A Science Adventure

Teri Roth's job isn't easy. She's responsible for making captive endangered species mate in order to preserve their species. What makes her job really difficult is that no one knows enough about some of these rare species to even know what their real needs are.

A Science Adventure in the Zoo

It was 7:45 A.M. when Teri Roth held out her ID badge as she drove through the employee gate of the Cincinnati Zoo. The thirty-eight-year-old zoological researcher parked in her spaced marked "Reserved for CREW Director." Clouds rolled thick and low over Cincinnati on October 9, 2000. The wind scurried through trees, gusting fiercely each time it had a chance to blow all the papers out of a person's hands.

Clutching her brief case and shoulder bag, Teri raced through the CREW (Center for Research of Endangered Wildlife) doors and past the receptionist heading toward her office.

Teri's assistant fell in step with her as she walked. "I put your phone messages on your desk. Bill Swanson of the Research Department wants to see you about Ewi. I think he wants to take more blood samples."

Teri sighed, *"Everybody* wants to talk to me about the Sumatran rhinos." (Sumatra is an island nation between Malaysia and the Indian Ocean.)

"And Mr. David Castiano is waiting in your office."

Teri groaned. "Not the finance committee . . . " She sucked in one deep breath, opened her office door, beamed her most confident smile, and extended her hand, "Mr. Castiano, so good to see you."

"It's budget review time, Dr. Roth," he said, lips seriously pursed. "And you have considerably overspent again."

Teri shrugged, "It was Ipuh."

"*What* is an Ipuh?" Castiano demanded.

"Not a what, a very rare *male* Sumatran rhino. One of only two in captivity available for breeding stock."

"Go on," said Castiano.

Teri Roth sank into the high-backed chair behind her desk. "First he developed eye problems we feared would leave him blind. When we realized he's used to the deep shade of the understory in the Sumatran rain forest, we built special polarized shade screens to protect his eyes."

Castiano interrupted, "You mean polarized like sun glasses?"

"Yes. We had to block glare as well as direct sunlight. Next he stopped eating. He lost several hundred pounds and could have died—do you realize the blow to our program such a loss would be? Luckily, one of our biologists discovered a variety of fresh ficus that could be flown in fresh every day from California and Florida and that closely matched the native species Ipuh was used to eating in the wild. Ipuh has now recovered quite nicely . . . "

"At a cost of $100,000 to the zoo!" Castiano scoffed.

Teri said, "You must understand. There are only three hundred Sumatran rhinos left in the world. Twelve are in captivity. We have three of those, including one of only two captive males—Ipuh."

Castiano countered, "That's all well and good, Dr. Roth. But we have to give priority to the zoo."

Dr. Roth pointed her finger at the accountant. "This endangered species breeding program enables humans to preserve diversity on the planet as well as in the zoo. We must recreate the key elements of natural habitat—even when we don't know which ones are 'key.' We try to encourage natural mating and reproduction—even when we don't know the details of that ritual and process for most species—and believe me, most species are both unique and creative in what they require in order to mate. When natural mating fails, we have to assist in whatever ways we can to maintain the gene pool for each endangered species."

Her intercom buzzed. "Dr. Roth?"

Teri pressed the talk switch. "Go ahead."

"The logs are in from yesterday. Neither Ewi nor Ipuh showed any interest."

Teri rapped her knuckles on the desk. "Why won't they mate?" She pressed the talk switch. "Show me last night's ultrasound on Ewi."

Her assistant entered the office carrying Ewi's file and a series of Polaroids of the ultrasound image. Teri held up the pictures. "Look! Her follicles just keep growing *bigger.* Why don't they pop and release a fertile egg so we can begin to encourage Ipuh to mate?"

Castiano peered over her shoulder at Ipuh's and Ewi's files. "They're sure *ugly* critters."

Teri answered, "Perhaps so. But each carries almost three pounds of horn."

"So?"

"Sumatran rhino horn is worth over twenty-five thousand dollars a pound on the black market as a magic cure-all."

Castiano stammered, "A rhino is worth seventy-five thousand dollars just for its *horn?!*"

"And that's why there are only three hundred left in the wild."

The intercom buzzed again. "Dr. Roth? Dr. Lewis from the Lexington, Kentucky, Zoo on line three."

A minute later, Dr. Roth hung up the phone and turned to her assistant. "We leave in ten minutes for Lexington. Today we'll get to test the new probe." Turning to Castiano, she explained, "They're going to operate on an Indian rhino this morning in Lexington."

"And?"

"We have developed a system for capturing sperm from male rhinos. But we need to test the probe."

"So, test it here."

Teri laughed. "First, the rhino must be anesthetized—always a tricky and dangerous procedure. Second, do you think I should make the first test of an experimental probe on one of the only two male Sumatran rhinos in captivity?"

Castiano stammered, "Well . . . since you put it that way . . . "

"The Lexington zoo is going to operate on a common Indian rhino this morning. While he's out, we'll test the probe and make sure it's safe. Good day, Mr. Castiano."

He rose to leave. "How you manage your program is your business, Dr. Roth. Still, I will need hard budget data for the next cycle. And I need it this week."

She shook his hand. "And I will give them to you as soon as you can give me hard data on the exact needs of each endangered species."

Two biologists met her outside her office door. "We have a problem with Tex." Tex was a female endangered whooping crane raised in Wisconsin who had never been introduced to male cranes. CREW was trying to get her to produce a fertile egg. "We're pretty sure she won't produce an egg unless she's paired with a mate."

"But she refuses to link with any of our male cranes," said Teri.

The two biologists glanced at each other. "But she's quite attached to George Archibald."

Teri's glance darted between the two staffers to make sure this wasn't a joke. "George Archibald, who runs the crane program?"

"He even agrees that she seems to feel paired to him."

Teri asked, "And is he proposing to act paired with her to get her to produce an egg?" The staff biologists both nodded. "Does he know what's involved in crane mating?"

"He knows about the days of dancing and he says he will build an enclosure—if you okay it—to dance with her in private."

Teri laughed and shook her head at the image of balding, fifty-eight-year-old George Archibald imitating the crane mating dance. "You see what we have to put up with?" she said to David Castiano who had lingered with her in the hall. "How do I build *that* into my budget?"

A twenty-four-year-old graduate assistant ran toward Teri crying. "What's wrong, Sarah?"

The young woman sobbed, "Sheidra is dead."

"Dead?" Teri stammered. "Our female cheetah? What happened? We've spent eight months teaching her how to respond to males."

Between sobs the assistant explained, "Sheidra and Tisah were actually playing the other day. They were getting along fine. She went into heat, so we put them together this morning hoping that they'd mate. Everything was going fine until she made a mistake and flopped onto her side."

"Oh no," hissed Teri.

"What's wrong with *that?*" Castiano demanded.

Teri explained, "A flop is a submissive gesture to a cheetah. Not good during mating."

"Why?" he continued.

The assistant said, "It triggered an aggressive response from Tisah. He killed her."

Teri sighed, "And now we have only one breedable female cheetah."

The building front door opened. Teri's assistant poked her head in. "Dr. Roth? The car's ready and loaded. We have to leave right now."

At 5:00 P.M., the car returned to the CREW building. Teri and her assistant piled out and unloaded their equipment from the trunk. Two of the biologists working on the rhino program met them at the reception desk.

"It worked," Teri announced. "There are a few modifications I'd like to make now that I've seen the probe in action. But if Ipuh never shows interest in mating, we can still collect his sperm and artificially impregnate Ewi."

"No need," answered the biologists. "Ipuh started showing interest early this morning. He followed Ewi around the enclosure all day, rubbing her with his nose."

"Really?" asked Teri. "Have you done an ultra sound on Ewi?"

"Just did it. Look." One of the biologists handed Teri an image from the ultrasound.

Teri squinted at the line image. "She's released an egg!"

One of the biologists said, "Looks like we had it backwards. It wasn't that *he'd* become interested after *she* released an egg. His interest is what caused her to release the egg."

Teri nodded as she thought, and then shrugged. "Makes sense. Sumatran rhinos live solitary lives. No need for a female to produce an egg until a male shows up who could fertilize it."

Back in her office reviewing mail and phone messages, Teri said to her assistant, "We know so few of the all-important details of most species mating rituals and needs. I wonder if we'll learn in time to save them."

A half-hour later, Teri was ready to leave for the day. Biologist Bill Swanson marched into her office.

"Ah, Bill," she smiled. "I understand you want to take more blood from Ewi."

"Now that she's mated," he answered, "that will have to wait." He paused, frowning, struggling to find the right words. "However, I can't help but worry about what kind of a life these artificially created animals will have."

"Artificially created?" Teri asked.

"We prod and test, and maneuver them together. We feed them and clean up after them. They won't be able to pass on basic life and survival skills to their offspring because we do the work they should be doing in the wild. In another generation or two they'll only be able to survive when humans wait on them hand and foot."

"What other choice do we have?" Teri asked. "We have to save these species even though we're stumbling in the dark to do it."

Bill shook his head. "But what we save won't be the same, self-sufficient, able-to-survive-on-its-own Sumatran rhino." Then he added, "Plus, with only two breeding males, the gene pool will be too small for them to successfully survive."

Teri threw up her hands. "*That* is a problem for another day." At 6:10 P.M., she locked her office door and wearily headed for home.

After Words

Zoo breeding programs, like that of Dr. Teri Roth, have sheltered and maintained endangered species from the California condor to the Sumatran rhino. As worldwide extinction rates soar, and as scientists struggle to devise methods to maintain essential diversity, these zoo breeding programs provide a critical stop-gap method of preserving important species until ways to successfully reestablish their populations in the wild can be found.

* * *

Suggested Topics to Explore

This story deals with endangered species and animal mating. Here are starting questions that will help you discuss and research both.

1. Each species needs to maintain a viable gene pool in order to survive. What is a gene pool? Why is a big gene pool better? Why do most states have laws against marrying siblings and close cousins? Do these laws have anything to do with maintaining a diverse gene pool?

2. What makes a species an "endangered species?" Is "endangered" the only designation for a species whose survival has been threatened by human activity? What other categories are there? Research each of these categories and list the plant and animal species on each list that exist in your area.

For Further Reading About This Story

Dekoster, Katie. *Endangered Species.* San Diego, CA: Greenhaven Press, 1998.

Ehrlich, Paul. *Extinction.* New York: Random House, 1991.

Johns, June. *The Mating Game.* New York: St. Martin's Press, 1990.

Keene, Ann. *Earth Keepers.* London: Oxford University Press, 1994.

Sparks, John. *The Sexual Connection.* New York: McGraw-Hill, 1987.

Walters, Mark. *The Dance of Life.* New York: William Morrow, 1998.

Vera Cooper Rubin

Missing Matter: Astronomer
A Science Adventure

She had only meant to test a new piece of equipment. But what Vera Rubin discovered was that the *actual* motion of stars and galaxies appeared to prove that Newton's laws—the most fundamental principles of all of astronomy—were wrong. Either that, or every astronomer in the world was wrong in that they had missed 90 percent of the mass of the universe!

A Science Adventure in an Astronomy Observatory

March 28, 1970, was a bitter day for forty-three-year-old astronomer Vera Rubin. She had worked in the observatory all night with telescope, spectrograph, and microscope. She had then spent the morning guzzling coffee and calculating her results instead of sleeping. Now, in the afternoon, her boss was yelling at her, insisting that she had made a mistake.

Worst of all, Vera was beginning to think that he was right. Of course, she had made a mistake . . . somewhere. She must have. How could she, in one night, prove that Isaac Newton's theories—the very basic of modern astronomy—were wrong?

Vera worked at the tucked-away, tree-shrouded Department of Terrestrial Magnetism (DTM) at the Carnegie Institute of Washington. DTM's director, astronomer Kent Ford, had just created a new high-speed, wide-band spectrograph that could complete eight to ten spectrographs in a single night, while existing models were lucky to complete one in a day. Vera was itching for a clear night when she could see what Ford's invention could do.

But March had been wet and bitter in Washington, DC, that year. Because a dense cloud cover had hung over Washington all month,

Vera couldn't accurately aim DTM's telescope or pick out appropriate targets on which to test the spectrograph.

On the morning of March 27, Ford announced that the forecast called for clear skies, and that the DTM telescope and spectrograph were Vera's for the night.

By 9:00 P.M., Vera had focused the DTM telescope on Andromeda, the nearest galaxy to our own. Like the Milky Way, Andromeda is a spiral galaxy that spins like a pinwheel at a sharp angle to the Milky Way. This lets astronomers look "down" on Andromeda sort of from the top.

Vera planned to focus on small clusters of stars near Andromeda's center and others near its outer edges and check the velocity (speed) of these stars—to see if Andromeda's millions of stars really moved as existing theory said they were supposed to.

When attached to powerful telescopes, spectrographs detect the presence of different elements in a distant star and display what they detect on chart paper. Each element emits bursts of energy at unique and very specific frequencies when it burns in the fiery cauldron of a star. By measuring the exact frequency of each spike of energy detected by the spectrograph, researchers can determine which elements are present in that distant star.

Vera rigged a high-power microscope to read the charts created by Ford's spectrograph. Most researchers, who simply wanted to identify the mix of elements in a star, didn't need to use microscopes to read their charts. But Vera had another project in mind that would require far greater accuracy than the human eye could produce.

Vera knew that those frequencies that astronomers measure on a spectrograph shift a tiny bit higher or lower depending on whether the star is moving toward the Earth or away from it. The greater that shift, the greater the star's speed. A human eye couldn't detect these shifts on a spectrograph chart. But a microscope could.

This frequency shift is called a Doppler shift. The same kind of a shift happens with sound waves. When a car speeds toward you, its sounds like the engine whines at a high pitch (frequency). As it passes, the sound of the engine seems to drop to a lower pitch (frequency). That's also a Doppler shift.

That night Vera completed nine spectrographs of different spots in Andromeda—nine in one night! Vera was elated. In the past she had felt lucky to complete one. The next day she analyzed the spectrographs with her microscope measuring frequency shifts.

When she finished and calculated the stars' velocities from the Doppler shifts she measured, she found that the stars near the outer edge of Andromeda were moving just as fast as the stars near the galaxy's center. That wasn't the way it was supposed to be. Vera assumed that she'd made a mistake, so she recalibrated the microscope and remeasured each of her spectrographs. Her results were the same.

Ford scowled as Vera presented her results to him. "It can't be, Vera. The outer stars *can't* travel as fast as stars close to the center of the galaxy. They would escape the pull of gravity and fly off into space."

Vera shrugged. The same conclusion had occurred to her before she re-checked her results for the fourth time. "But that's what I measured."

Ford shook his head. "Be reasonable, Vera. The planet Mercury travels around the Sun ten times faster than Pluto because Pluto is one hundred times farther away. Gravity is weaker at Pluto's distance, so it *has* to travel slower to keep gravity and its momentum in balance. That's simple physics, Vera. You know that."

Vera did not back down. "But it's not what I saw when I measured Andromeda."

Ford pounded his fist on the DTM office metal desk. "Then you must have made a mistake. You did something wrong!"

"I did not," Vera bristled. "You know that I am exceptionally careful with both telescope and spectrograph. And you know I am the best at reading Doppler shifts."

Again Ford scowled. Clearly, *something* is very wrong here. "Check the equipment."

"I did. The spectrograph and microscope are perfect. I ran tests on closer, well-known stars. The results I got perfectly match results from other spectrographs."

Ford drummed his fingers as he thought. "Do the experiment again tonight."

Vera nodded. "I already planned to—just as soon as you approve my time on the telescope and spectrograph."

As Vera reached the door of Ford's office, he scowled. "*Something* has to be wrong because this cannot happen. It defies the laws of physics! Figure it out!"

Vera's results the next night—and the night after—exactly matched her first results.

Baffled, Rubin and Ford decided to make spectrographs of other galaxies. Maybe some explanation would appear when they studied these more distant objects. Spectrographic charts had only been prepared for about 100 of the millions of available galaxies. Maybe their answer lay in the many uncharted systems.

Over a period of two months the two scientists completed 200 new spectrographs. For every galaxy it was the same. The velocity of stars they measured came out all wrong. Stars farther from the galaxy's center were supposed to travel slower. They didn't. Sometimes the outer stars actually traveled faster! According to every known law of physics, some of those stars were moving too fast for gravity to hold them in their galaxy and they should fly off into space.

But they didn't.

Vera began to feel that her findings were part of a personal nightmare, and soon she'd wake up and the universe would make sense again. When she let herself think about it, she got a sinking feeling in her stomach. She began to believe that someone was playing a practical joke on her and that everyone was laughing at her behind her back.

Then it got worse. Vera noticed that whole galaxies—whole *groups* of galaxies—weren't moving as they were supposed to. After the Big Bang explosion that began the universe sixteen billion years ago, the motion of stars and galaxies was supposedly directed by gravity—as defined by Newton's Laws of Motion. But here were giant groups of galaxies that moved in ways and at speeds that Newton's laws couldn't explain.

Ford groaned, "Now *everything* is wrong and *nothing* makes sense!" He glanced accusingly at Vera. "What have you done to my universe?"

For a long moment Ford pawed through the charts and graphs showing their calculations and results. "Either Newton and every other astronomer and scientist in the world are wrong, or we're wrong. Frankly, I don't like those odds." He glared hard at Vera and asked, "How sure are you of these findings, Vera?"

"You've seen my work," she answered. "You've watched me make spectrographs and interpret the charts. You know I've double-checked and rechecked every figure. There are no errors in our work."

He rocked back in his chair. "Do you realize what you're saying? You're saying Newton—*the* Isaac Newton—was wrong ... *is* wrong!" He shuttered, "And I am too old to take on *that* fight. We'll be skinned alive!"

"There's a chance we may not be at odds with Sir Isaac," Vera answered. She had been thinking about this ever since her first baffling spectrograph.

"But the numbers . . . "

Vera shoved her glasses back up the bridge of her nose and raised a finger. "What if," she began. "What if there were lots more matter in the universe than anyone has yet seen. And what if that extra matter were scattered about in our galaxies and between the stars—even in our own solar system—in such a way that their extra mass would make Newton's laws *correctly* predict the real motion of stars and galaxies that we have measured?"

Ford blurted, "Are you suggesting all the astronomers in history have simply *missed* a number of stars and galaxies?!"

She smiled, nodded, and adjusted her glasses. "What if that extra matter couldn't be seen? It would still be ordinary matter. It would still be part of our known universe—just not visible to human eyes."

"Invisible matter?" he scoffed. "This sounds like a science fiction story, Vera."

She answered, "Some have called it 'missing matter'."

Ford's face lit with recognition. "Ahhh, the 'missing matter' theory. I remember when the theory that there was matter in the universe we couldn't see drifted through the university twenty years ago. Everyone laughed."

Vera nodded. "I think we just proved it exists, and I can guess at where it has to be. So it's not truly missing any longer. We should call it 'dark matter' since it gives off no light."

"Dark matter . . . " Ford grimaced. "You want me to announce to the scientific community that we have discovered the existence of matter that no one can see?"

Vera nodded. "Exactly that."

"But what *is* this . . . dark matter?"

"I don't know because I can't see it," she answered. "Probably it is free-floating small particles—maybe even subatomic particles that hover like a fine mist through all the galaxies of the universe."

Ford thoughtfully rubbed his chin. "How much 'dark matter' would there have to be in order to make Newton's Laws of Motion correctly predict the movement of the visible universe?"

Vera's face flushed as she shuffled through her papers. "I have made some preliminary calculations." She winced, then slid her final page of numbers over to her boss. "Ninety percent of the matter in the universe has to be dark matter."

"Ninety percent?" he exploded. "You're telling me that *ninety percent* of the universe is matter that's there, that creates gravitational forces, but just cannot be seen. And no astronomer—other than you—ever noticed or detected it?"

Vera smiled and shrugged. "I know it sounds astounding. But it's the only explanation we have—unless you want to claim that Newton was wrong."

After Words

It took the rest of the scientific community a full decade to grudgingly accept Vera Rubin's results and the reality that most of the matter in the universe cannot be seen or detected by any means available to humans. For much of that decade, Rubin and Ford were laughed at and shunned by mainstream astronomers.

However, Vera Rubin's work from that summer of 1970 changed every calculation and theory about the structure and origins of our universe. It vastly improved astronomers' ability to correctly calculate the distribution and motion of matter. Meanwhile, Newton's Laws of Motion, luckily, still survive.

* * *

Suggested Topics to Explore

This story deals with astronomy and dark matter. Here are starting questions that will help you discuss and research both.

1. Vera Brown used Doppler shifts to measure the motion of distant stars. Research Doppler shifts to make sure you understand how they work. Then try an experiment. You'll see that the faster an object moves past you, the greater the Doppler shift of its sound as it passes.

   On a tape recorder, record the sound of a car as it drives past you at 20 mph, at 40 mph, and at 60 mph. Back in the classroom play the tape and use a piano to match the tones and tonal shift you recorded as the car drove past. Now you have translated a car's Doppler shift into notes on a piano.

   The sound of the car never changed. It only appeared to because of a Doppler shift. Did the shift grow bigger as the car's speed increased?

2. What is dark matter? Is it really matter—with mass and substance? What's the difference between dark matter and anti-matter?

3. What is a spectrograph? Are they still used by modern astronomers? How do they work and what information do they provide for scientists?

For Further Reading About This Story

Bartusiak, Marcia. *Through a Universe Darkly.* New York: Harper Collins, 1993.

Golway, James. *Where is the Rest of the Universe?* Los Angeles: KCET, 1991.

Kraus, Lawrence. *The Fifth Essence: The Search for Dark Matter.* New York: Basic Books, 1993.

———. *The Mystery of Missing Mass in the Universe.* New York: Basic Books, 2000.

Rubin, Vera. *Bright Galaxies, Dark Matter.* New York: American Institute of Physics, 1997.

Tucker, Wallace. *The Dark Matter.* New York: Morrow Books, 1988.

Yount, Lisa. *Contemporary Women Scientists.* New York: Facts on File, 1994.

Florence Sabin

Blood Work:
A Science Adventure

Histologist/
Biologist

Florence Sabin started with a simple question: Where does blood first come from in a developing embryo? That question ended with Florence becoming the first human to watch the first cells of a new embryo begin to divide and to specialize to form organs and arteries, and then—magically—the first drop of blood.

A Science Adventure in the Lab

Forty-seven-year-old professor Florence Sabin sat in her bright-yellow laboratory on the third floor of a plain three story brick building on the Johns Hopkins University campus in Baltimore, MD. Her ever-present wire-rimmed glasses perched over her square, plain face.

"I have failed again," she admitted.

Sitting across the cramped metal lab table from her on this crisp October evening in 1918, Mabel Mull (widow of former Anatomy Department Chairman, Franklin Mull) scowled. "You need not face this shameful slight alone, Florence. We will all fight with you"

"Slight?" Dr. Sabin repeated. "It's just an experimental problem."

"*Experiment?!* This is your *life!* And I say it is unacceptable that you were pushed aside into this insignificant department." Mabel jabbed the table with a finger for emphasis as she spoke.

Florence leaned back, confused. "I'm talking about a lab experiment, Mabel. What are you talking about?"

"That you were not appointed head of the Anatomy Department, of course! A shameful slight to you and to all women."

Florence waved her hands to protest. "I'm *glad* to be head of the Histology Department."

Mabel scraped back her chair and began to pace. "I hardly even know what *Histology* is."

"It's the study of blood. Very important, actually."

But Mabel wasn't listening. "We will not stand for this cruel slap in the face. Anatomy is the premier department at this university. You should have taken my husband's place when he passed on." Mabel paused to gather herself and concluded, "You'll resign in outraged protest, of course."

"I will not. I have a department to run, and I have research in progress."

Mabel drew her hand to her chest in shock. "You can't be serious."

Florence shuffled through a stack of articles and reports searching for one she had just read and had heavily underlined. "Quite serious. I have been mulling over a new question. Histology is the perfect place to pursue it: Where does blood come from?"

Mabel scoffed, "From veins and arteries, of course. Really, Florence . . . "

"No. I mean, where does blood *originally* come from?" Sabin's earlier work had proved that the entire lymphatic system arose from blood vessels as tiny sprouts that grew into lymph glands and canals. Now she was asking: What is the origin of our circulatory system? White cells, red cells, blood vessels—when and from where do they first appear as an embryo develops?

"Why could you possibly care?" asked Mabel.

"Blood is the lifeline of all beings. A better understanding of blood will better aid all life."

Mabel raised her hands toward the ceiling. "Fine. Do your blood study, Florence." She lowered her hands and wagged a finger at her friend. "But, mark my words, if you let them get away with this . . . "

"Of course . . . there *is* a problem . . . " Florence admitted.

"A problem?"

"There doesn't seem to be a way to do the study. Each time I try, I fail."

Mabel's eyes danced with indignant energy. "Has someone at this university prevented you from doing it? Someone in the Anatomy Department?"

Florence laughed. "Nothing like that. Just a scientific dilemma. Last night was my nineteenth straight failure and, frankly, I've run out of ideas. If I stain cells so I can see them through a microscope, I kill the cells so I can't watch them grow. But if I don't stain them I can't see them at all."

The technology available in 1918 required tissue samples to be stained with special dyes so that the individual cells would be visible through a microscope. However, existing dyes and staining technique were not useable on live tissue. The stains affected and damaged the tissue. Thus, the process a researcher wanted to watch would no longer happen normally once the sample was stained to make it visible.

Florence continued, "I've searched for cell types that are resistant to the stains. But the few that are, tend to be from simple organisms that don't specialize into complex beings as their early cells divide. I've tried all five available stains. I've varied my technique for staining the cells. Nothing works. Staining always inhibits the normal cell growth and division I need to watch."

Florence smiled and held up the report for which she had searched. "Ah, here it is. Coincidentally, this morning I received a report of a new development in Germany that might give me a new chance."

A research team in Leipzig, Germany, developed a "live staining" technique that used harmless dyes. Live tissue samples could now be stained for microscopic observation without affecting the tissue or its normal development in any way.

"If this new staining process works as the Germans claim it does, I should be able to watch every moment of an embryo's early development. With a bit of luck, I will actually see the circulatory system begin."

Florence decided to use a chicken embryo for her study. They developed quickly. Their development and physiology were well known. And they were inexpensive—within the budget of even the small Histology Department.

On her first try, Florence used too much dye. It blurred her vision through the microscope and she saw nothing of importance. She spent two frustrating hours frantically adjusting her scope but could never bring the cells she needed to see into sharp focus. By the time the stain had dissipated enough for her to see, veins, arteries, and flowing blood already existed.

On her second try, two days later, she focused on the wrong set of dividing cells. Again, arteries, veins, and blood already existed when she realized that the cells she was intently watching were forming into bone and shifted her microscope's focus.

The same frustrating disappointment happened on her third and fourth attempts. Florence began to fear that the process she wanted to watch happened too fast for her to find before it had already occurred. She feared that she would never learn how to interpret initial cell divisions in a way that would guide her to know where and when to direct her microscope.

At 7:30 P.M. on November 6, 1918, Florence's fifth set of embryonic chick cells were delivered. She placed them on a glass slide and stained them using the Leipzig method. Florence carefully focused her microscope and settled into a comfortable chair to watch. Her wall clock read 9:45 P.M.

From her earlier failed attempts, Florence had a better sense of what to look for and where to look for it. Ignoring the cramps in her shoulders and neck, she kept her eyes jammed against the microscope lenses, searching for the first signs and patterns of specialization she had learned to recognize from her earlier failed attempts. Her hands rested on the microscope control knobs, slowly shifting the position of the glass slide and the delicate focus of the microscope.

Florence felt like a space traveler visiting an alien world, drifting between blobs of matter, gliding among the soft, oval inhabitants, searching for one particular cell that would blossom into a vast complex of tubes and blood cells. She sipped tea and nibbled sandwiches as the hours past and her eyes roamed across the mass of dividing cells.

At 11:50 P.M., she detected the first tiny blood vessels beginning to form from the thick serum, called the endothelium, which lined the embryo's body cavity. Dividing cells began to form a tiny arch, leaving a hollow space beneath. In a matter of minutes, the arch expanded into a complete circle and then extended into a tunnel or tub—a vein. It reminded Florence of the tunnel construction she had watched one summer as workers drilled a round hole deeper and deeper through the mountainside.

Fascinated by the delicacy and complexity of this newly forming and dividing life, Florence stared through her microscope lenses. The high-power lights that illuminate the slide shimmered with radiant heat. Perspiration dampened her face. Yet she didn't dare turn on fans for fear of jiggling the embryo and the cells she needed to study.

Around 1:00 A.M., the blood vessels spread to form a simple system of interconnecting canals—growing like sprawling suburban streets, like the spreading roots of a tree, like the tendrils of a spreading spider web. She witnessed the creation of a maze of empty tubes. But where was the blood?

At 2:00 A.M., something unexpected happened. Florence was so riveted by this drama of an emerging life that she was unaware of how cramped and bleary-eyed she had become. The cells forming the inner walls along one section of an artery swelled, bloating like a slowly filling water balloon. Then one of the cell membranes snapped back leaving a new liquid cell—a tiny drop—behind to glide with gravity along the tunnel. Florence recognized its shape and structure. It was a white blood cell. Moments later others followed—white cells, red cells—both were created by splitting from the walls of these initial blood vessels. Soon a flood of them filled the tubes, each liquid blood cell created in the same fashion.

Florence watched in awe as those first cells became the blood supply of this new chick. The circulatory system was born. Florence had watched it happen and now knew precisely which cells lay at the root of both arteries and blood cells.

At 5:45 A.M., the summer sun crept through Florence's lab windows and crawled across her yellow laboratory walls. Florence Sabin never noticed. Her attention was riveted on the chick embryo. Blood cells now filled a rapidly expanding network of arteries and veins. A tiny heart had formed. And then, before her eyes, just as most in Baltimore were sleepily stumbling from their beds to start another day, Florence saw the heart make its very first beat. Blood cells streamed down the tiny arteries and flowed back through even smaller veins.

Another beat, and another. A new life began. Florence Sabin had stayed up all night to watch, so absorbed in this miracle of miracles, with this dawning of a new life, that she was unaware of the passage of time or the dawning of a new day.

More thrilled than on any other day of her life, Florence Sabin hastily jotted down her profound and valuable discoveries.

After Words

Blood vessels form from the cells of the endothelium. The very first blood plasma cells develop from the liquid portions of the cells that form the walls of the first blood vessels. This groundbreaking work by Florence Sabin helped guide other researchers to the conquest of Tuberculosis and several deadly blood disorders, and enhanced science's understanding of the circulatory and immune systems.

Florence Sabin continued her research on blood and embryonic development at Johns Hopkins University and at the Rockefeller Institute until 1938 when she retired and moved to Denver, Colorado. There she became a major force in the advancement of public health issues until her death in 1953.

* * *

Suggested Topics to Explore

This story deals with blood supply and embryonic development. Here are starting questions that will help you discuss and research both.

1. Why would anyone care how, and from where, the blood vessels and blood cells are formed? Are there genetic and developmental diseases that would be easier to correct once researchers knew how normal blood vessels and blood cells formed?

2. If each being begins as one single cell, how do different cells decide to specialize and turn into different organs, blood cells, hair, or other body parts? What tells one cell to become a heart muscle and another to become a tooth?

3. What does blood do for your body? What is its role? Research both the components of, and function of, blood. Decide how you'd complete this simile: Blood is to the body as _____ is to a great city.

For Further Reading About This Story

Bluemel, Elinor. *Florence Sabin, Colorado Woman of the Century.* Boulder: University of Colorado Press, 1969.

Haber, Louis. *Women Pioneers of Science.* New York: Harcourt Brace, 1991.

Kronstadt, Janet. *Florence Sabin: Medical Researcher.* New York: Chelsea House Publishers, 1990.

Phelan, Mary K. *Probing the Unknown: The Story of Dr. Florence Sabin.* New York: Crowell, 1989.

Sabin, Florence. *An Atlas of the Medulla and Midbrain.* Baltimore, MD: Friedenwald, 1901.

Stille, Darlene R. *Extraordinary Women Scientists.* Chicago, IL: Children's Press, 1995.

Karen Tejunga

What a "Croc!"   Biologist
A Science Adventure

Drifting among the reeds of a shallow lake in her small, flat-bottom skiff in the dark of night, Karen Tejunga bumped into a fierce eighteen-foot long South American crocodile (called a caiman). Karen wasn't surprised—after all, she had done it on purpose.

A Science Adventure in the Amazon Rain Forest

It's 10:30 at night in the remote Amazon rain forest of Brazil. Twenty-nine-year-old Karen Tejunga rides in the front of a small skiff winding its way through narrow channels toward Lake Mamiraua. Her assistant sits in the back and controls the outboard motor.

Over 200 miles from the nearest road, this part of Amazonia is one of the wettest and wildest places on Earth—a land of myth and story passed through countless generations. Here, the story of the caiman (the largest and most vicious predator in the Amazon and largest crocodile in the Western hemisphere) is frightfully short. "Caiman kill. They are the devil."

The nighttime symphony of sounds almost overpowers the whine of the tiny outboard motor—cicada, crickets, howler monkeys, birds, the howls of predators, the screams of victims, and the excited chatter of those that escape.

Lake Mamiraua only exists during the wet season. As rivers flood, the lake fills a shallow grassland between two branches of the Amazon over 1,800 miles west of the great river's mouth. Mamiraua is choked with floating pads, mats of tangled vegetation, and great tufts of reeds and grasses. It's the perfect place for caiman to hide, and from which to ambush and attack.

It is the night of April 17, 1997. Scattered clouds cause the moonlight to fall in blotches across the rippling waters of the lake. Mosquitoes and gnats swarm in clouds over the lake's surface.

Karen switches on the skiff's main headlamp. Light stabs across the lake. At first it finds only water and tufts of reeds. Then the light falls on glowing dots of unearthly yellow-green. The dots always come in pairs. Karen slowly swings the light. Five, six, a dozen, then several dozen pairs of glowing dots stare back—the distant eyes of giant caiman waiting for their next meal.

Over her shoulder Karen calls, "They're thick tonight. We should be able to tag a couple."

Karen's hair is pulled back in a ponytail under the miner's helmet she wears because of its strong headlamp. She wears catcher's shin guards, heavy gloves, and a thickly padded leather jacket—even in this oppressive heat. She now stands barefoot in the skiff's bow, panning the light, deciding which caiman she'll go after.

Caiman were slaughtered by the millions earlier in this century when alligator shoes, boots, and bags were in fashion. Their skins were stripped and the carcasses were left to rot in the jungle. By 1970, caiman were extinct in ninety-nine percent of their historical range. Then Brazil passed laws to protect the remaining giant predators.

Now these South American crocodiles are making a dramatic comeback. But science knows almost nothing about the life cycle and habits of these mighty creatures. Black and almost invisible at night when the nocturnal killers emerge from hiding, caiman can reach twenty-two feet long and have four-foot hydraulic jaws that can tear a buffalo in two—or that could crush Karen's skiff like a soda can. Cold-blooded, lurking, vicious menaces, unseen and unheard until the moment of attack, caiman represent all that is terrifying about the jungle. And caiman can live for a hundred years and eat any- and everything they meet.

In the skiff Karen carries a minicassette recorder for notes, extra batteries for the lights, two gas cans, a wire noose on an eight-foot bamboo pole to snare caiman, lots of rope, and a bucket of tags and radio collars. By capturing, measuring, and tagging caiman, Karen and a few others like her hope to develop an accurate population profile. By attaching radio collars to caiman, Karen hopes to learn these animals' migration patterns.

But to do anything, she first has to catch them—at night.

"*That* one," decides Karen, pointing at the glowing eyes of a giant male forty yards ahead.

Her assistant increases the gas. The outboard whines louder. A small wake spreads out behind the skiff. Karen flexes her knees to keep her balance, her toes curling around the lip of the wooden front seat, as she shines the light on the glowing yellow-green eyes that are her target.

The caiman glides across the lake, gently swishing its thick tail that stretches almost sixteen feet behind the eerie eyes. The skiff turns to approach from behind on a parallel course. The skiff's rails ride only ten inches above the waterline. This caiman is several feet longer than Karen's whole skiff.

The skiff gently pulls along side. The croc is a massive male— almost twenty feet long—algae encrusted and ancient looking, as if from a long gone era of monsters. Deadly teeth protrude from a mouth turned up into a permanent smirk. The caiman almost seems to know who is the *real* hunter here and who is the prey.

Inching closer and closer, Karen lifts the bamboo pole and feels an electric tingle in the air. The jungle grows quiet as if all are focused on this battle of giants. Over her shoulder she says, "They don't chew, you know. Just rip off huge hunks and swallow them whole."

If the caiman turns on the skiff, he'll easily crush it. Karen wouldn't last three minutes in this water at night. If and when Karen nooses the caiman, its tail is equally deadly until her assistant ropes and immobilizes it. Any mistake now means death.

Karen glances back and nods. Her assistant grabs a loop of rope, ready to lasso the tail. Karen dangles the noose just in front of the caiman. Then she hesitates. He's big enough to pull her under—even after he's noosed and tied.

Maybe she should pass . . . No! She's always wanted to snag a *big* one.

Karen's muscles tense. Her jaw tightens as she lowers the noose almost to water level.

With a final quick glance back, she sees that her assistant's eyes have grown wide with fear. This is the biggest caiman they have ever tried to snare.

And then, like a ghost, the caiman sinks into the depths and is gone.

Karen flops onto a seat, panting from the tension of her hunt. Her hands tremble. Her heart pounds. "Nuts . . . " But she is also relieved that this caiman vanished into the dark.

They steer the skiff nearer to the shore. Karen stands and clears her throat. She breathes deeply and imitates the deep, throaty call of a caiman bull. *Bwaaa, bwaaa, bwaaa!*

They hear a replying challenge from the dark. First one, then a second and a third. Then a soft plop as something large slips into the water. The glowing eyes of a young male are caught in the glare of Karen's light.

"*That* one!" Karen calls and points with her light.

The skiff leaps forward as the motor whines. Karen grabs her wire noose and again curls her toes around the edge of the front seat as she braces for the attack.

The motor putters back to idle as the skiff glides along side of a ten-foot youth. Its eyes seem to glow from deep within. It appears to be sizing up Karen and the skiff for a quick meal.

Karen lowers the noose so that the bottom end of the wire loop skims along the water surface just in front of the caiman's deadly jaws. Her assistant leans over the back with a rope loop ready to snare the caiman's tail. The skiff's rail dips dangerously near to water level.

Karen lowers the noose, pulls back, and then yanks up as hard as she can in a quick and well-rehearsed motion. Her assistant loops the tail, hoists it out of the water, and throws a quick knot through an oarlock to secure it.

The caiman thrashes like a bucking Brahma bull. Water sprays as if from a fire hose. The deadly jaws, held shut by the wire noose, gnash and grind. Claws scrap at the skiff's metal side. The great body smacks against the water after it arches above the surface. The skiff rocks violently. Water sloshes over the side and flows along the flat bottom plating.

Sometimes the team wraps the caiman's jaws in duct tape and drag it to shore for more extensive measurements. But not tonight.

Karen speaks quickly into her recorder. "Male. Approximately eleven feet. No more than eight years. Standard mottled black pattern. No unique markings." Louder she calls, "Help me with a collar and tag."

Her assistant kneels and reaches over the side to yank up one front leg. Karen uses a rivet gun to attach a metal tag to a loose fold of skin just above the foot. The skiff pitches and rocks as if it were caught in a violent, stormy sea. The assistant reaches into a bucket and hands Karen a radio transmitter collar that looks like an oversized dog collar. Karen loops it around the caiman's neck while her assistant bear hugs her around the waist to keep her from pitching overboard.

"Prepare to release," Karen calls. Her assistant releases his knot in the tail rope. Karen picks up the bamboo noose pole. "Ready. One . . . two . . . three!" Both ends of the caiman are released. It snaps once and sinks out of sight below the surface.

Both humans sink onto the skiff's wooden bench seats to pant and thrill at their success—and their survival. Karen bails with a plastic bucket.

Gas is running low. It is after midnight. Karen signals to turn back. The outboard putters to life and they begin the hour trip back down river to the town of Tefe, where Karen has set up her study camp.

She'll be back out tomorrow night to hunt and tag again. Maybe next time she'll catch a really *big* one. Maybe . . .

After Words

As caiman populations grow, Brazilian governmental decisions will be made on their future based now on a strong scientific database, thanks to Karen and other researchers in the deep Amazon jungle. Soon her work will have produced enough data to document the importance of the caiman to the jungle environment.

* * *

Suggested Topics to Explore

This story deals with caiman biology and jungle ecology. Here are starting questions that will help you discuss and research both.

1. Tagging and studying caiman is very dangerous. Why would someone want to do it?

2. Why did Karen Tejunga study caiman in their natural environment? Why not study caiman that have been captured and live in a zoo, where it would be easier and safer?

3. Why is it important to study the rain forests of the world? What discoveries have been made in the rain forests? Research these discoveries and their importance to humans.

4. Caiman are a member of the crocodile family. What other types of crocodiles are there, and where do they live? Are any endangered?

For Further Reading About This Story

Castern, James. *Layers of Life.* New York: Benchmark Press, 2001.

———. *Rainforest Researchers.* New York: Benchmark Press, 2000.

———. *River Life.* New York: Benchmark Press, 2000.

———. *Surviving in the Rain Forest.* New York: Benchmark Press, 2000.

Dollar, Sam. *Caimans.* New York: Steadwell Books, 2000.

Dorst, Jean. *The Amazon.* New York: Steck-Vaughn Library. 1992.

Lewington, Anne. *Rainforest.* New York: Raintree, Steck-Vaughn, 1999.

Untley, Beth. *Amazon Adventure.* New York: Garth Stevens, 1990.

Helen Thayer

Chilling Challenge: Climatologist
A Science Adventure

Trudging alone across the Arctic sea ice for a month with temperatures down to minus one hundred degrees (–100° F)—with her eyelashes frozen solid and snapped off by the hurricane-force wind, with her eyes swollen shut by flying shavings of ice—Helen Thayer suffered great hardships in her endeavors to gather data about Arctic ice. But she returned with all the data she needed for an important study.

A Science Adventure on the Arctic Ice

Helen Thayer looked up with a start. It was quiet—too quiet. She realized it was the first pure silence in days. The wind had died. The sea ice didn't groan and crack. The temperature was –48° F. But the sudden silence—not the cold—made her shiver.

The date was March 17, 1988, the eighteenth day of Helen's solo trek on skis and snow shoes across the Arctic ice sheet from Resolute Bay, Canada to the magnetic North Pole near King Christian Island, and then south to Cape Halkett on the northern tip of Greenland.

The fifty-one-year-old scientist had stopped to take readings and ice and snow samples for Canadian Government climate scientists. She unsnapped the nylon cover over her eight-foot long, sky-blue sled. At this temperature, even the nylon seemed frozen stiff, and reluctant to fold and crinkle. Helen lifted out her mini-weather station and measured air temperature, humidity, and barometric pressure. A fist-sized machine calculated oxygen levels in the air—but only after Helen cupped it in her gloved hands long enough to warm it up to the point at which it would work.

The hairs at the back of Helen's neck—buried deep beneath layers of neoprene and fur—began to tingle. Although she was over 200 miles from the nearest human, Helen felt that she was being watched. She twisted left and right, scanning the horizon. But all she saw was an endless sheet of flat, slightly buckled ice and deep blue sky laced with streaks of white clouds.

Nothing . . . unless it was a polar bear who watched. They were said to be virtually invisible until the moment of attack. Helen tried to convince herself that it was her imagination, and she returned to work.

She scooped a sample of the powder-dry surface snow that coated the vast sheets of sea ice and poured it into a labeled Ziplock bag. She chuckled, remembering her pretrek concern about preserving samples. "How will I keep them frozen?" The temperature hadn't risen above −28° F since she set out seventeen days ago. Keeping snow and ice samples frozen had not been a problem.

Using a corkscrewlike metal core sampler, she drilled two feet down into the ice, carefully sealing that thin cylinder of ice into another prelabeled bag. A surge of fear always washed over her when she drilled ice cores. It reminded her that she was miles away from land, walking on a frozen ice sheet over deep and deadly frigid water. It was creepy to know that she stood, skied, ate, and slept over water two miles deep, held up only by a creaking, groaning, shifting, treacherous—and often thin—layer of ice.

Scientists would use Helen's data and samples to gaze thousands of years into the Arctic past and compare the ancient Arctic climate and environment to the present that Helen measured daily. She had agreed to take samples and readings once every twenty miles along her 350-mile solo trek across the frozen Arctic wasteland. The governmental scientists had been eager for her to volunteer for the trek, since the only way for them to get their needed data was for *someone* to walk or ski to each spot and collect it.

Each time Helen stopped to collect samples or to set up her evening camp, she couldn't shake the eerie feeling of being watched. Even though she could see for miles—when the wind and blowing ice permitted her to see at all—each time she stopped she found herself twisting one direction and then another half expecting to come face to face with . . . with . . . something.

When she was on the move, the mind-numbing cold and endless drudgery of pulling her hundred-pound sled across the rough ice kept her mind from wandering far from the most basic concerns of survival and progress. The sled carried her fuel, food, water, tent, sleeping bag, clothes, samples, scientific equipment, extensive camera equipment for photo documentation, and a loaded Winchester rifle.

The rumpled surface of the sea ice was shaped into small, wave-like ice ridges called *sastrugi,* which often trapped her skis and held them like clamps. Each time, Helen had to climb out of her skies and claw them free with a pick before she could start up again.

And each time she stopped, she was almost overwhelmed by the feeling that something was closing in on her. Mostly, she worried that that something was going to be a polar bear. Polar bears were huge, hulking, and fast. The Arctic ice belonged to *them,* not to flimsy humans. Polar bears had long and lethal claws. They were called Arctic ghosts. Massive, lumbering beasts, polar bears moved invisibly and silently in their pure white world. A victim never heard or saw a polar bear until the actual moment of attack.

Even before the trek began, Helen couldn't stop herself from wondering: what would happen if a polar bear came upon her tent at night? How long would it take those six-inch claws to rip through a nylon tent? Through her? It was hard to sleep while feeling terrified at what might be just outside her tent. For the entire trip, Helen slept with her sleeping bag only half zipped. It was much colder but felt safer.

Fear of nighttime bear attacks is what finally convinced Helen to take one stalwart husky with her—Charlie. Four-year-old Charlie was a veteran dog sledder and seemed thrilled to trot solo next to Helen pulling his own eighty-five-pound child's blue plastic sled, which carried extra water and dog food.

As afternoon shadows stretched long across the barren ice on this eighteenth afternoon of her trip, Helen crossed a pair of polar bear tracks. By the sharp edges of the prints, she could tell they were recent. These were the fourth sets of tracks she had crossed today. Nervous sweat trickled down Helen's spine. Her body twitched. Helen knew for certain that polar bears were near, and it was almost time to stop for the night. That meant the noise of unpacking and pitching her tent and the smell of cooking. It felt like hanging out a neon sign that flashed "Good Eats" for miles across the ice.

Through most of that bitter night Helen sat bundled at the entrance of her tent next to Charlie, Winchester across her lap, eyes straining to see through the midnight dark. She was afraid to flop into her bag and zip herself in, so she sat shivering through the $-65°$ F cold made worse by the constant wind moaning through the night, snapping the stiffly frozen sides of her nylon tent. A ridge of blown ice slowly gathered to cover Charlie's side where he peacefully slept.

In the morning Helen was bleary-eyed from lack of sleep and she didn't bother to cook breakfast. Instead, she went straight to the high-fat, whole-wheat crackers she munched like candy on the trail along with cashews, walnuts, and granola.

Meals were simple even when she took the time to make camp and cook: peanut butter, rice, potato flakes, and powdered milk. Each meal and snack was followed by chocolate. Unfortunately, chocolate lost most of its flavor when chilled well below zero. Helen had to burn precious fuel just to melt her drinking water. It seemed to take forever to boil her simple mealtime gruel. There wasn't enough extra fuel to warm her chocolate bars along the trail.

But if meals felt like a necessary drudgery, the stark and barren beauty and isolation of the Arctic thrilled Helen. On this nineteenth day of her trek she skied past her second island, a small lump of wind swept, ice-covered rock called Helena. She had passed the larger Sherador Osborn five days earlier.

Helen was tempted to ski over to and across Helena. The comfort of standing on solid land beckoned her like a siren. But land was too rugged and difficult to traverse. She'd have to walk instead of ski. She'd easily lose a day—just for the comfort of standing on snow-covered rock instead of on snow-covered ice. She reluctantly skirted around Helena on sea ice. She felt like a turtle, hitched permanently to her blue plastic shell.

In the total isolation and stillness of the endless glistening jumble of Arctic ice that looked exactly the same every minute of every day no matter how far she skied, even the wind became a welcome companion and a pleasant break from the monotony of sameness. Helen found herself babbling one-sided conversations with the moaning wind through her neoprene facemask.

She also found an eerie "aliveness" to the ice as each shift or contraction made low groans, drawn-out squeals, and sharp cracks. It felt as if the ice were trying to barge into her private conversation with the wind. Ice and air slowly changed from parts of the physical environment into living and mischievous hikers on her trail.

On the next day, the temperature dipped sharply below $-80°$ F, the point at which Helen's neoprene facemask froze and lost much of its protective qualities. When the temperature reached $-100°$, the camera mechanisms froze and her thermometer pegged. Helen stopped worrying about the polar bears, and began focusing on protecting herself from the elements.

Then the wind began to howl and thick gray clouds and blinding ice and snow obscured the sky. A violent and raging wind flung shotgun pellets of ice and snow at her. Helen could find no way to protect her face from the driving ice that stuck like a sand blaster. Her eyelashes and eyebrows froze and were chipped off by the flying grains of ice. Both her corneas were painfully scratched. Her eyes swelled shut.

Helen huddled next to the sled with her back to the raging storm, unable to see. The wind tore at her sled cover, shredding the heavy nylon. It blew away most of the rest of her food and her clothes. Helen couldn't even hear herself scream as the howling wind ravaged her meager camp through the night.

By morning, little was left of Helen's equipment and supplies. All that remained from her sled were half of her samples, a little frozen water, and one pack of walnut meat. The storm had stolen everything else.

The storm also seemed to have attacked Helen's strength and body. The fierce cold had formed painful blood blisters on most of her fingertips. At best, Helen could see only blurry shapes. Charlie became a seeing-eye dog as well as bear guard for the final assault on the magnetic north pole.

The final three miles slid by over smooth ice and under clear skies with the temperature a brisk –45° F. Even though her vision slowly improved, Helen had trouble focusing on her compass.

As she neared the magnetic pole, her compass needle seemed to wander turning thirty and forty degrees in a single swing, leading her to ski first one way and then another. She reached the actual spot of the magnetic North Pole in a meandering spiral rather than in a straight line. The compass needle lazily turned, not caring which way it pointed.

It was the twenty-first day of her trek. Helen was bone weary, injured, and already gnawingly hungry. With no fuel left, she would have to eat snow and stretch her meager hoard of walnut meat over the final three days of skiing to reach her take-out point.

Nothing existed at this spot, other than her drifting compass needle to tell her she stood at the magnetic North Pole. The landscape here looked no different than on any other day or any other mile of the trek. The wind swirled and moaned the same as always. The ice stretched forever, slightly buckled—just like the last 300 miles.

Helen set up her tripod and snapped a picture of herself and Charlie. She took a final weather reading and core sample, turned and started the final fifty-mile ski to her lift-out point near Greenland.

After Words

Helen's data are being used by scientists to build more accurate models of the Arctic ice cap and its affect on, and its response to, global climactic changes over the past 10,000 years. This model will then help predict the interaction of Arctic ice, oceans, and air in the presence of a globally warming climate.

* * *

Suggested Topics to Explore

This story deals with the Arctic environment and weather research. Here are starting questions that will help you discuss and research both.

1. Can you think of the value of ice core samples and weather data to scientist trying to compare the present to past Arctic conditions? Research this topic and see if you can find out how scientists use core samples to peer into the past.

2. If you were going to make a long solo trek across the Arctic, what would be most important for you to take? Why? Make a list of items necessary for a monthlong Arctic trek.

3. Polar bears are the real kings of the Arctic. Research these magnificent animals. Find out about their life styles, their diet, and their territorial range. How many polar bears are still alive in the Arctic?

For Further Reading About This Story

Curlee, Lynn. *Into the Ice.* New York: Houghton-Mifflin, 1998.
Fleming, Fergus. *Ninety Degrees North.* New York: Grove Press, 2002.
Friedman, Kathleen. *What if the Polar Ice Cap Melted?* Danbury, CT: Children's Press, 2002.

Gibbons, Gail. *Polar Bears.* New York: Holiday House, 2001.

Hemstock, Annie. *The Polar Bear.* McLean, VA: Capstone Press, 1999.

Patent, Dorothy. *Polar Bears.* Minneapolis, MN: Carolrhoda Books, 2000.

Slung, Michele. *Living with Cannibals and Other Women's Adventures.* Washington, DC: National Geographic Society, 2000.

Cindy Lee Van Dover

Trailing Snails and Shrimp: Marine
A Science Adventure   Ecologist

It was an ecosystem in a part of the world that no one had ever studied before—under 15,000 feet of ocean water. Cindy Lee Van Dover and her scientific team had secured the funding—now they had to produce dramatic results from their venture into the unknown.

A Science Adventure on the Bottom of the Indian Ocean

At 24° South, 70.2° East, the research ship *Knorr* glided above the Indian Ocean's mid-ocean ridge on the afternoon of April 10, 2001. In the control van mounted on the rear deck, chemists watched the readings of sensors being towed 1,000 feet below the ship. "Temperature is up point-oh-eight degrees. I've got a slight rise in sulfur." Bob Collier yelled out the control van door. "We think we've found a vent!" All on deck cheered.

Cindy Lee Van Dover raced to the control van. At age forty-three, the senior biologist and senior scientist on board had written the many proposals to fund this thirty-day excursion in the Indian Ocean.

Cindy hoped to study biogeography (the distribution of life) at new vent sites along the Indian Ocean mid-ocean ridge. The mid-ocean ridge is a mountainous chain that extends around the globe through every ocean and marks where crustal plates split apart. Volcanic and geothermal vents dot this ridgeline.

However, at the dawn of the twenty-first century, still less than 1 percent of these mid-ocean ridgelines have been mapped. Humankind knows less about Earth's deep oceans than about Mars or deep space. No human had studied the Indian Ocean floor. Van Dover's team would be the first and they were to start by studying the ecosystems around ridge vents.

But even ferociously boiling vents spewing plumes of noxious gas were almost impossible to detect through 15,000 feet of ocean water. A temperature rise of 0.08 degrees was as strong an indicator as they were likely to get. Onboard computers accounted for current and drift and spit out the most probable coordinates of the vent.

Cranes lowered a small, unmanned submarine, *Jason* (called a submersible), and its power platform, *Medea* (called a submerged tender), into the choppy sea. Both *Jason* and *Medea* would sink to the ocean floor. *Medea,* a stationary platform, was attached to the *Knorr* by a bundle of cables. *Jason* explored the depths tethered to *Medea.* A line of dark clouds smeared the western horizon as *Jason* and *Medea* disappeared into the Indian Ocean depths.

Three hours later *Jason* reached the ocean floor. Only senior scientists were allowed into the control van to watch *Jason's* progress 15,000 feet below.

"Headlights on," announced *Jason's* pilot, Andy Weller, flipping a switch. "Camera on." The seven scientists jammed around two black-and-white monitors, staring, mesmerized, as a cone of light stabbed through the blackness three miles below. Cindy Lee Van Dover hunched over a straight-backed chair in the front row.

"Pan left," ordered one of the crew members who was reading sonar and radar screens. *Jason's* cone of light swept left as the unmanned submersible glided above the ocean floor revealing a lifeless moonscape of rippled sand, silt, and small boulders.

Each scientist became riveted to the screens, as if viewing pictures of an alien world. "No human has ever seen the floor of the Indian Ocean," said Cindy, hushed and reverent. "We're the first."

Time crept by as Jason's electric motor whirred.

"That's a *Rimicaris,* a vent shrimp!" Van Dover exclaimed, tapping a TV monitor. "There's another." The shrimp actually bounced off Jason's camera before scurrying away.

"There! Ahead to the right!" shouted another scientist.

Andy Weller turned the control wheel and shifted the motor to neutral. Jason's camera panned across an alien and sinister-looking forest of eighty-foot high needlelike spikes of rock. It looked like a Dr. Seuss-style fortress built on the flat plain of the ocean floor. Hot smoke and gasses boiled from crevices that snaked among the spires. Swarms of pink shrimp jostled for the best positions in the smoke as if the boiling gases were Jacuzzi bubbles. Fields of snails, mussels, anemones, shrub- and fanlike plants, polychaetes, and worms—red ones, bristly ones, fat ones, fuzzy ones—densely carpeted the ocean floor, which turned back into a barren desert a few yards away from the vents.

"We found a vent!" one scientist shouted out the van door. The crowd on deck cheered. The decks transformed into a buzz of activity. The biology team raced below to open their lab and unbolt lab equipment from storage straps attached to bulkheads.

Using a stern-mounted crane, *Knorr* crewmen lowered the Elevator—a six-foot square platform stacked with buckets, jars, and coolers to haul deep-sea samples up to waiting biologists and chemists.

Chief engineer Andy Bowen poked his head into the control van. "Whatever you do, do it fast. A storm's rolling in. In ninety minutes it'll be too rough to retrieve the elevator."

Outside, clouds streamed out of the west, thick and black. Waves bunched like menacing giants. The ship began to roll and creek.

Cindy pointed at Andy Weller. "I want samples of the snails, amoebae, fans, polychaetes, worms, and *lots* of the shrimp. Load and lock the coolers and buckets and get that Elevator up here! We'll worry about geology and water samples later."

Using remote-control steering levers, Andy maneuvered *Jason* through turbulent vent water. He used a joystick to direct the movement of *Jason*'s front scoop and basket. Each sample he captured had to be carried forty yards to the elevator and carefully dumped into one of its containers. Andy used *Jason*'s claw arm to seal and lock filled sample jars.

He carefully directed *Jason* in loading the elevator with plant and animal samples. Each movement seemed torturously slow to Cindy as she felt the pressure to retrieve as much as possible before the storm hit. When *Jason*'s scoop slipped, a dozen snails tumbled in slow motion back to the ocean floor in a cloud of sand and silt. Andy muttered, "Drat!" and glided *Jason* back down to try again.

Cindy staggered across the rolling deck to Andy Bowen, who was waiting by the Elevator crane. She had to shout to be heard over the howling wind. "We need another hour to finish sampling the entire ecosystem down there."

Bowen shook his head and shouted back, "In twenty minutes it'll be too rough to hook the Elevator and lift it back on board."

"Elevator comin' up!" called the crew chief five minutes later.

Crew wearing bright yellow rain slickers hooked the crane's cable to the Elevator when it bobbed back to the surface between giant gray-green waves and hoisted it onto the *Knorr's* deck, sea-water streaming like waterfalls off its sides.

Twenty-foot swells towered over the *Knorr's* rail and slammed into the red-painted hull. The whole ship trembled with each blow. Stinging spray blasted across the ship like shotgun pellets. Scientists and crew lurched across the pitching deck.

Biologists rushed at the Elevator like bargain table shoppers elbowing to snatch a sample bucket of their own. Cindy was knocked out of the way by two eager junior biologists. Any basket might contain a great discovery, an unknown species. The scientist who found it would be famous forever. Besides, there were only a few hours to catalog, process, and preserve these samples before deterioration destroyed their usefulness.

The main biology lab sat one deck down. Biologists had to adjust to the violent rocking motion of the ship and still quickly complete their initial washing, sorting, identifying, and counting. Each move had to be timed to the bucking motion of the ship. Water sloshed from sinks and buckets to run across the floor in rivulets.

One team member cursed as the ship rocked over a larger wave and the pile of worms she had already sorted and counted sloshed back to mix with the uncounted pile.

"Anything new?" Cindy called, and then glanced up to see head after head sadly shake "no." So far, this Indian Ocean vent ecosystem appeared to match what they expected to find—what had been found in other oceans at other vents.

Most of the samples were logged in, placed on steel trays, and wheeled into the freezers (meat lockers) for storage until they could be analyzed back on land. Some were selected for immediate analysis.

Lab techs held razor-sharp scalpels in one hand and braced with the other in the pitching cabin in order to make precise incisions and remove specific organs. Tissues were sliced into thin cross-sections and laid on glass plates. Stomach contents were collected in beakers for chemical composition analysis. Blenders and grinders whined. Sample dryers whirred. Dishes of ground stomach, gill, and skin cells were arranged and labeled on long trays. The lights on high-powered microscopes softly hummed as technicians carefully—almost reverently—fawned over each organ and tissue sample from this new and alien world.

One biologist fired up a gas chromatograph, a machine used to identify the chemical composition of the original sample. Liquefied tissue samples were injected into its helium-filled glass tube and heated. The line-chart printout identified which chemicals were present in the sample. Another biologist turned on a mass spectrometer that identified gaseous ions based on their behavior in an electromagnetic field. Biologists studied the graphic readouts looking for spikes that indicated chemicals and compounds present in the sample. This would help them determine how the creatures in this system grew and lived.

Bob Collier peered over Cindy's shoulder. "What are you looking for?"

"Just the basics for now," Cindy answered without looking up from her microscope. "What do they eat? What are their energy and nutrient sources? How do they grow without light and oxygen? What are the species relationships in this ecosystem?"

She sat back, rubbed her eyes, and sighed. "Nothing glamorous." Then her eyes brightened. "Now, the discovery of a new species or of a new kind of vent ecosystem . . . *that* would be about as glitzy as it gets." She slowly shook her head. "But no such luck today."

The motion of the ship slowed each step in every process and forced innumerable mistakes. Precious time was wasted painstakingly redoing processes that were almost automatic on land. A beaker of acid tipped over when the ship twisted and dipped. Hissing acid flowed across an entire tray of samples that then had to be thrown out and replaced. When the ship rolled unexpectedly and two biologists were thrown across the cabin, they had to be helped to the infirmary—one with a head gash and one with a twisted knee. A thousand-dollar microscope tumbled off a counter and shattered, spraying glass slivers across the lab. Trays of frozen samples in the meat locker rattled like distant thunder.

Still, each biologist worked on, acutely aware of the pressure for speed. Once pulled from their native depths to the surface, biological samples deteriorate quickly. If they weren't processed and preserved within a few hours, they would be worthless.

Over fifteen hours after she entered the lab, Cindy snapped off her rubber gloves and stepped wearily to the lab door. Behind her, others still ground, mixed, centrifuged, labeled, and stored samples for later analysis. They each had aching backs and arms from long, intense hours of tedious work—sifting through every specimen, every clue, trying to reconstruct a picture of the ecosystem around this vent where life flourished without any sunlight or oxygen. Her hair and skin reeked of strong laboratory chemicals. The odor swirled past her into the ship's hallway.

One of the chemists passed her and raised a hopeful eyebrow. Cindy sighed and shook her head. "Nothing new. Nothing we didn't expect to find."

Outside, hidden beneath 15,000 feet of water, a tantalizing and unknown world waited to be discovered. Cindy Lee Van Dover longed to explore that world like the famed land explorers of 500 years ago. Inside the *Knorr,* which lurched and shuttered as waves slammed across her bow, the meticulous lab work of science ground on.

After Words

The continuing work of Dr. Van Dover and other deep sea scientists has begun to create a picture of the biological, chemical, and physical processes that occur in the deep oceans, the last unexplored preserve on Earth. Because the world's oceans are a major source of food, energy, and fresh water, and are also our primary dumping ground, understanding the oceans is vitally important to human survival. Cindy Lee Van Dover remains at the cutting edge of the effort to chart, explore, and study the ocean depths.

* * *

Suggested Topics to Explore

This story deals with researching the biology around mid-ocean vents and with the process of discovering new deep ocean vents. Here are starting questions that will help you research in these areas.

1. What are mid-ocean ridges? Map this mountain ridge that meanders around the world and through every ocean. Which parts of this ridge system have it been studied? Which parts have been mapped? What created the mountainous ridge?

2. What flows out of deep ocean vents? How do these gasses support an ecosystem that flourishes around the vents? What animals and plants live in vent communities?

3. When was the first deep-sea submersible built? How many are in current use? How deep can they go? How many can carry

human passengers? Why is a deep-sea submersible harder to build than a spaceship?

4. What is new Earth crust made of? Where does it come from? Why is it created deep in the oceans? How do the mid-ocean ridge lines relate to Earth's tectonic plates?

5. What lives in the lightless ocean below 2,000 feet? Are the deep oceans more or less densely populated than the surface waters? Why?

For Further Reading About This Story

Blair, Carvel. *Exploring the Sea: Oceanography Today.* New York: Random House, 1995.

Broad, William. *The Universe Below.* New York: Simon & Schuster, 1997.

Gibbons, Gail. *Exploring the Deep, Dark Sea.* Boston: Little, Brown & Company, 1999.

Markle, Sandra. *Pioneering Ocean Depths.* New York: Atheneum Books for Young Readers, 1995.

McGovern, Ann. *The Desert Beneath the Sea.* New York: Scholastic, 1991.

Rice, A. L. *The Deep Ocean.* Washington, DC: Smithsonian Institution, 2000.

Stowe, Keith. *Exploring Ocean Sciences.* New York: John Wiley, 1996.

Wallace, Joseph. *The Deep Sea.* New York: Gallery Books, 1987.

Waters, Sandra. *Deep Sea Vents.* Sarasota, FL: Cobblehill Books, 1994.

Annie Wauneka

Tradition Transition:
A Science Adventure

Community
Health Worker

Annie Wauneka wanted to save her people from the devastating epidemic of tuberculosis. Her real fight, however, wasn't against the disease, but against the traditions, beliefs, lifestyle, suspicions—and anger—of her own people.

A Science Adventure on a Navajo Reservation

Forty-year-old Annie Wauneka stood tall, addressing the Navajo Tribal Council in June 1951. "My father, Chee Dodge, led this council for many years. For all of those years, he spoke of the need for better education for our people. But I see a different need, a more important need."

Annie was the first woman ever elected to sit on the council. This was her first council meeting. This was her first speech to the council. Many of those gathered in the lodge hall eyed her with suspicion. Traditions were important to the Navajo, and her presence there as a council member shattered traditions that went back to the beginning of time.

Outside the traditional hogan used for the meeting, a fierce sun flung its relentless heat at the parched desert of the Northeast Arizona Navajo reservation. Hogans were earth-covered dwellings, typically with no windows and a smoke hole in the center of the roof.

When working on her ranch and with her herds of sheep and horses, Annie wore jeans and cotton work shirts. Here, she wore traditional Navajo dress—full, flowing skirt of cotton with colorful geometric pattern of desert tones, velveteen blouse, and as much silver and turquoise jewelry as her forearms would bear. Her black hair was pulled back and tied with yarn. Standing almost six feet tall, she appeared both invitingly friendly and imposing.

"You look like you're going to a wedding," laughed her oldest daughter as Annie had left the house that morning. (Annie had six children ranging from ages five to eighteen.)

"Why don't you dress western or in a business suit?" suggested her son.

"I want the council members to know that I value traditional ways," Annie replied.

Both children chortled, "Mom! You argue and fight *against* traditional ways all the time. You're the first woman on the council. How untraditional can you get?"

Now Annie continued her speech to the council in a strong, forceful voice. "Education is not what must come first. Education will not help the sick and dying. The health of our people must improve or nothing else matters."

An elderly councilman with white, flowing hair nodded. "This TB [tuberculosis] is a curse from the white man. We should not have let them come. We should not believe or listen to them now."

Deadly tuberculosis, a respiratory disease unknown to the Navajo until introduced by whites, had reached epidemic proportions all across the sprawling Navajo reservations spread across parts of three western states. Its rattling cough could be heard in every village. Its raging fevers and radical weight loss had been experienced in almost every family.

Annie responded, "Tuberculosis will not go away if we hide from it. When I was eight, the influenza epidemic wiped out thousands of Navajos. The blindness disease came a few years later. Not one family here lives without at least one blind member from that plague. When these epidemics plague our people, we are not healthy enough to successfully fight them. How many have already died from TB? When TB finally goes away, it will be something else tomorrow if we do not act to improve the health of all our people."

A tribal elder said, "Medicine men have always taken care of our people. They, not we, should decide on health matters." Most of the council nodded and murmured in agreement.

Annie answered, "But now we need more care than they can provide."

Angry silence followed. Annie could feel the fire from twenty pairs of eyes boring into her. "Council Member Wauneka," cautioned the council leader. "Our faith in tribal medicine is one of our strongest and oldest traditions."

But Annie Wauneka—as she always had—stood her ground. "Perhaps it is time for us to create new traditions."

Annie felt as much as heard the deep rumbles of anger and resentment being whispered all around her at the council circle and in the gallery behind where tribal members could watch. Nothing was said out loud, in the open. That was not the Navajo way. Still, Annie could tell she had just made many powerful enemies.

The head of the council called for a recess for food and thought. During the break, one council member who had been a close friend of Annie's father, drew her aside. "Let us take a short walk." Once they were away from the crowd, he asked, "Are you sure your words here are wise and carefully chosen?"

Annie answered, "If they will improve our people's health, I will use any new technology or idea—no matter where it comes from."

"But we as a people *are* our traditions and values. How can you improve the people by destroying who we are?"

Annie snapped, "Tuberculosis is the enemy, not me."

He sighed, "But if you make them angry, Annie, aren't you making *yourself* the enemy?"

As she returned to the meeting hogan, Annie was pained to overhear several muttered personal attacks. She saw two council members shake their heads and scowl. She thought her heard one say, "How can we trust someone who flaunts her wealth and luxury?" It was true, Annie's father had been a wealthy and successful rancher. But Navajo tradition said it was improper to make yourself stand out or to show off in any way.

As the meeting resumed, Annie quickly finished her remarks with a plea for improved health and sat down. By meeting's end, Annie had been appointed to head the Health Committee. It was a minor assignment, offered more out of respect to Annie's deceased father than to her own accomplishments.

That night Annie sat with her sister-in-law, Shirlee Wauneka, who said, "I'm sorry that the council meeting did not go well."

"Why do you say that?" Annie asked. "I said my central message and was appointed to the Health Committee."

"You *said* your message, but did anyone *hear* it?"

Annie said, "They all heard me. I saw their reactions."

"Their *ears* heard. But not their hearts and minds." When Annie's face saddened, Shirlee added, "You're a council woman! You'll figure it out."

Annie decided she would have to take her message directly to the Navajo people. Her goal was to stop the spread of tuberculosis. In village after village, she gathered with the community adults. By the time she visited the village of Klagetoh in September, she had learned to make her message simple and direct.

"If we are healthier, we will live better. To be healthier, we must do three things. First, improve cleanliness and washing—with soap and water—every day."

Someone countered, "That is white man's way."

Annie nodded in agreement. "It is the way to stay healthy now that the whites have come to share our lands."

Some heads nodded in understanding and acceptance. Many scowled, feeling that Annie was trying to do way with Navajo culture.

Annie continued, "Second, stop living on dirt floors." All traditional hogans had dirt floors. As soon as she said it, she knew the argument would begin.

"We've always had dirt floors."

"A wood floor is better for your health."

Angrily, someone shouted, "My grandparents and their grandparents before them lived on dirt floors. Are you saying that my ancestors and their ways were foolish and that they did not live properly?"

In the first few villages Annie stammered without a good counterargument. Now she had learned to say, "The dirt is not as healthy for our people now that whites have come. We cannot treat life the same as our grandfathers did."

Annie was relieved to see a few more nods of agreement and understanding. She paused to breathe and gather herself for her third point. This was the one that always found the most anger and opposition. "The sick should not stay at home with the healthy. They should go to hospitals and use government doctors." Annie knew that this statement would summon forth the most bitter argument of all.

"The government can't be trusted. They lie and cheat!"

"Not for our health," Annie protested.

"For everything. They burned our villages and fields and forced us to march hundreds of miles to these reservations."

"That was forty years ago," Annie pleaded.

"And it has been bad for our health ever since. *That's* how much the government cares for our health!"

Someone said, "Traditional medicine men have cared for us since the beginning of time. Why should we listen to you instead of to them?"

Annie answered. "Because our people are dying of a white man's disease that medicine men can't cure. White man's medicine must cure white man's diseases."

As it had in past meetings, that answer brought out more anger in Klagetoh. "We were fine until the whites came. We shouldn't trust them or their medicine!"

Another villager said, "People go to the white hospital and die. We are better off with our own medicine men."

Annie was regularly snubbed and created more anger and resentment than understanding. She felt shut out by the very people she was trying to help. She was ignored and dismissed. Sadness and anger swirled in her heart. Even those about to die from the epidemic would not listen to the truth in her words.

"It's not working," Annie told Shirlee in early 1952. "The people don't want to hear what I have to tell them."

"They don't understand your words," answered Shirlee.

"My words?"

"Tuberculosis, sanatorium, injection, epidemic. These are white man's words—English words—and mean only mistrust and resentment to Navajo people."

"But that's what they're called."

"By the whites," Shirlee added.

Annie thought for some time before answering. "Then I'll invent new words that sound Navajo so the people can understand."

Shirlee smiled in agreement. "And you must make the medicine man your friend, not your enemy." She grew more somber. "How did it happen that the Navajo have become weak and sick? We were once a mighty people."

"It doesn't matter," Annie answered. "It is what we must live with today."

"It didn't use to be like this when we lived in traditional villages with traditional ways."

"It's not the old days any more," Annie sighed. "Whites are here and we must adjust. I must make our people *want* to adjust, or epidemic by epidemic we will surely die." She sighed and paused. "You're right. I must start with the tribal medicine men."

For weeks she worked on her presentation to the tribal council of medicine men. She had come to see that she could never win the people if she did not win this anchor of the traditional ways. She could not sleep the night before her talk.

Twenty medicine men were in the hogan when Annie made her plea. "Our people suffer not from traditional illnesses, but from white man's diseases. Whites came and brought white diseases from outside our traditional life and ways. White man's diseases must be fought with white man's medicine."

She paused to see if they had taken offense. She saw none of the smiles that would mean she had won support. But neither did she see any scowls or anger.

"I am here to ask that you strengthen and expand your role. Our people need you more than ever in these desperate times. You need to hold to traditional ways, but also to learn enough of whites' medicine to use both it and the white doctors to fight sickness and disease caused by the coming of the whites."

Annie could see that, by emphasizing their role and importance, she had struck a supportive chord with the fierce pride of the medicine men. She concluded, "It is a job of great responsibility. Great honor will be given by the medicine men to those who can do it."

Annie saw the first hint of a smile and a nod from several of the gathered medicine men, and she knew she would win her fight.

After Words

It took all of the rest of the year for Annie Wauneka to convince her people to use Western medical technology. By late 1953, new tuberculosis cases were down over 80 percent. The tribal medicine men publicly supported the lifestyle changes needed to improve tribal health—all thanks to Wauneka's efforts.

Annie Dodge Wauneka was one of the most influential and inspiring community health activists of the American twentieth century. She successfully bridged traditional Navajo medicine and beliefs with modern (Western) medicine and single-handedly led the fight to conquer a long-standing tuberculosis epidemic on the Navajo reservation.

* * *

Suggested Topics to Explore

This story deals with public health and modern versus traditional ways. Here are starting questions that will help you discuss and research both.

1. Annie Wauneka risked the anger and resentment of those in her tribe that she was trying to help because she advocated change and new ways of thinking. Have other scientists made people angry with their discoveries? Research this idea and see how many scientists you can find.

2. Research the life and work of Annie Wauneka. What else did she accomplish for her people? What about her makes her unique among her people?

3. Do all cultures and societies benefit from traditions? Are traditional ways valuable to modern American society? Is it also important to incorporate new ways into our traditions? What new ideas and concepts have been introduced into our society in the past twenty years?

For Further Reading About This Story

Bataille, Gretchen, (ed.) *Native American Women*. New York: Garland Publishing, 1993.

Gridley, Marion. *American Indian Women*. New York: Hawthorn, 1974.

Nelson, Mary. *Annie Wauneka*. Minneapolis, MN: Dillon, 1972.

Steiner, Stan. *The New Indians*. New York: Harper Row, 1968.

Waltrip, Lela. *Indian Women*. New York: David McKay, 1964.

Witt, Shirley. "An Interview with Dr. Annie Wauneka," *Frontiers* 6 (Fall 1981): 64–67.

Chien-Shiung Wu

Expert Experimenter: Physicist
A Science Adventure

If you conducted a single experiment that proved one of the fundamental law of nature to be wrong—a law that was accepted by every
great physicist in the world, a law that was the basis for much of
modern nuclear physics—what would you think? What would you
do with your experiment and results?

A Science Adventure in the Physics Lab

A beautiful October afternoon in 1956 spread fall colors across
New York City. Columbia University Physics Department graduate
assistant, Henry Tom, leaned against forty-five-year-old associate
professor Chien-shiung Wu's office doorframe. "Uh-oh," he muttered. "I've seen *that* look before."

Professor Wu sat erect at her well-ordered metal desk, focused,
absorbed—almost mesmerized—by the journal article she was reading. But it was the eager gleam radiating from her face that drew
Tom's attention.

Henry Tom's job was to assist with the seemingly endless stream
of complex experiments Wu designed to test physics theories. She
was considered one of the top subatomic experimenters in the world.

"Have you read this paper, Henry?" she asked without glancing up.

He stepped into the office and peered over her shoulder. It was a
paper by Tsung Dao Lee and Chen Ning Yang of Chicago on their
revolutionary theory to explain the "tau-theta puzzle."

Still without looking up, she continued. "They claim that the law
of parity is wrong."

Tom glanced at his boss to see if it was a joke. She looked serious. "But the law of parity is a fundamental law of nature," he stam-

mered. "Many of the accepted theories of subatomic physics—some by the most famous physicists of the twentieth century—are based on that law. It *can't* be . . . wrong."

Wu shrugged and smiled. "Lee and Yang propose that the tau-theta puzzle is not a problem with experiments and detection equipment but with the law of parity itself."

If you look in the mirror, you see a mirror image that is an exact match of you, but backwards. Subatomic particles also have mirror images, like twins that look and act exactly like the original particle, but spin in the opposite direction. The laws of physics said that a particle and its mirror twin acted the same. It was called the law of conservation of parity (law of parity for short) and it was one of the fundamental building blocks of subatomic physics.

Lee and Yang had been studying the tau-theta puzzle. In 1952, scientists discovered that when certain atomic nuclei broke apart, short-lived particles, called mesons, flew out. There were two kinds of mesons (tau and theta). They were mirror images of each other. According to the law of parity, they should act the same. But they didn't. Tau particles broke down into *three* smaller and even shorter-lived particles (called pi-mesons). Theta particles broke down into only *two* particles.

Virtually every physicist in the world had shrugged, and claimed it was a problem with our ability to conduct subatomic experiments on such tiny, submicroscopic particles that only existed for a tiny fraction of a microsecond. Lee and Yang said the experiments were fine—it was the law of parity that was wrong.

Henry Tom repeated, "We—you—can't challenge the law of parity."

Wu smiled. "But has anyone ever *proved* it?"

"You'll have every physicist in the world breathing down our necks!"

Wu turns back to the article, fingers of one hand idly drumming on her desk.

Tom groaned, "Let Lee and Yang do their own experiment and prove their own theory."

"They're mathematicians, not laboratory experimenters. Besides, I'm not trying to prove or disprove anything. I think it's about time someone tested the law of parity in the lab. Isn't it exciting to take on one of the fundamental laws?"

Tom grimaced. "Terrifying is the word I'd use." Then he added, "Did you know Lee and Yang when you lived in China?"

Chien-shiung Wu had been born in China in 1912 near Shanghai. She was one of the few Chinese women to gain an education, graduating in 1935 from the National Central University in Nanking before moving to Berkeley, California, for graduate studies. After war came to China—followed by the Communist takeover—Wu had not been able to return to her native country.

Wu shook her head. Then she cocked her chin and smiled. "Relax, Henry. I just want to make sure we can depend on the physical laws we use in our theories."

Chien-shiung consulted with Lee and Yang both by phone and by letter. From these conversations she decided that Cobalt 60 (the radioactive form of the element Cobalt) would be an ideal element for her test.

Wu planned to surround a small sample of radioactive Cobalt 60 with a dozen giant, high-power strip magnets to create a massive magnetic field. This field would force the Cobalt 60 nuclei to align like rows of tiny magnets all spinning to point the same direction. When these nuclei naturally broke apart, mesons would shoot out— and should all travel in the same direction, because all of the nuclei were aligned in the same direction.

Mesons from *original* particles should fly off in the direction of the magnetic field's spin. Those from *mirror twins* should fly off in the opposite way. Wu would count the number of mesons emitted in each direction. The law of parity predicted that the same number would shoot out in each direction. If Lee and Tang were right, the numbers would be radically different.

It was a simple, elegant experimental plan. It was, however, massively awkward and difficult to do. Each strip magnet weighed several tons, stood over eight feet tall, and had to be maneuvered into place with fork lifts and them bolted and aligned to within 1/100th of an inch to create a uniform magnetic field. Handling radioactive samples required shielding and protective equipment that had the nasty habit of disrupting the uniformity of that magnetic field.

Wu installed detectors called scintillation counters to detect the short-lived mesons. But the counters had to be painstakingly calibrated to the background radiation in the lab room, and then recalibrated to the magnetic field.

It took three weeks to assemble and prepare the test on a campus concrete loading dock (the only open space big enough). Wu then made twenty runs of her test over a three-day period.

Her results were disappointing. At room temperature, Cobalt 60 nuclei possessed too much energy. Their natural motion overpowered the magnetic field. Nuclei did not align with the field and mesons scattered out in all directions. That same problem had been encountered by the other experimenters who had attempted to test the law of parity.

Chien-shiung realized she needed to cool the Cobalt 60 to reduce the energy and motion of its nuclei.

She contacted the National Bureau of Standards in Washington DC and arranged to use their lab with an installed super cooler. This added a new set of equipment to her experiment site. The Cobalt 60 would now be confined inside a freon super-cooling unit. Magnets and counters had to be trucked to Washington and realigned and recalibrated to the new conditions.

Wu lowered the temperature of her sample to $-100°$ C (far colder than the coldest temperature ever recorded on Earth) and repeated her tests. Results were still inconclusive. Cobalt nuclei were *still* too active and broke from alignment with the magnetic field. Mesons were still scattering in many different directions.

Reluctantly, Wu concluded that she would have to cool her radioactive metal further—almost down to absolute zero. Additionally, she would have to increase the strength of her magnetic field. These changes would double the difficulty and cost of her experiment.

Wu ordered additional strip magnets. To make room for the additional cooling tubes and thermal shielding, she had to relocate the entire experiment to a larger, hangerlike concrete room about the size of most school multipurpose rooms. She needed to bring additional electric circuits into the room to power the massive machinery. She also needed to use three technicians from the National Bureau of Standards to round out her team.

More weeks were spent aligning and calibrating the equipment. Each step involved endless climbing and moving of twelve-foot stepladders to reach different sets of controls for magnetic units and freon coolers.

Wu planned to cool her Cobalt sample to $-273.15°$ C, just $0.1°$ C above absolute zero (that temperature where all motion inside an atom stops). The work became deadly dangerous. Even momentary exposure to this extreme cold could be deadly and would certainly destroy any tissue it touched. The team had to wear thick protective suits and padded gloves. Wu had to find special thermometers capable of accurately measuring temperatures as low as $-273°$ C.

The room filled with noise on every test run—the roar of giant exhaust fans, the deep hum (almost a rumble) of super powerful magnets, the hiss of expanding coolant as it sprayed through jet nozzles.

At Wu's command, enough power surged into this room to power a small city. She could almost feel the magnets pull on her skin as if the lines of her magnetic field were thick and strong as spider webs strung through the air. All watches, calculators, computers, and other electronic equipment had to be stored in an adjacent room. Each could be destroyed by the room's magnetic power.

Chien-shiung ran her experiment twenty times as preliminary runs to test her methodology and equipment setup. Then she ran it using other sample elements to create background and baseline checks on her procedure.

Finally, she was ready to conduct the experiment for real. It took over an hour to cool each sample to $0.1°$ C above absolute zero and then twenty minutes to power and align her magnets and confirm that the Cobalt nuclei were aligned with the unified magnetic field. For each test, Wu climbed an average of 800 stairs up and down ladders.

When monitors, gauges, and meters told her that all was perfect, Wu began her test run simply by switching on her two scintillation counters. Each was programmed to run for precisely one minute and to then calculate the density of mesons emitted per second. The test itself always seemed anticlimactic after such lengthy and elaborate preparation.

Following each run, Wu rechecked all of her equipment and verified her meson counts. Then she warmed the sample to room temperature—and was ready to start the test all over again. Twenty times she ran the test to ensure that her results were valid and consistent. For the last three days of testing, she averaged less than four hours of sleep each night. Her legs and arms ached from climbing and hauling.

The end of her experiment seemed to come so suddenly. Finally, Chien-shiung had her results. With the final test run complete, meson counts were compiled and averaged over her twenty tests. Other researchers reviewed and verified the data to establish that her methods and set up were valid. The work was over except for Chien-shiung to write her report and journal articles describing her experiment and findings.

After Words

Lee and Yang were right. Parity did not exist within the structure of an atomic nucleus. The law of parity was wrong. It did not describe the way real particles acted in nature. It seemed so simple and obvious a statement after months of careful work.

With that one experiment and with that simple statement of her results, Chien-shiung Wu toppled one of the fundamental pillars of nuclear physics into the dust of fiction. She shook every corner of the international physics community, rattled every theory concerning subatomic behavior.

Subatomic physicists worldwide scrambled to rethink their theories and to reevaluate their work and findings compiled over the previous twenty years. Rather than pause to shine in the glory of her startling success, Chien-shiung was already back at Columbia University, beginning the design of her next science adventure.

* * *

Suggested Topics to Explore

This story deals with subatomic physics and accepted laws of physics. Here are some starting questions that will help you discuss and research both.

1. This story describes a "natural law" that was disproved. Can you find other concepts that were once believed to be "natural laws," but which were later disproved? Do you think any of the "natural laws" scientists currently believe to be true will be eventually shown to be wrong?

2. Chien-shiung Wu repeated her experiments many times. Why? What does she gain by repeating her experiments? How many times must a scientist repeat an experiment to be sure of her results?

3. Chien-shiung Wu was an experimenter. Lee and Yang were theorists. What is the difference between theory and experi-

ment? What is the relationship between the two? Do the two activities use different skills and bodies of knowledge?

For Further Reading About This Story

Marton, L. L., and Claire Marton. *Methods of Experimental Physics: Nuclear Methods in Solid State Physics, Vol. 2.* New York: Academic Press, 1983.

McGrayne, Sharon Bertsch. *Nobel Prize Women in Science: Their Lives, Struggles, and Momentous Discoveries.* New York: Carol Publishing Group, A Birch Lane Press Book, 1993.

Shriprakas, Patel B. *Nuclear Physics: An Introduction.* New York: Halsted Press, 1991.

Wu, Chien-Shiung, and Luke C. Yuan, eds. *Elementary Particles: Science, Technology and Society.* Berkeley: University of California Press, 1981.

Yount, Lisa. *Contemporary Women Scientists.* New York: Facts on File, 1994.

Index

About the Author

KENDALL HAVEN is a nationally recognized master storyteller and the author of numerous books, including *Marvels of Math, Write Right!,* and *Close Encounters with Deadly Dangers.* A former research scientist, he is based in Fulton, California.